THE
FAMILY
SABBATICAL
HANDBOOK

"How can a committed parent find adventure in a life cluttered with soccer practice, PTA, and play dates? With equal parts storytelling and "how-to" *The Family Sabbatical Handbook* provides a blueprint for any mom or dad who dreams of adventure yet still puts family first. It motivates those of us who may have been afraid to take our families to faraway parts of the world and then tells us how to get there. The happy result is a family-enriching experience wherein everybody grows both closer to each other and as world citizens. Every American parent should read this book."

     – Dan Buettner, explorer, travel journalist and founder of
      Quest Network

"As someone who has long been intrigued with the idea of an extended stay abroad, I was impressed by *The Family Sabbatical Handbook*. The subject matter is well organized with a descriptive table of contents that makes it easy to find exactly what you need, and if there is anything about living abroad with children that Bernick hasn't covered, I certainly didn't find it. From locating an apartment to coping with homesickness to seeking medical care, she has the information you'll need. Presented in a down-to-earth, conversational style, with anecdotes from expat friends, *The Family Sabbatical Handbook* is a must-read for anyone planning an overseas adventure."

     – Janice Macdonald, author and travel writer

"Elisa Bernick has written an impeccable, step-by-step guide for getting out of Dodge. I mean, really getting out of Dodge — how to move your family to another country for 18 months. Equally important, she offers an articulate and fascinating examination of why you might want to do that and the consequences of doing just that. This is not only an excellent handbook; it's also an affecting story of the rewards that accrue to parents with the imagination and courage to change their lives as well as the lives of their children. Perhaps forever."

     – Rudy Maxa, Contributing Editor, *National Geographic Traveler*,
      Public Radio's "Savvy Traveler," and star of the PBS series *Smart*
      Travels

THE FAMILY SABBATICAL HANDBOOK

THE BUDGET GUIDE TO LIVING ABROAD WITH YOUR FAMILY

— ELISA BERNICK —

The Family Sabbatical Handbook:
The Budget Guide To Living Abroad With Your Family

Published by
The Intrepid Traveler
P.O. Box 531
Branford, CT 06405
http://www.intrepidtraveler.com

First Edition
Printed in the U.S.A.
Cover design by Foster & Foster
Interior design by Alfonso Robinson
Photos by Jean-Michel Batty, www.betterthanwords.com. All rights reserved.

Some of the information in Chapter 8 appeared in "Schooling Abroad: How to Make the Best Choice For Your Children" in the July/August 2005 issue of *Transitions Abroad* magazine.

ISBN: 978-1-887140-69-0
Library of Congress Control Number: 2006939940

10 9 8 7 6 5 4 3 2 1

DEDICATION

For Michael, Cleome, and Asher. *Mi familia intrépida.*
Without you, *no vale la pena.*

ABOUT THE AUTHOR

Elisa Bernick spent the first 12 years of her life lying on a hill in her suburban Minnesota backyard staring up at the sky wondering what life was like outside her tiny spot on the globe. She has spent the next 35 years doing her best to find out. At 17, she headed off to travel around the world and worked with fire-eaters in Paris, inoculated turkeys on a kibbutz in Israel, fed truckers on a boat to Greece, rode the Magic Bus to London, and sold camping supplies in Edinburgh. During college in Madison, Wisconsin, she sat down on a bench next to a 23-year-old man named Michael. He had a long blond ponytail, a quick smile, and excellent traveling stories of his own. They decided to try some adventures together (including having a couple of kids) and have been traveling together ever since.

Elisa is an award-winning writer and journalist. During her 25-year career, she has worked as a reporter and producer for radio, broadcast television, and cable stations that include Minnesota Public Radio, PBS, WCCO-TV, and Twin Cities Public Television. Her freelance magazine articles on travel and parenting have been published by *Parents Magazine*, *Minnesota Parent*, and *Transitions Abroad*. She is the author of *Cyberos*, a romantic thriller set in the mysterious world of virtual reality, and *Exit Strategies*, which traces the adventures of a Jewish family that moves to the Protestant Midwestern suburbs in the 1960s and '70s.

Elisa has taught creative and broadcast writing at Syracuse University, the University of Minnesota, and in San Miguel de Allende, Mexico. She is an avid gardener and lives with her husband and two children in St. Paul, Minnesota.

ACKNOWLEDGEMENTS

I would like to thank all of the friends and family who supported us during our family sabbatical and during the writing of this book. And a special *gracias* to those families who shared their own family sabbatical stories and wisdom with us. Some are named in this book and some are not, but you will travel forever in our hearts.

Table of Contents

INTRODUCTION

". . . The search for lost things is hindered by routine habits and that is why it is so difficult to find them."
Gabriel Garcia Marquez
One Hundred Years of Solitude

"The tattered, oft-consulted, never-to-be-correctly-folded-again roadmap of the world only seems to yield up the small red bullet indicating 'YOU ARE NOT HERE.'"
El Grito #3

Cuidado! Popo! "Careful! Poop!" is one of the first Spanish phrases our family learned in January of 2002 when my husband and I quit our jobs and moved with our two young children to San Miguel de Allende, Mexico. For 18 months we sidestepped dog and burro poop, studied Spanish, worked on novels, sent the kids to Mexican schools, and spent intensive time together as a family. It wasn't a spur of the moment decision. We spent nearly three years paying off our debts, saving money, and preparing for our "family sabbatical," as we dubbed our grand adventure. Our plan, simply put, was to lease our house in St. Paul and use the monthly rental income, along with $35,000 in savings, to live without working for 18 months abroad with our kids. We didn't know a soul in the city we moved to. We couldn't speak Spanish. We weren't sure our money would last. And we'd never traveled with our children for anything longer than a two-week family vacation. But we decided to leave everything else up to chance and see where the adventure took us.

If this type of adventure seems intriguing and you're thinking, "Wow, I'd love to do that with my kids." Or, "What a cool idea." Or even, "I'd never be able to do that with my kids," then read on. By the time you finish this book, you'll have a much better sense of what's involved in taking a family sabbatical, how to start preparing for it, and why it might well be the right adventure for you and your family too.

When I began researching our family sabbatical I was surprised and disappointed to find almost nothing written about living abroad for an extended period of time as a family. I turned up numerous general guides (many of them excellent) to retiring abroad, finding good air-fares, living on a budget, simplifying our lives, and maintaining my sanity during family vacations. I also found a few interesting and helpful books specifically geared toward traveling with children (see *Resources*). But these were either limited in scope to basic travel tips or they were travelogues with lots of interesting anecdotes about the *wheres* of *traveling* with children, but very little nuts and bolts information as to the *why's*, *wherefores*, and *hows* of actually *living abroad* with kids.

We wanted to know what it was like to pick up your family and move to another place to actually live, not just to visit or sign on for a few interesting adventures. Obviously, the type of travel a person chooses has a tremendous impact on the nature of the experience. If you move around a lot, you learn a lot about moving around but probably very little about what it's like to actually plant yourselves in another locale. I couldn't believe the paucity of information on this topic. Ours wasn't the only family doing this. We knew several others from the Twin Cities area who had made the decision to jump off the U.S. career treadmill and move with their family to some wonderfully different place. But these families had prearranged jobs or were using an existing volunteer organization to help them navigate the details of their new lives abroad. We were heading out cold: two parents, two young children, a limited budget, and the world.

Because we decided to move to a place where they didn't speak English and we assumed we would have to do without many familiar comforts, all sorts of interesting questions occurred to us. How would we learn the language? How would we deal with finances back home and abroad? What if we ran out of money? How much would we need to live on? What cultural differences might exist and how might we prepare for them? And perhaps most importantly, how would an adventure of this type change the nature of our family itself? Would it draw us closer together? Rip us apart? Would we look at each other a month into the adventure and say, what in the hell were we thinking? And if that did happen, what then? Well, I couldn't find a book out there that touched on these issues in any depth, so I decided to write it myself.

Another reason I wrote this book is that while living abroad we began running into more and more families like ourselves. Families who had traded busy lives back home for a simpler, cheaper, and slower life abroad where their kids could experience a different culture, a different pace, and in many cases, a different language. Many of these parents had traveled when they were younger or had always aspired to live elsewhere on the globe. They had finally moved abroad with their adorable, precious offspring only to feel like strangling them a week into their journey.

Obviously, there's no guarantee that this book will help you avoid all the rocky parts of living abroad with your kids. Kids are kids and no matter where you live in the world, rocky parts are inevitable (and a sign that you're actually spending "quality" time together). The only guarantee I can make is that you and your kids will have to deal with the unexpected every day — unexpected difficulties as well as unexpected joys. It's my hope that this book will allow you to sidestep a few of the difficulties on the way to those joys. And also, perhaps, that it will help you move through the inevitable difficulties with your sense of humor intact. In our experience, one of the greatest unexpected joys of living abroad is developing a sense of humor as a family.

What follows is not strictly a guidebook although I do include very detailed advice about everything from sabbatical locations and finances to packing and preparations, vaccinations and visas, foreign schools, bi-lingual vs. immersion education, long-distance communication, medi-cal care abroad, coping with homesickness, cultural differences, visitors, growing together as a family, returning to the states, and much, much more. You'll find humorous (and occasionally harrowing) anecdotes, suggestions and advice not only from our family but from fifteen other ex-pat families who lived or are living with their children in China, Europe, Central America, and Mexico and who, in some cases, had very different experiences from our own. Throughout the book you'll also find excerpts from "El Grito," the family website we maintained for the duration of our trip.

This adventure changed our family forever and perhaps that's also the reason I decided to write this book. Consider it a gift from our fam-ily to yours; a place to begin if you're contemplating setting off on a similar adventure with your own family. It's partly a record of how we came to do this, partly a survey of other families we met along the way, and partly the guide we wish we'd had when we started the process. I hope these thoughts and experiences will offer you insight, concrete advice, and inspiration as you start to plan your own family sabbatical.

– Elisa Bernick

1. WHY LIVE ABROAD
WITH YOUR KIDS?

"The whole point of this sojourn is to enhance creativity: in our lives, our relationships, our work — in everything. It's about having the space in which to awaken to the possibilities not just in our lives — but of our lives — and developing the skills to en- gage those possibilities. Establishing ourselves in a new environment with a controlled mixture of the familiar and strange, of comfort and alienation, is a crucial part of this effort. Creativity is simply possibility in action; and possibility is about what happens at the boundary between the known and the unknown."　　　　　　El Grito #4

You might (rightly) ask, why bother? What's the point of harnessing the energy, saving the money, and coping with the challenges of moving to another country to live with your children? Why wade through the health concerns, the language and cultural barriers, and all the inevita- ble difficulties of dealing with children and then raise the bar exponen- tially by doing it in a different country? If your kids are very young, will they even remember living abroad? Why not wait until they're older and you've got more money, more leeway, and more confidence in your children's ability to handle themselves in challenging situations?

Why indeed? Let me start by telling you why Michael and I did it. For as long as we've been a family, we've been trying to figure out how to live more intensely and creatively *as* a family and how to forge the kind of elusive, intimate bonds that seem to us the very essence of *be- ing* a family. We had assumed this bonding would come naturally. But when we looked around for role models, we didn't find them. Amidst the corrosive effects of the hectic lives we all seemed to lead, everyone we knew had similar complaints. There was a vague sense that the best of life was slipping away and we were powerless to do anything about it. There was simply never enough time or psychic space to savor the marriages, the children, and the good lives we were all working so hard to make. It began to sink in that we would never find this time unless we created it for ourselves.

We're obviously not the first or only ones to feel this way, but that feeling was the prime motivation for Michael and me to *do something different*. Otherwise, we figured we could easily continue to work at our pleasant jobs and have our pleasant lives while our children grew up, moved away, and . . . that would be that. The unique and fleeting opportunity for intensive interaction with our children would be gone.

After a lot of discussion, we decided to quit our jobs and take what we dubbed a "family sabbatical" to distinguish it from a "mere" break or vacation. We thought of it as a family retreat, a time to concentrate on our own creative projects and to develop more creative and passionate relationships with our children and each other. Quite honestly, it's one of the best decisions our family ever made.

Our kids were seven and two at the time, pretty young for such a big adventure. But we felt that there were as many reasons to do it when they were young as there were reasons to wait until they got older. The reality is that you'll cope with a set of difficulties whenever you go, whatever the ages of your children; it will just be a different set (see below).

Hmmm, you think to yourself. Interesting. But you're probably still wondering why *your family* should undertake such an adventure. Ten of the chief reasons follow, along with comments from other parents who have taken family sabbaticals with their children.

1. Forge strong family bonds by creating a family history and mythology.

Life in the U.S. doesn't necessarily encourage family togetherness. Everyone's so busy at work, school, and various "enrichment" activities that it often feels like we're less a family than roommates wandering around the house, sharing the same space and refrigerator. Often, the most we manage to do together as a family is sit around watching television or a movie.

Traveling, on the other hand, is not a spectator sport and it creates a bond like no other. Not only do you spend more time together and learn to rely on each other in a different way, you also go through fun, unusual, and occasionally frightening experiences together. These experiences take on a myth-like status and create the heart of a family story that everyone is an indelible part of forever.

Our children will always talk about the beach trip where we nearly lost our lives after the pick-up truck we were riding in veered off a mountain pass and almost flipped over. They'll often bring up the midnight visit of "the *alacrán*," the scorpion that dropped from our palapa roof and decided the back of my leg was a perfect place to snooze. And then, of course, no one will forget the fat, drunk, naked lady snoring contentedly behind the mosquito netting in the bed we were supposed to occupy the first night of our arrival in our new home.

There were difficult moments during our adventure when it felt like it was our family against the world. And there were astonishingly beautiful moments when we turned to each other and shook our heads at the mystery of what was unfolding in front of us. These adventures have become a rich part of our family story, a story we continue to build on and one that each of us now feels exists concretely. We're not roommates who just happen to inhabit the same house. We're a *family*. And that now feels like a powerful entity, indeed.

> *"I lived in Brussels, Belgium, for four years when I was between the ages of seven and eleven, when our family was transferred there by my Dad's company. It had such a huge influence on our family. It made us more adventuresome, open to other cultures and ways of thinking, and it made us closer as a family. I wanted to duplicate that experience on a smaller scale with my own family."*
>
> — Kim with Andy and Derek (9), Kyle (11), and Drew (13), who lived in San Miguel de Allende, Mexico, for seven months

2. Spend extended time with your children.

A reason to live abroad for a while when your kids are young is that you actually get to spend a bunch of time with them when they're still genuinely interested in spending time with you. Remember back to your teens. Wasn't there always one cool family on the block where everyone, including their own kids, actually wanted to hang out because the parents were so much cooler than everyone else's? We wanted to be that family and those parents for our own kids.

Before our sabbatical, Michael and the kids and I ran from morning until night doing, doing, doing, and whether working or playing, it was still hard work. The pace just kept heating up no matter how we tried to prevent it. We realized, like so many others, that we saw our kids awake for only a few hours a day. Michael, in particular, was working 50 to 60 hours a week as an architect and rarely saw the kids except on the weekends. And much of that time, the kids begged to be with their friends instead of with these strangers claiming to be their parents.

In addition, despite our best efforts to limit it to the "good" stuff, the U.S. media's inescapable influence contributes to a sense of frenzy. Everything competes for our attention and that reinforces the feeling of living our lives in sound bytes and sidebars — grabbing 15 minutes to eat or chat on the way to the next regularly scheduled program. It isn't necessarily unpleasant. It's just too fast. And it's hard to fathom changing anything specific because it all feels so overwhelming. We figured that the way we were headed, we wouldn't know our kids or they us — much less enjoy spending time together (or even know how to) — when they hit their teen years. The time to spend time together was *now*.

> "We loved the slow pace of life and the fact that we had so much time together as a family. We played chess, played cards, talked and wandered together. We strolled to "el jardín" in the town center and ate dinner together. We relied on each other a lot, in a way that drew us very close, especially when we were traveling."
>
> — Julie and Marc, with Kaya (8) and Ari (4),
> who lived in Guanajuato City, Mexico, for five months

"We did everything together, which was nice. And the kids liked it too — we were there to help them out, facilitate things, and play with them. They knew they needed us. It's amazing how life in the U.S. just seems to separate people inside a family."
— Marline and Rob, with Lilly (11) and Emory (13),
who lived in Guanajuato City, Mexico, for six months

3. Explore and enhance your own creativity.

Throughout our lives Michael and I have pursued creative projects in music, theater, writing, and film, trying to fit them in as best we could amidst all the other projects and people vying for our time and attention. Michael played his guitar and I worked on a book in fits and starts, but it never felt like we had the large chunks of time required to really dig into our creative selves. It was our own fault, of course. We just never found the time. But we finally decided to *make* it. We wanted our children to see us as creative beings and to learn to value exploring their own creativity as well.

Getting away was the key to making that happen. One of the most empowering aspects of moving abroad with your children is that you start with a clean slate. Your time is largely your own. You can have a life with no commitments outside of those you actively choose. Nobody knows you and nobody expects anything from you. You have the opportunity to throw out the old rules and make decisions as a family about the new ones. Which media will you allow in your house abroad? How many activities will the kids be involved in each day? How many chores will you take on? How many friendships will you cultivate?

We also found that living in an unfamiliar place actively encourages you to touch pieces of yourselves that you simply don't back home. While living abroad, your senses are heightened by the newness and differentness of everything around you. Forgotten or rarely used bits of gray matter can be re-energized and tapped to explore yourselves and your children in more interesting and creative ways.

"We were pleasantly surprised by how much our kids loved the museums and other tourist sites. They were much more curious about the culture and history than we had expected." — Julie and Marc

4. Create a strong bond between (and among) your kids.

Something that was totally unexpected but, in retrospect, is probably one of the most valuable and long-lasting benefits of our trip is that our kids developed an amazing relationship with each other. Sibling relationships can change drastically when you take kids away from all their friends, activities, and distractions and plop them down somewhere where they're deprived, quite frankly, of nearly everything else except each other. They suddenly and joyfully discover how wonderful it is to be and to have a sibling.

In our case, there's a five-year age difference as well as a gender difference between our two kids. I'll wager that if we'd spent the years when the younger was two to four and the elder seven to nine at home, they never would have developed the kind of closeness and care they have for one another now. The elder would have undoubtedly spent every moment with her own friends or involved in her own activities; playing the Memory Game with her younger brother would have been as welcome as a trip to the dentist.

In Mexico, they had each other and, for the most part, that was pretty much it. They each had friends at school and occasional play dates, but those were much rarer in Mexico than at home. They largely played with each other and devised games that each could play at whatever level they were capable. An easily packed inflatable swimming pool was one of the best investments in toys that we made. That, along with art supplies, a few computer games, videos, DVDs, soap bubbles, balls, a bunch of plastic animals and little figures, and a couple of colanders that they could use to sift sand, float toys, and fling water around creatively, kept them busy for hours. Kicking a ball together, playing house in a giant box, messing around in the park — they did it all together and, for the most part, had a great time. Asher, our younger, was thrilled to have his older sister to play with. And while Cleome did sometimes miss playing with kids her own age, she developed such a strong love and real enjoyment of Asher that she rarely complained about having him as her only playmate most of the time.

5. Learn another language.

Numerous studies confirm the advantages bilingual children have in the areas of higher abstraction and concentration. In terms of brain development, optimal language learning happens before kids turn 12. The natural ability of young children to learn a second or third language relatively quickly and without an accent is something you can take advantage of by spending time in another country. Even very young children, who may not do much speaking in any language while they're living abroad, will benefit. Their ears will become finely tuned to the nuances of pronunciation and rhythm so that when they do begin speaking the new language, it may very well be without a strong American accent.

That said, however, it takes longer that you might think to learn to speak another language, even when you are immersed in it. It wasn't until about halfway through our trip that Asher, then three, finally started speaking an interesting mix of English and Spanish. Getting dressed in the morning, he would say "I want to wear my *verde pantalones* and my *playera* with the *patos* on it." ("I want to wear my green pants and the t-shirt with the ducks on it.") I suspect he no longer knew or cared which language a word belonged to. From there it wasn't a long leap to speaking Spanish when he was with Spanish speakers and flipping to English when necessary. By giving your children the opportunity to learn another language relatively effortlessly, you're giving them a lifetime passport to the world.

"We decided early on that the very best thing we could do for our children, over and above piano lessons, ballet classes, and so on, was give them the opportunity to learn a second language and learn it at an early age, so that the learning process was easier.

The little one-hour Spanish playgroup classes we were doing back in Nashville weren't cutting it. Thus we decided to move abroad to really and truly accomplish this. And then we not only accomplished learning a second language via immersion, but we got the benefit of living in and experiencing another culture as well."

— Jody and Jordan, with Conor (13), Kirby (11),
and Wyatt (8), who are living in San Miguel de Allende, Mexico

Learning another language as a family has a special advantage for parents; it helps motivate us comparatively dim-witted adults to master the language along with our children. Although Michael and I each speak another Romance language (French and Italian, respectively) it wasn't easy for us to learn Spanish. Our brains weren't nearly as flexible as our children's and I, for one, was often tempted to throw in the towel. But being in a place where you need to chat with the garbage man, question the butcher, and find out from your child's teacher exactly what kind of costume is needed for the Mother's Day program provides enormous motivation to communicate.

6. Give your children the gift of self-discovery.

Part of the value of living in a different culture is allowing your children to meet and cope with difficult feelings. Isolation, homesickness, fear, and boredom are an important part of this experience. So is the elation and power your kids will feel when they make a new friend, begin to communicate in another language, and master difficult moments. Cleome was the only *gringa* in a class of 47 Mexican children (and in the whole school as well). She was obviously nervous the first few days but discovered surprisingly quickly how skilled she was at making new friends and operating in a completely different culture and language.

Both our children had the luxury of exploring their own imaginations through the many hours they spent alone reading, drawing, and daydreaming. I know these discoveries have permanently changed their self-perceptions, especially our daughter's. She's much more independent now and less prone to self-doubt and lack of confidence. During difficult moments here, a gentle reminder of all the challenges she met in Mexico visibly lifts her spirits.

"It did lots for the kids' self-concept. In Mexico, both girls felt gutsier about asking questions and talking. Something about operating in a different language sort of gave them a cover of confidence. They told us it felt it okay to 'mess up' because everyone would know it wasn't their language. As a result, they seem more outgoing and confident now." — Marline and Rob

"One of the things I wanted to accomplish with this sabbatical was to expose our kids to a heavy dose of change. In the U.S. we live in a very sheltered, homogenous, 'Leave it to Beaver' type of community. It is so nice here that a lot of kids don't want to leave. Also I had noticed that some kids had difficulty dealing with change and our middle son Kyle was one of them; he was definitely not thrilled with change. I really believe after this experience that all three know they are capable of dealing with dramatic change." — Kim and Andy

7. Experience another culture through your kids' eyes.

Young children open doors that might otherwise stay closed when you're living in another country. It's not always easy to bridge cultural and language gaps with local families and children are often the best ambassadors. Thanks to your kids' relationships with local children, your family will be welcomed into the local world through birthday parties, soccer games, dinner invitations, and more.

Seeing a new place through your children's eyes can also be startling and wonderful. "Why are those children begging, Daddy, shouldn't they be in school?" "Kids have to work really hard here. It's not like at home." "I tried a really cool new fruit called mamey. It tastes sort of like chocolate and sort of like an apricot." "I made a new friend, Mom. We're invited to their house for dinner." (Which turned out to be cactus tacos served from the back of their pick-up truck.)

Not only do young children walk around with their brains wide open, but their eyes are open wider than ours in many ways as well.

They don't avoid looking at unpleasant or difficult things as we've been taught to. They want to talk about why the fruit vendor has a withered sixth finger . . . why there's dog, cat, and burro poop everywhere . . . why people live with so little when the churches are coated in gold leaf. They question the treatment of the less fortunate and make sure that every outstretched hand is met with a coin, no matter how small the denomination.

8. Make the world your child's classroom.

There's tremendous value in broadening your children's education beyond the classroom to include other cultures and languages. But it's hard to give kids a real sense of what those cultures are like through books, movies, two-week vacations, and PBS specials alone, no matter how diligently we may try. Without exposure to the real thing, other cultures are too easily reduced to stereotypes and varieties of take-out food. A culture, like a language, contains elements that are untranslatable. To really experience another culture you have to interact with it over time as it unfolds around you and envelops you within it. The lessons of living abroad are both obvious and subtle. There will be those "aha" moments where your kids suddenly understand a phrase or concept they didn't the day before. And there will also be more subtle lessons learned from being at a critical distance from their own culture; moments that can spark a kind of intelligent curiosity about themselves and others in the world.

"We met people from Poland, Scotland, Japan, Canada, the Netherlands, Ireland, and other places. The children are now curious about geography and international relations in a concrete way because they can relate what they are learning or have questions about to specific people they have met from various countries." — Marc and Julie

"Our kids became more aware and sensitive to how differently people can live – they saw people living in shacks made of straw, living in crowded one-room apartments with bathrooms down the block. They learned about how little money so many people

around the world have and what a rich country the U.S. is. I think they began to see ways in which the U.S. is not the center of the world and also ways in which, to many people, it is."   — Rachel and Orin, with Isaiah (9) and Stanley (4),
who lived in Nanjing, China, for two years

9. Prepare your kids to be citizens of the world.

The events of September 11, 2001, opened the eyes of many Americans to the fact that beyond U.S. borders, many people view the world and the U.S. government and its citizens and culture differently from the way we perceive them ourselves. One of the hardest lessons to learn — and absorb — is other people think and do things differently and that difference is okay. Living abroad gently introduces children to points of view that are different from their own, without the implicit threat that's often part of the news coverage of tumultuous world events here at home.

"We think the exposure to the Mexican culture and to Spanish will give our children a lifetime appreciation for things that are different. They will have learned that there sometimes is not a right way and a wrong way but two different ways for things to be done or expressed. We also think our kids have a better sense of how fortunate they are and how most people in our world live with a lot less."   — Kim and Andy

10. Find what you never knew you'd lost.

Leaving home gives you a much deeper appreciation for what you've left. Living in the same place day after day makes the world around you largely invisible. Traveling the same path over and over, thinking the same thoughts, and seeing the same things can have an anesthetizing affect. Living abroad is such a re-energizing experience that you and your kids will be looking at the world around you through different eyes after your sabbatical, whether you go back to where you came from, head somewhere else, or decide to settle down in your sabbatical home for a more extended stay.

"I think our travels gave our children a great sense of self-confidence (if I could survive going to school there, I can survive anything!). I also think that they understand, in a way words alone could never adequately describe, what real poverty is. They know that there are families who live in cardboard shacks and children in rags who beg in the streets to eat. They are also aware of how much we have in the way of material goods and comforts." — Julie

"I loved that my children learned to be comfortable with being on the move, they learned to think about what was most important for them to bring with them – books, pencils, CD player, etc. And they learned how much they would be able to carry themselves. They learned how to make transitions, that change was not something they had to fear, even if in the moment they might feel nervous. They learned how lucky they are. In summary, one of the biggest joys was watching my children grow amidst other lands and turning them on to the amazing world we live in." — Rachel

ARE THE KIDS OLD ENOUGH? TOO OLD?

I'd be lying if I said that living abroad with kids is always one big picnic. But one of the most surprising and important things we discovered during our sabbatical is that when children are young, they're amazingly flexible travelers. They're willing to live in the here and now and they're easy to please as long they're provided with a few basics. Give them a friend to play with (siblings count), some sort of daily routine in terms of waking and going to sleep, a couple of familiar foods that can be had for each and every meal if necessary, and your attention. Toss in an occasional swimming pool visit and a video, and young travelers become amazingly pleasant, at least in the short term.

Obviously, there will be difficult moments and each age brings with it a different set of challenges in terms of living abroad:

• **Challenges with babies and toddlers.** Asher was a very active two-year-old when we arrived in Mexico, and life anywhere with babies and toddlers can be tough. Letting your nine-month-old crawl around in the backyard at home is a bit different from finding him examining burro poop in a Mexican barrio. And it's not as easy to cope with a sudden nighttime illness without a Walgreen's nearby. (But there's probably a *farmacia* or its equivalent on the corner staffed with someone who can sell you — and inject — a shot of penicillin or other extremely cheap antibiotic.) Finding a babysitter for a much-needed night out can be an interesting experience. The first time we did it, the sitter let Asher stay up until midnight and consume an entire bag of candy, so we spent the rest of the night cleaning vomit off his bedsheets. Also, what we consider basic necessities, such as diapers and wipes, can be expensive abroad. Baby food, juices, formula, macaroni and cheese, peanut butter, and so on, can be either difficult to find, pricey, or filled with added sugar and preservatives. And certainly, it's much easier to actually explore the sights of a new place with slightly older children. (This is probably one of the biggest drawbacks of traveling with very young children, other than babies who will just nap).

For those reasons you may want to wait until your kids are out of diapers and past needing constant infusions of treats and snacks to round out their days. (Does that ever happen?) But the upside is that babies are wonderfully relaxed travelers. And toddlers are so spirited and curious they'll definitely take you to places you've never been before — like the back of every restaurant you venture into and the interior of every bathroom you can imagine. (See *Chapter 10: We're Here!* for a discussion of sanitation issues, basic shopping tips, suggested daypack supplies, and the ups and downs of strollers, backpacks, and other equipment.)

• **Challenges with children in elementary and middle school.** Generally kids this age are terrific travelers. They're flexible, interested in everything, and will usually do what you say. They're also good at meeting other children and making friends, which, as I mentioned earlier, can be your entrée to meeting their parents. However, older kids may focus more on what they lack, instead of what they have. And some would rather walk through hot coals than leave their friends to go on some crazy adventure halfway around the world with their parents.

"Two of our children hope never to return to San Miguel at this point, while the youngest one loved it and would go back anytime. The older two missed their comfort stuff from home. They also missed the American school system and all the bells and whistles that go with it (just the things I wanted them to be without for a while). We do still feel strongly that the experience will ultimately be a great one for them, and we are actually thinking of returning next fall for one semester."
— Karen and Rick, with Remington (7), Austin (10), and Tyler (11), who lived in San Miguel de Allende, Mexico, for four months

• **Challenges with children in junior high and high school.** Once they hit 13 or 14, it can be really hard for parents to pry kids away from home without subjecting themselves to continuous griping. The child may not be able to appreciate much of anything except a good Internet line to instant message friends all day long. An adventurous teen, of course, might consider spending six months or a year abroad the coolest thing you've ever done.

"At 11 and 13, our kids are old enough to do everything with us and appreciate it. They loved experiencing the differences and really enjoyed the 'smaller world' of Mexico. They came to appreciate the new rhythms and basically ignored the lack of modern amenities. Other pluses of this age are that they're old enough to stay home by themselves so we could go out by ourselves. And finally, they're old enough to remember this experience."

— Rob and Marline

Practically speaking, pulling kids out of school and ensuring their place when you return is much easier when they are younger. Not only will your kids miss less academically, but also school administrators are more flexible when specific graduation credits and requirements are not at stake. (See *Chapters* 7 and *8: School Daze Parts One* and *Two*, for more on ensuring your children's place in school back home and finding schools abroad.)

"Both the elementary and the middle school were very supportive. They suggested home schooling in math and making sure our kids continued to read a lot and to try and encourage writing. They said the kids wouldn't miss much and if they did, they could pick it up when they returned, like kids who are transferred in."

— Kim and Andy

2. Where to Go and For How Long?

"There are a ton of interesting folks down here, each with a fascinating story to tell of how or why they made their way here and why they never left. San Miguel has a way of doing that to you. You come for a week and still find yourself here two years later, never quite managing to make it back to wherever you used to call home. Part of it's the climate, which is nigh perfect. Part of it's the city itself, which is quite Mexican but offers enough creature comforts that gringos can feel very much at home. And part of it is the energy from the long history of art and revolution created in this part of Mexico. We put the kids to bed and sip wine in the dark cool of the evening wondering, how did we get here? How did we find our way to this magnificent house and city? What forces magically came together and set us down here in this warm and friendly place?" El Grito #1

As you begin to contemplate your sabbatical plans, deciding where to go seems enormously important and it might be. But then again, it might not. Obviously if you've already got a job or a housing situation waiting for you somewhere, that's where you're likely to go. But if you're starting out cold with the whole world at your disposal, you could resolve that issue by closing your eyes and touching a finger to a spot on a spinning globe and end up having a perfectly magical time. On the other hand, you could be extremely thoughtful about it, invest a lot of time and energy researching exactly the right place to satisfy all your detailed requirements, and then go on to have a perfectly awful time.

After considering the haphazard and circuitous paths we and others took to finding sabbatical destinations, I think the decision about where to go is an arbitrary one; it won't necessarily make or break your sabbatical. This goes back to realizing that the adventure is less about moving somewhere specific and more about shaking up your and your family's routines and predictable responses to the world and each other. It's less about where you are, and more about where you are not. And even though your sabbatical planning may start years in advance of your actual departure date, it constitutes the true beginning of your journey and sets the tone for what's to come.

As you start considering your adventure, I urge you to keep in mind that your plans are more about preparing for a host of unknown possibilities than establishing a specific agenda.

"Our first criterion was to go to a Spanish-speaking country. We both strongly felt that Spanish would be most helpful to our kids in the future with the growing Hispanic population in the U.S. We settled on Barcelona originally because it was in northern Spain with good access to the rest of Europe but I ran into big problems with getting a visa for us for more than 90 days. They wanted financial papers, proof of housing, and so on. I also had great difficulty in finding info on schools other than the American schools. I even tried emailing the American Women's Club in Barcelona and Madrid and the response I got was that they were not a relocation service! A friend of ours who grew up in Mexico City suggested San Miguel de Allende. After two hours on the Internet, I began getting responses back from people, and within 48 hours I felt I could find housing and schools. Two weeks later I was on a plane to San Miguel to finalize housing and choose schools." — Kim

Make a List of Essential Requirements

A great way to start narrowing down potential sabbatical locations is to make a list of requirements that you and your family believe are essential to the success of your sabbatical. I'm defining the word "requirements" loosely. The list should start out as a sort of "wish list" that includes your most extravagant and even contradictory desires as well as all the basics you feel are necessary to keep you safe and comfortable during your sabbatical. You may also want to include the things you *don't* want to encounter or deal with along the way. It may seem like a simple exercise, but until you share these thoughts and write them down, you run the risk of imagining very different sabbaticals, which can create tension and conflict around something that should be enormously exciting and unifying. Also, once you articulate the inevitable differences in your visions of this adventure, you have a tool you can use to negotiate those differences and arrive at a truly shared set of priorities. You may want to begin with individual lists and then merge them gradually. Or try creating your list out of family brainstorming sessions. As you search for suitable destinations, your list will continue to evolve and become the primary tool you'll use to winnow down all the possible locations for your sabbatical.

Is there a part of the world that's intrigued you since you read about it in *National Geographic* as a kid? Put it down on your list. Maybe there's a topographical wonder that's caught your imagination and you want to live on, near, or under it for a while. Jot it down. Is there somewhere wonderful you once vacationed and you'd like the opportunity to explore it more fully? Is there a particular language or culture, cuisine, or climate that interests you? Do you just like the sound of Timbuktu?

There are as many reasons to move to one place rather than another as there are people and places in the world. Your list of essential requirements will help you cull through all the potential sabbatical locations to find a place that's right for your family. The older your kids are, the more involved they can be with compiling the list. You and your spouse may want to come up with an initial list and then have your kids add their own ideas at the end. Just the exercise of drawing up the list can be profoundly instructive because it requires you to revisit and refine the idea of a family sabbatical and to think consciously about what it means to be a family moving through the world together.

"I wanted to move to a Spanish-speaking country and improve on my own Spanish-speaking skills. Spain is just too far away; it's harder to think about moving there in

reality. Mexico is closer and had a lot more real potential for us. After deciding that this could be a reality for us I started asking a lot of questions to find out which part of Mexico would be best suited for our family. My uncle taught Spanish in high school and every summer he would take kids on a tour of Mexico, so I asked him for places that he thought would be good for us. Our criteria were that it had to be near an international airport, have plenty of schools to choose from, and be a safe environment. He listed several areas to check into. So the next step was to go to a few areas in person and check out schools, communities, and places to live, as well as cost of living. My friend and I did that in the fall (which gave us almost a year to plan) and we chose San Miguel [de Allende]." — Julie

Our List of Essential Requirements:

It's quite possible that once you've got your list and you begin researching potential locations, your first-choice spot may not be where you ultimately end up. Michael and I are Europhiles and our first choice was Italy. Our second choice was Spain; our last, Portugal. In the end, we moved to Mexico. The reason this happened gets us back to my list idea. When we first started discussing our adventure, we drew up this list of essential requirements for our sabbatical destination:

- *Lifestyle.* Must be able to live and write for 18 months in relative comfort. (This essentially meant having comfortable housing, basic sanitation facilities, child care, and reasonably priced quality food and wine readily available.)

- *Budget.* Must be able to live in the above mentioned relative comfort on $35,000 in savings and $900 a month in rental income without working for at least a full year. (We imagined we might need to work after the year was up to sustain us for the remaining months of our trip, but we didn't plan to work unless absolutely necessary.)

- *Kid Friendly.* Must be someplace where children are welcomed and enjoyed.

• *Language.* Must be someplace where English is not the first language.

• *Technology.* Must be hooked up to the Internet or at least offer Internet access without great difficulty.

• *Climate.* Must be someplace with year-round warmth that never gets too hot or humid.

• *Accessibility.* Must be located someplace friends and family can visit with relative ease.

• *Schools/Medical Facilities.* Must have adequate schools, day-care options, and medical facilities.

In retrospect, I would add one more thing to the list because this item proved to have the greatest impact on our lives abroad overall . . .

• *Pedestrian Friendly.* Should be small enough and/or offer enough cheap mass transportation that a car isn't necessary on a daily basis.

Depending on your priorities and goals, your family's sabbatical requirements might be profoundly different. Perhaps you could care less about learning another language or what the weather is like. Maybe living close to an ocean or a university is an essential requirement for you. Maybe you'll only consider a destination that will welcome your pet (see below). The important thing is to sit down with your family and create your list before starting the process of choosing your sabbatical destination.

"We wanted a small enough city to be able to get to know it. We feared we'd just be lost in a large city. Besides, we wanted a 'community' type experience for our kids. We

wanted a change from mass society USA. However, we didn't want it so small that we'd go bonkers. A city of 100,000 with a university would be perfect." — Marline

What About Fluffy?

If you have pets, you'll obviously have to decide whether you want to be able to bring them along on your sabbatical, which will, in turn, affect your choice of destination. Pet entry requirements vary country by country. Some countries quarantine all incoming animals for up to six months. Some don't admit certain breeds of dogs. And some cultures or communities don't have a tradition of companion animals and may react oddly if you choose to bring along a pet. In the Middle East, for example, dogs are not perceived as house-pets. Other countries are pet friendly but lack the necessary resources to care for pets responsibly. Consider whether veterinary care, medicines, and pet supplies will be readily available, and be alert to health concerns affecting animals abroad that aren't issues for your pet back home. If you can't drink the water in your sabbatical destination, neither can your pet. You'll want to make sure your pet has purified or otherwise safe drinking water available and doesn't drink from puddles or toilets around the house.

Consider, too, that sterilization, preventive check-ups, and vaccinations may not be available or affordable for the general pet population, which could put your own pet at risk. San Miguel de Allende, Mexico, for example, is a very pet-friendly city. But it has a stray dog population of 15,000 and one of the highest incidences of rabies in the region. You'll also want to think about how your pet is likely to react to hazardous critters in its environment. A tussle with a scorpion or a black widow isn't fun for anyone.

Thinking about these issues may give you pause, but they needn't deter you from bringing your beloved pet along so long as your sabbatical destination welcomes pets (see *Chapter 5: Get Ready, Get Set . . .*). Having the family pet at your side can make your sabbatical more fun and can even help break the ice when meeting new friends. We know many families who brought their pets on their sabbaticals without much difficulty (especially if they drove to their destinations). It's simply important to be aware of the issues when you are choosing your sabbatical destination.

Communications

One criterion that will definitely influence where to live abroad is your ability to maintain easy communication with everyone back home. If you're conducting business while living abroad or have a lot of financial details to attend to, you'll need to locate in a city that provides fast and reliable Internet service to your home, offers overnight package delivery and predictable mail service, and allows you to send and receive faxes. If your communication needs are less rigorous and an occasional jaunt to an Internet café will suffice, then your options for living abroad are that much wider.

The Possibilities Are (thankfully) Not Endless

Given our family's general interests and list of requirements, the areas of the world that initially attracted us were Europe and Central America. We'd traveled extensively in Europe, and between Michael and me, we spoke two European languages. The culture wasn't too different from our own and none of the requirements on our list presented a problem except one, our budget. France, Italy, and Spain immediately dropped off the list of possibilities after I spent a few days on the Internet looking at the basic costs of lodging, food, and airplane tickets. It became obvious that we wouldn't be able to swing six months in any of those countries with our paltry budget, much less a year. Not unless we abandoned the idea of not working during our sabbatical.

Well, that was a possibility, but it really moved us away from one of our prime motivations for this trip: the opportunity to live a creative life for at least a year unhindered by the pressures of work. So we turned our sights to Portugal. It was still Europe, but it was the least touristed, the cheapest, and somehow the most mysterious European country on our list. We'd never been there and we didn't know anyone who'd ever lived there. We got to work immediately researching it.

"Cost was the first criterion. Europe sounded more interesting than Mexico. However, Mexico did offer plenty of history and art, and we could drive instead of fly."

— Karen

Finding Answers to Questions You Don't Have (yet)

There's so much travel information out there that initially it's more a matter of sifting through all the available resources than of tracking down elusive facts and figures. Begin your investigation with a trip to the library and the bookstore. Grab an armful of travel books and a cup of coffee and start reading. When something strikes your fancy, jot it down in your sabbatical notebook for follow-up later. Check the bibliographies for specific titles about ideas and places you're becoming more interested in. Hit the Internet and start checking travel chat boards, blogs, and websites for factual information, opinions, and links to other sites about specific cities and countries around the globe. Talk with friends, acquaintances, and even strangers standing next to you in the grocery line about their various travel adventures. People love to talk about places they've been to, especially places they love (or hate).

Michael was chatting with an old friend about our newest destination idea, Portugal, and it turned out his friend's family had an amazing (abandoned) vacation home located in the Algarve, Portugal's sunny southern coast. For an exciting two weeks, before the whole deal fell through, we spun dreams about spending the chilly Minnesota winter perched on a Portuguese cliff in a house with a pool and private garden. Not long after that dream fizzled, Michael found out through the grapevine at work that a colleague had spent two weeks in Portugal with his family the previous Christmas. Michael emailed him out of the blue, took him to lunch, and debriefed him over sushi. His colleague raved about an ancient university town in the north of Portugal called Coimbra. That really whetted our appetite and gave us a specific city (other than Lisbon) to focus on. We loved the idea of living in a university town and I contacted various university language programs in Minnesota and Wisconsin to see if I could talk with anyone about Coimbra with the specific goal of getting information on lodging and living costs.

I didn't have a speck of luck finding anyone who knew anything about Coimbra, but from my general research we figured we could initially splurge on a house in the Algarve for the winter, and then head north to Coimbra as it warmed up. We knew it was cheaper and less touristed the further north you went, and we didn't think we'd have any problem finding someplace to live. We ordered some Portuguese language CD-ROMs and laughed ourselves silly trying to learn the alphabet and how to count to ten. Our plans began to solidify and I roamed the Internet for good deals on lodging in the Algarve. I had a series of increasingly unpleasant emails with a woman in New York who advertised her vacation home for $400 a week and then, the old bait and switch, upped the price to $600 a week because we weren't staying "long term." I eventually understood that "long term" was always longer than your intended stay.

> *"We had visited Barcelona a few times before and knew it was a great city. We felt for the ages of our children it was important they be in an international school, so that cut out smaller cities. Our older son studies bass and we connected with a teacher there. The food and architecture are beautiful. It was better located than Madrid for visiting other places in Europe."* — Frances and Steve, with Henry (11) and John (9), who lived in Barcelona for 13 months

Decide on Your Bottom Line

By now it was September. We were planning to leave right after New Year's and I was starting to get into the nitty-gritty of preparations. I wrote the Portuguese consulate for visa applications for our intended long-term stay. They responded promptly with impossibly difficult and detailed application forms requesting information about our reasons for spending a year plus there, where we would be living, how we would be financing our stay, and so on. We needed medical forms, police forms, school records, and extensive financial records proving we could support ourselves there without working. All of this had to be typed, notarized, and then sent back for translation into Portuguese by consulate officials. For each page of translation, we would be charged $25. We figured that when all was said and done, our application forms would total around 50 pages for our entire family. So even before paying the cost of the visa itself (which would run about $600 for our family), we would be required to spend more than $1,000 just to have the application translated! Add to that the cost of plane tickets and the fact that even though it's the cheapest European country to live in, it's still Europe and not exactly cheap, and we started to have second and third thoughts.

We knew we could swing it financially but only if we lived in some tiny apartment and fretted about every dime and dollar. Suddenly, the whole thing started to sound like work instead of fun. We didn't want to set ourselves up for a bad time or one that we had to cut short because we'd run out of money. So, just a few months before we were slated to leave, we found ourselves destination-less once again.

Our experience is a good example of why it's so important to remain open to unforeseen problems and possibilities that will present themselves during your search process. Opening your lives to the unforeseen is central to the idea of a family sabbatical abroad. And on a more practical note, if you get fixed on something and it falls through, it could drive you nuts!

We briefly considered moving to India at this point. I had been working with Indian colleagues for several years and Indian culture and food had always intrigued us. Our money would certainly have gone a long way there. But after some discussion we ruled it out for several reasons: the long plane ride over with a two-year-old, our concerns about the availability of adequate medical care, and mostly because picking up Urdu or Hindi wasn't something that we could really sink our teeth into. We examined our list once again and turned our sights to Central and South America.

"Rich wanted to live in a Latin American country because of a love of Hispanic culture and music and an interest in what's in our backyard. We had friends and family members who had spent time in Ecuador and had good reports. And we looked at the relative stability of the country. Despite there being a new government every two years, Ecuador is pretty calm." — Tani and Rich, with Kira (16), Ellen (14), David (12), and Jack (10), who lived in Quito, Ecuador, for a year

"There were times I thought during planning that it would be nice to be in a smaller city where you could really get connected and feel like you had a handle on the place. But the considerations of school won out. We considered South America too, but several countries where we wanted to visit (Venezuela, Argentina) were not particularly stable at that point." — Frances

Why We Chose Mexico

We began looking south of the border because a number of our friends had spent time there in the past few years and most of them had really liked it. One family we knew had had an awful time in Ecuador but we chalked that up to the family's lack of planning and travel expertise rather than the country. No one we knew had stayed without working for as long as we planned to, and no one we knew had kids as young as Asher (he was two when we left). But we knew it was completely doable, and the more research we did, the more we knew we'd found the right area of the world. Now all we had to do was choose the country, the city, find housing and schools . . .

As I've said, the whole thing can be rather arbitrary. That's why your list of essential requirements is so helpful; it's what finally narrows things down. We ultimately decided on Mexico rather than, say, Ecuador or Guatemala because of our list of requirements. Internet access was a biggie for us. We're writers and we needed reliable online access for research. Plus, it was important for us to be able to stay in touch and manage our money and other financial dealings online. People would be able to visit us in Mexico without too much difficulty or expense, and the climate was a deciding factor. We wanted someplace relatively temperate so we wouldn't have to sweat over our computers or move around constantly trying to escape oppressive heat and bothersome insects.

So in mid-fall, with only a few months remaining before our scheduled departure, I once again scoured the Internet, the library, and bookstores, and talked to everyone we met about life in Mexico. Travel books were quite helpful in providing general information and Internet websites and chat boards were an invaluable source of up-to-date information and opinions about everything under the sun. You can find all sorts of specific, accurate legal information online without making costly telephone calls (see *Resources* for a list of helpful travel websites) and we quickly discovered that Mexico's long-term visa requirements were much less onerous than Portugal's. Best of all, we didn't need to translate the required visa documents into Spanish.

> *"Originally we came to San Miguel in the summers. I discovered it when asking a university professor for his recommendations on immersion programs in Mexico. A school in San Miguel offered summer programs to children as young as two. Once we were here, we fell in love with the smallness of the community, the ease with which you can get around, the beauty of the place, and all the academic opportunities available. I just wish it were closer to an airport because my husband commutes."* — Jody

Ultimately, the most fruitful avenues of research were the spontaneous conversations we had with other people. It was during one of these conversations that a close friend suddenly remembered that her old college roommate's mother had a house in San Miguel de Allende, Mexico. The small hillside town of San Miguel had popped up numerous times during my general research, so I tracked down the college roommate's mother simply to chat about that part of Mexico. Three telephone conversations later she'd convinced us to rent her house in San Miguel for the first six months of our sabbatical. Many people we know had similar experiences with a chance conversation setting them on a path to their sabbatical location. A chat here and there leads you to one thing which leads you to something else, and suddenly, you've got it narrowed down to a couple of potential cities.

One more conversation leads you to someone who knows someone with a house in one of those cities and voila . . . you're on your way. (See *Chapter 4: Finding a Home Away From Home* for more on locating long-term housing.)

All it takes to get going is getting started. So pull out that atlas, make that list, and start talking to people. The world's out there waiting for you.

> *"We wanted to learn Spanish, so we started by looking at Spanish-speaking countries. We were also looking for a place that would be affordable, have a good medical system, and not have too many tourists from the United States. Mexico seemed to be the most reasonable choice from an economic standpoint. We were still undecided, though, when serendipity seemed to take hold. Trusted friends suggested Guanajuato in the highlands of Mexico without hesitation when they heard that we were going to take a sabbatical. Then, in the same week, another friend gave me a book about nearby San Miguel de Allende called 'Living on Mexican Time.' The book really sparked our desire for an adventure. On the Internet, we found a Spanish language school in Guanajuato with apartments for rent. The website also said that there was a nearby elementary school for our children to attend, which really appealed to us. Then to top it off, a Mexican friend of ours in Madison got us in touch with his cousins who live in Guanajuato. Their children attended the same elementary school we had just learned about over the Internet. Because having local contacts was important to us as a way to find our way into the culture, that sealed our decision."* — Julie

How Long Should Your Sabbatical Be?

The length of your sabbatical will depend on a variety of factors including your job situation, available income, school affairs, your family's goals for your sabbatical, and your sabbatical location. Economics will undoubtedly play the largest role in your decision and fortunately, this is an area where there is a tremendous amount of flexibility. It all depends on what your family can live with and without. If you're willing to live with a bit more in terms of daily inconvenience and a bit less in terms of daily luxury, you can live somewhere else for a whole lot longer. The word luxury, however, can be terribly misleading. In San Miguel we lived in two different houses and each was three times the size of our house in Minnesota. A maid came in three times a week. We had gorgeous views, a sunken courtyard garden, and a very relaxed and comfortable lifestyle in terms of material comforts. But of course, we couldn't drink the tap water, we lived with an occasional cockroach and scorpion, and our first house had erratic plumbing. We had to stand in long lines to pay our bills rather than put them in the mail. (Tedious, but a great way to meet the locals and learn how to grumble in a foreign language.) But given those relatively minor inconveniences, we were able to live in beautiful San Miguel de Allende, Mexico, for 18 months very comfortably on our savings and rental income — without working at all. So you can see that it comes down to what your family can live with and what it can live without. You'd be surprised at how quickly and easily everyone adapts to the new surroundings and those petty inconveniences. Making conscious sacrifices in a few nonessential areas can truly mean the difference between taking a 6-month or a 16-month family sabbatical.

> *"It doesn't really feel like we 'chose' where to move. In some ways, what we chose was a travel experience that had a job attached. Although we might not have accepted any job overseas, depending on the location and circumstances, China spoke to us because it was so unknown, so far, so difficult to travel to without a job like this. We wouldn't have even considered undertaking going to China independently."* — Rachel

Staying put means staying longer

Living in one place for the duration of your sabbatical is dramatically less expensive than traveling around. If you intend to do some serious traveling during your sabbatical, the costs for transportation, meals, and lodging will affect your budget significantly. In fact, depending on the type of travel you plan to do, it can easily double the cost of your sabbatical. This will obviously impact the amount of time you can afford to take off. So if you want to stay away for a significant period of time, ask yourselves if the sabbatical destination you're considering is a place where you're likely to be comfortable staying for the entire time (with an occasional jaunt away here and there). Or might you be more interested in moving around and experiencing life in a new city every few months? The answer to these questions will help you determine both how long you can stay and where. (See *Chapter 4: Finding a Home Away From Home* for more on this topic.)

Time is money

Job flexibility will also impact the length of your sabbatical. The amount and type of financial flexibility you will have during your sabbatical depends on the kind of job you have, the state of the economy at the time of your departure, your comfort level with the vagaries of the job market, your debt load, the flexibility of your position (and that of your employer), if you can lease your house and how much you can get for it, and how much you're able to squirrel away in savings for your sabbatical. (See *Chapter 6: The Money Thing* for more on financing your adventure.) Michael's company offered him unpaid leave for the duration of our sabbatical but that wouldn't have helped us financially and Michael didn't want to feel pressured to return at any specific time. Since both of us have relatively portable professions, we decided to quit our jobs, feeling confident that we could always find something to come back to. This may sound radical and it may not fit your life situation at all. The point is to be as thoughtful and as open as possible regarding your job options. You may be surprised at how flexible an employer is willing to be if you're willing to do some bending as well. And as it turned out, I was laid off a couple months before we left.

> *"Steve was teaching Internet courses for the university back home. This was a great way to avoid the hassle of finding a local job, which would have been very difficult. His students in the States never knew he wasn't in the country."*
>
> — Frances

"Marc and I had to ask for leaves of absence from our jobs. Though we both were granted permission to go (and would have quit if they'd refused), we were both the first to receive permission to do something like this at each of our workplaces. It was a big hurdle." — Julie

How long is long enough?

The answer to this question really depends on your family's goals. Six months may sound like a long time to live abroad but quite honestly, it's not. If learning a second language is one of your priorities, you'll need a sabbatical of a year or longer. Any shorter, and you may be surprised and disappointed at how relatively little you and your kids will come home with in terms of language acquisition. This may surprise you, but in our experience and that of many other families we've spoken with, this is definitely the case. (For more discussion on this topic, see *Chapter 8: School Daze Part Two*.)

It's also very difficult to really live in your new home if your sabbatical is too short. The first month or two of living abroad is spent getting to know the place and learning to relax and slow down. The next month or two is spent "not living" back home but not quite actually "living" in your new home. By month four or so, you're finally living where you are, making new friends, and digging into new projects. So you can see that if your sabbatical is only six months long, the remaining two months are going to fly by, and much of that time, you'll be looking at where you're headed rather than where you are.

Of course the reality is that you and your family will benefit no matter how long your sabbatical. You'll just have to adjust your goals accordingly and be realistic about how much you can do in the time you have available.

"We had only five months because we did this on unpaid leave. Our sense was that if you want to become fluent, seven months is about the minimum. At four months you feel you're really breaking in and three months to practice and reinforce would be ideal. If we had it to do over, we'd try to figure out a way to stay a complete school year. It

was sad to leave just as things were starting to come together and friendships were established. However, we gained enormously from the five months, and many people just don't have the luxury of more time. You get what you can get. The nice thing about choosing Mexico is that it's not that far to come back to for shorter stays."

— Marline

"I would suggest staying the entire school year. My kids did not allow themselves to get totally involved, knowing we were leaving after Christmas. They also didn't master the language in the way we had hoped, because we only stayed one semester."

— Karen

Additional Considerations — When to Leave and Return

One other thing to consider is when it makes the most sense to leave for your sabbatical and when to return. Take into account things like job cycles, sabbatical goals, the school year (at home and where you are headed), the seasons, combining your sabbatical with vacations, tax ramifications, and seasonal airfares. The primary reason our family's departure date was January 15, 2002, is that Michael needed to work up until January 1 to receive his yearly bonus. This money was critical for our sabbatical and we definitely timed our departure around it. We also wanted to miss two Minnesota winters! We didn't want to come back from our warm and wonderful Mexican sabbatical only to land in four feet of snow. (How depressing!) So our stay had to be either shorter or longer than a year if we were leaving in mid-January. In addition, we factored in the way the school year works in Mexico as well as the needs and availability of the person who was going to rent our home, to come up with the most logical exit and return dates.

I encourage you to think outside the box. The best departure and return dates for your family's sabbatical are determined by your own unique situation. If a year makes sense, by all means do it. You'll have a blast. But if 14 months is possible, consider that. If you can only take a leave from work for four months, do it. Will your children's school be more flexible if you leave after the first semester? Plan around that.

Will return flights be cheaper in the fall rather than in the summer? Take that into consideration. There's no right or wrong way to do it. Just do it.

3. You're Gonna Do What? Reactions of Friends and Family

"There is a growing familiarity with the way the light falls through the streets at different times of day; the faces of clerks with brooms standing in doorways; the cats that loiter on the roofs and parapets; the feel of cobblestones through my shoes, and the acquired habit of knowing where and when to look so as not to trip or step in shit; the feel of the language in our ears; the warm saturated ochres and the cool cobalt filling in our eyes; the smells of cooking and diesel and cleaning water tossed from buckets and evaporating from the stones . . ."
El Grito #2

When you first mention this notion of yours to move away from your lifelong home and steal away your precious children (grandchildren, nieces and nephews, best friends, cousins, soccer buddies, swim-team leaders, etc.), not everyone will be as intrigued by the idea as you are. Try casually bringing it up at a party or a family gathering and see what happens.

We commonly received two reactions. "What? Are you nuts? Why do you want to do that?" Or "Wow! What a cool idea! I'm so jealous! We've always wanted to do that!" The excited ones used phrases like, "You guys are so brave" and "We've been talking about doing that for years, but you guys are really doing it!" The opposite camp voiced their concerns about us stepping off the career track; our kids falling behind at school; and myriad worries about finances, healthcare, and housing arrangements.

> *"Most of our friends and family thought we were crazy. They didn't see what the big deal was about having our children learn a second language and couldn't imagine why we would want to up and move to another country, of all things! There were, however, a very few who thought what we were doing was fabulous, and for them we seemed inspirational."* — Jody

> *"Most people were supportive; some were wildly enthusiastic. One family even decided to do what we had done after they learned about our experiences. Some older members of our extended families were worried about the economic implications of our decision to leave — and not work — for an extended period of time."* — Julie

The Big Chill

My father thought we were nuts. But he quickly caught family sabbatical fever when he came to visit us in Mexico a couple of months after we left. He had a blast roaming the cobbled streets of San Miguel and listening to the kids try out their Spanish on the fruit vendor in the open-air market. He did catch us off guard one day when he cautiously inquired if everything was OK with our relationship. He said something like, "Friends of mine were wondering whether you'd gone on this trip to try to shore up your marriage." I think Michael and I actually laughed out loud at the idea that a family sabbatical could prove the ideal cure for a rocky marriage. I suppose some people do embark on these types of adventures thinking it will bring them closer together. Usually, however, a sort of "magnifying effect" happens: good relationships get better and shaky relationships get shakier. Even the best relationships undergo tough moments abroad. So I urge you to reconsider embarking on this sort of adventure if your relationship is on the skids. Everyone we know, including ourselves, felt a bit of additional stress on their relationship at times during their sabbatical. (See *Chapter 19: The*

Good, the Bad and the Ugly for more about marital stress.)

My dad's well-meaning query into the health of our marriage was a good reminder that a number of our friends and relatives remained uncomfortable with our decision to spend extended time abroad, even after we'd left.

"Our friends and family thought we were crazy. But we had American friends who had lived in Lucca for a year and we had visited the area before. We knew it was a good size city for a family and was close to a lot of activities as well as to other Italian regions."
— Channing, who moved with her husband Jim and daughter Claire (2 1/2) to Lucca, Italy, for 20 months when she was 7 months pregnant

"Some friends questioned the safety, either fearing that we'd get sick from the food or worrying about kidnappings. Many could not see the appeal of Mexico. They expressed disbelief when we told them we'd be driving three days with three kids, the dog, three bikes, and a trailer."
— Kim

No matter how diligently or patiently you try to put your loved ones at ease, some people will perceive your sabbatical as foolhardy or downright dangerous. You'll encounter many who are not in the least excited or jealous about an adventure of this type. In fact, they're profoundly relieved that it's you and not they who are going. The whole idea makes them so uncomfortable that they can't even discuss it.

One of my closest friends shut down completely and refused to discuss any part of our plans with me. This is a woman I chat with every day about our kids, recipes, worries, the weather. It's not that she ever came out and said, "I don't ever want to talk about this thing you're going to do with your family." It's just that she never once brought it up. No questions, no comments, no excitement. At first, I was oblivious to her discomfort and blithely reported our latest trial or tribulation: "You won't believe how much the Portuguese embassy wants to translate visa documents from English to Portuguese!" She'd just sort of stare at me blankly and wonder out loud why a neighbor down the street was watering her lawn when it was obviously going to rain later.

I couldn't figure out what was going on until I realized that the whole idea of packing away all your belongings and trooping off with your husband and kids to another country was truly her idea of a living hell. It's not that she lacks imagination or curiosity about the world. It's just that her soul doesn't cry out for that kind of adventure; there is nothing innately intriguing or even interesting about it for her. I also think her disinterest was a way of protecting herself from the pain of saying goodbye to us.

It was a bit unsettling not having someone so close to me excited about our trip when I was jumping out of my skin. But it was also a bit of a relief to spend time with someone who never asked about it. I'd walk over to her house knowing that we'd be discussing the kids or what was for dinner rather than whether the peso was moving up or down against the dollar.

"My family was fairly enthused until I told them we were putting our kids in private Mexican schools. When we'd lived abroad as children, we had attended the English-speaking school. My parents were very concerned about the stress and difficulty our kids would have adjusting to a Spanish-speaking school, even though we had picked a bilingual school. My mother (who has traveled to over 150 countries and even drove to Mexico in the 1940s with her mother and aunt) was concerned about whether the kids would like it and very concerned that we were renting our house. She asked, 'What will you do if you decide you don't like it and want to come back early?' I told her part of renting the house was to make the firm commitment that we were going to stay seven months. Our friends either thought it was exciting and said they were envious (about 30% of them) or they thought it was weird and outrageous and just could not relate." — Kim

"People thought it was great that our son would naturally learn a second language. But those who know a bit more about our destination, Guatemala, raised health and safety concerns, especially as our youngest would be just five months old on arrival.

However, people were very supportive and admiring of our plan to work abroad in a poverty relief nonprofit organization. A colleague of Ward's even arranged to come out for three weeks to assist with the project, with financial support from his firm, which also gave Ward some financial support."

— Sarah and Ward, with Saskia (5 months) and Zeb (4),
who moved to Antigua, Guatemala, for a year

Rebellion on the Home Front

And let's not forget about the reactions of those living under your very own roof. Don't be surprised if your kids or your spouse are initially a bit cool to the idea of your family sabbatical. You may have to spearhead the effort yourself at first until everyone understands that you are really serious about doing this. Eventually, your infectious excitement will win them over despite their concerns or hesitation about embarking on this crazy adventure of yours.

"Our middle son Kyle (11), who doesn't like change and is very close to his friends, was devastated that we were leaving for seven months. He reminded us that he got homesick on a two-week vacation. In contrast, our oldest, Drew (13), was very excited even though he was the one who would be giving up the most: Middle School Jazz Band, his own growing rock band, eighth grade graduation, and the eighth grade trip to Washington, D.C. He even wondered whether seven months was long enough. Derek, our-nine-year-old, was excited when he saw Drew's reaction and scared when he saw Kyle's." — Kim

Enlisting Allies on the Ground

Once you've announced your plans and gotten a sense of which of your loved ones are allies and which you'll just have to let come around on their own, it's time to get organized. You need to sit down with a One-Year Countdown List (see *Chapter 5: Get Ready, Get Set . . .*) and figure out which items you'll need help with and who among your friends and family can provide it. Don't hesitate to involve them in your adventure. Most will love to be asked to contribute in some way. Whether it's helping to find a temporary home for an animal, forwarding your mail, or planning your family's goodbye party, many friends and relatives will eagerly offer their services. Knowing they're helping make your trip easier in some small way lets them live your dream vicariously.

4. Finding a Home Away From Home
Be It Ever So Humble . . .

"We've found a lovely house on the outskirts of town in a very Mexican neighborhood (grittier and more desolate—though we prefer to think of it as more authentic) called Colonia Independencia. The house we're living in now is gorgeous and we'll especially miss the lush courtyard and sunken garden (at the moment we've got a white Bird of Paradise blooming among all the orchids, amaryllis, and calla lilies—we didn't even know there was such a thing!), not to mention the handful of scorpions and museum-quality cockroaches we've encountered and dispatched in a variety of heartless ways. But we're looking forward to living among more Mexicanos and speaking more español on a daily basis. The new hacienda is a three-story, three-bedroom, three-bath house with two studio/writing/guest rooms, an autonomous little casita out back, and a roof deck with a cantina and industrial-sized barbecue from which there are sweeping views of the desert and mountains to the west, and the most picturesque part of San Miguel to the east, laid out in all its glory, climbing the hillside to which most of it clings."   El Grito #3

Once you have a sense of the city you'll be moving to, it's time to think about finding a place to live for at least the initial leg of your sabbatical. There are two primary strategies to consider when locating a house or an apartment to rent abroad. One is to find a short-term rental (for a month or so) and look around for something longer-term once you arrive. The other is to rent something long-term and hope for the best. In either case, the Internet is probably the best place to start.

You can usually get a fairly good sense of what's available in your price range on the Web and begin to gather information about your sabbatical city in general, getting an idea of its various neighborhoods and finding out where parks and other amenities are located in the town. You'll find listings for short- and long-term vacation rentals in your chosen city on a variety of Internet sites, including bulletin boards for specific regions of a country, vacation-lodging sites, sites sponsored by the local chambers of commerce and realtors, and sites targeting tourists interested in a specific area.

Tip: Even if you don't plan to rent something with five bathrooms and a pool, it can be a ton of fun to check out the photographs on these sites to drool over all the properties you couldn't afford in a million years.

Be aware, however, that no matter how humble your housing requirements, booking a rental property over the Internet can be an expensive way to go. Individuals or companies with the education and funds to advertise on the Net typically charge a lot more than those who don't have the wherewithal to use the Web commercially. Booking a rental over the Web also means you're committing to something sight unseen, and you really can't be too careful when committing to something from afar. Despite that lovely description and those carefully chosen photos, a "charming, cozy living room" might be a couch and chair pushed into a large closet. So if you do find a listing online (or through a classified ad) and you don't plan to visit the city beforehand to actually see the property, it usually makes sense to commit to something relatively short term. That way you have the option of extending your lease or finding something else when it is up.

Finding Housing for the Short-Term

You'll find listings for short-term lodging, such as hotel rooms, rental apartments, and rental homes, on the Internet and in the classified section of larger U.S. and foreign newspapers. Sometimes you'll also hear about them through word of mouth.

Home exchanges

If your sabbatical is very short, say three months or less, or you want to experience your sabbatical country by moving from place to place during an extended stay, you might consider a home exchange. That's provided you live someplace that's considered relatively desirable. (Our Minnesota home in mid-January didn't qualify.) A short-term home exchange can be a good way to minimize your sabbatical costs because you don't have to lease a home abroad.

Generally speaking, the way a home exchange works is that you pay to become a member of a service (online or via snail mail) that allows you to list your home and to access the listings of other members' homes in cities all over the globe. You communicate directly with the owners of the homes you're interested in to inquire about availability, references, and so on.

I've heard of many families having good experiences with home exchanges. Since both parties in an exchange open their homes to strangers, each tends to be respectful of the other's property and the agreements they've made. That said, it's obviously important to check references carefully and have a very clear understanding regarding the use of one another's vehicles, recreational equipment, and the like before exchanging homes. You also need to feel comfortable with the ideas of opening your home up to people you've never met and living in a stranger's house without really being able to make it your own.

Note: The greatest potential downside of a home exchange is that, should you change your mind about wanting to move around during your sabbatical, you're locked in. (See "Other Useful Internet Sites: Accommodations" in *Resources* for some home exchange sites.)

"The Internet was great for looking over neighborhoods and getting an idea of prices, etc. We were able to narrow in on a few areas that would be close to the kids' school,

close to the metro, and close to parks. We were fortunate to be connected with a family from our town who had done the same thing the year before (and overlapped with us by a month). So we got their realtor's name and set up appointments to see some apartments in the areas we'd targeted." — Frances

In addition to searching the Internet, there are a number of options for researching housing abroad:

• ***Realty agents.*** Most towns of any size have at least one real estate agency. It can be very helpful to contact someone there and ask if they know of any rentals. They won't provide this service for free, of course, but usually the price isn't too steep. In fact, it may be much cheaper than finding something over the Internet. Working with a realtor also offers a terrific advantage: you'll see things you might otherwise miss. You can contact realty companies online beforehand to let them know your price and lodging requirements, length of stay, and your arrival dates. Armed with this information, a realtor can scout ahead and show you neighborhoods and properties around the city it would take you months to find on your own.

• ***Expats.*** Contacting expats online is another terrific way of locating short- and long-term housing. Search the web for bulletin boards for your destination city and post a query with your dates, price, and the type of housing you're looking for. You might be surprised at the number of replies you receive. You can also ask expats living in your destination city to send you copies of the classified section of the local newspaper.

Tip: Sometimes, you can access the local English-language newspaper online and scour the classifieds from the comfort of your own living room. Many cities abroad have such papers in one form or another.

• ***Location scouts.*** If you have the funds, paying a visit to your destination city to scout the location is a good way to go. Once on the ground, you can work with a realtor and also check bulletin boards in coffee shops, universities, tourist offices, ice cream shops, grocery stores, libraries, rec centers, and other tourist gathering spots for offers of available lodging. If you're lucky enough to find something you like during a scouting expedition, be aware that what you see may not always be exactly what you get once you arrive with your family. Friends of ours rented a furnished house for a year in San Miguel that they'd found during a pre-sabbatical visit. They'd walked through it, checked the kitchen cabinets, the mattresses, and so on, and felt confident about signing a rental agreement and handing over a damage deposit plus the first and last month's rent. Three months later, they arrived with bags carefully packed based on what had been in the house during their earlier visit — only to find that it had been stripped bare during the intervening months. No dishes, no silverware, no mattresses . . . nothing. None of these items, which they'd considered basic to a furnished house, had been specifically written into the rental agreement. The landlord eventually agreed to provide most of the things they needed and allowed them to deduct from the rent the cost of the kitchenware and assorted miscellaneous items they hurriedly bought. But they certainly hadn't counted on having to shop for silverware and drinking glasses on their first day in a brand new city.

Tip: The definition of "furnished" and "unfurnished" varies widely in cities around the world. Sometimes a "furnished" house or apartment may not even come equipped with appliances. So even if it feels uncomfortable, discuss the smallest details of your stay with your prospective landlord before signing the lease to make certain your expectations match.

"We had an apartment lined up for the first few months, so in the short-term we were fine. However, we realized quickly that there were plenty of regulations in Italy and getting around them is the trick to getting anything done (a phone hook-up, buying a car, renting a house, opening a bank account). It was important to have an Italian on your side if you wanted to get anything done, and it didn't help that we didn't speak much Italian!" — Channing

Talk Is Cheap (or can be if you get lucky)

If you can't send someone ahead to secure lodging and everything you find on the Net is simply too expensive, talk to everyone you run into back home about your plans. Share your dreams with perfect strangers. Post ads in language departments at nearby universities and colleges; maybe a visiting scholar will be able to help you figure something out or at least give you someone to contact in their hometown. Try contacting the local tourist offices and universities in the town you want to move to. They often have listings of possible rentals. Ask everyone you meet if they know of anyone currently living in your sabbatical destination — or even someone who once lived there. Over and over again, we've heard of people locating the perfect house or apartment by mentioning their search to someone who, it turned out, had a friend or relative living near their sabbatical destination.

Another Strategy — Wait Till You Arrive

If you can't afford to visit first, have trouble locating anything that sounds suitable, or simply don't feel comfortable signing a lease on a property you haven't walked through, you could rent yourselves a hotel room for the first couple weeks of life in your new city and start looking around once you get there. This may not be the ideal situation, however. It's hard to get to know a city that quickly and you'll be feeling pressured to find something you can call home, even if it may not be exactly what you're looking for. Be aware that it may be cheaper in the long run to fork over the big bucks to rent a "vacation house" for a month (living it up while you've got it) and then take your time about finding your permanent digs.

> *"My advice for families relocating to a foreign city is to find someone who has been there and question them about what you want to know. People who actually went through immigration, drove the same route we were planning to drive, and so on, were far more helpful than websites. When we were planning our move, they were our*

most valuable resources. If you don't know someone from where you are going, start with the real estate rental offices. They were a good source for me in finding people to connect with." — Jody

Furnished or Unfurnished?

We toyed with the notion at one point of renting an unfurnished place and quickly thought better of it. While finding a few things at garage sales and the Indian markets is fun, outfitting an entire house or apartment for a limited period of time and then figuring out what to do with everything when you leave is the makings of a nightmare in my opinion. For a bit more money (very little more, really), most of the furnished places we saw (or read about) came with nearly everything we needed. We knew it would be very easy to find the dishtowels, colander, and coffeepot that were lacking.

But we were lucky; we had a choice. San Miguel is a "snowbird" destination with an enormous number of furnished rentals that cater to the annual influx of retirees wintering south of the border. In many cities it can be difficult or even impossible to find furnished rentals.

If you have the choice, think hard about it. It's important for a lot of reasons. Depending on where you're planning to live, finding furniture, appliances, kitchenware, linens, and all the rest can be fun and easy or downright impossible. In Mexico, the latter was the case; the affordable appliances were of lousy quality and the name brands were at least twice the cost of those in the States. Transportation is another issue. For example, we didn't have a car and so finding housewares and dragging them home on the bus or in cabs was a pain. And then there is the problem I mentioned before of having to dispose of the furnishings when you leave.

If you do decide to rent an unfurnished place (or have no choice), just be aware that your assumptions about fixtures and so on may not match your new reality. In some places, unfurnished means no stove, refrigerator, lighting, or even ceiling fixtures. Walk through the place so that you have an accurate idea of just how unfurnished it really is.

Make sure you understand the situation with utilities. It's very common in Mexico and in other Latin American countries, for example, for residences not to have phone lines or to share lines with other houses and apartments. Also inquire about the availability of potable water and water in general. In some places, water is available to particular parts of a city only at specific times each day and it may or may not be potable.

If you decide to rent a furnished place, imagine your family really living in the place before you commit to it. Friends of ours couldn't believe their luck when they found a gorgeous furnished house for rent in their price range that belonged to an elderly expat couple who had spent their lives collecting exquisite Japanese pottery. It was an incredible deal and our friends were tempted to grab it. Then they asked themselves if they really wanted to spend seven months living with their three- and six-year-olds in a place with a white carpet and fine china. If you do happen upon something incredible, just make sure those collector-quality vases are stored out of the reach of your budding kung-fu artist's feet. And don't be so wowed by your potential new home's décor or amazing views that you forget to do a thorough check of the water pressure, electrical outlets, and other basic utilities before committing to the property. It's going to be a bit harder to really enjoy your new home away from home if you're constantly looking for a plumber to repair a backed-up toilet.

Tip: Take pictures of every room and any major pieces of furniture before you unpack. That way when you move out, there'll be no confusion about whether that crack in the kitchen table was there before you took up residence.

Longer Can Be Cheaper (and other tips for lowering the rental cost)

You can almost always work a better deal rent-wise by committing for the longer term because people who lease houses and apartments love stable tenants. So once you find a place you're comfortable committing to for six months or longer, press your advantage. In exchange for your long-term commitment, ask for $50 off each month's rent.

Does the city you're going to be living in have a high season and a low season? Search for your place during low season and you'll always get a better deal. San Miguel, for example, rocks between December and April. By May, everyone's gone and places are sitting empty all over town. Landlords are practically giving the houses away. Plan your arrival accordingly. In Europe, spring is the start of high season. You'd be better off arriving in the fall to find the best deals there.

The Comforts of Home

It can be hard to imagine living without your houseful of belongings — your artwork, your photographs, your carefully tended houseplants and beloved pots and pans. However, you may actually be quite surprised at what you can get along without during your sabbatical and even more surprised by how wonderful it feels to live with less of everything you've considered essential. Not that you have to live in a sensory deprivation tank, but traveling light and streamlining your existence will help open you up to the world of possibilities around you. It can also help to clarify which things are indispensable and which merely serve to clutter or distract your family from the truly essential things in your lives.

Be aware that border requirements will have a significant impact on what you'll be able to bring along. Some countries strictly limit the importation of specific items such as electronics and housewares. You can find the customs and import regulations for most countries on the Internet. Once you have a good idea of what you're legally allowed to bring with you, decide as a family on the things you absolutely must have to make your home away from home comfortable and fun. Then be prepared to cut your list in half. The list might include things like music equipment, toys, a VCR/DVD player, a television, coffeemaker, sports equipment, books, videos, and DVDs. (See *Chapter 5: Get Ready, Get Set . . .* for much more on packing and preparations.) Separate the items you want to bring along into "basic necessities" and "nice to haves" and then see what you ultimately have room for. (Is Sega really a necessity? If it's the difference between sanity and a year of whining, it is. Find a way to bring it.) Obviously, your mode of travel will have a significant impact on what you'll be able to tote along.

You will usually be able to buy what you need overseas. If there are specific brands or "essentials" that you're not sure will be available, bring along a one-month supply and look into it when you arrive. You can always ask a friend or relative to bring or send a care package of specific items if there are certain things you ultimately can't locate overseas.

If you're planning to drive to your sabbatical destination, it's tempting to stuff everything you can think of into the car and hope you don't have to open the trunk and/or car-top carrier until you get there. Friends of ours drove the three-day journey from Chicago to San Miguel with three boys, a large dog, and a trailer packed to the gills with bikes, a Sega Genesis, a television set, several computers, sports equipment, and a variety of other essentials. They had no problems getting everything across the border and they used everything they brought along. But on the return leg their trailer seemed to have shrunk a few sizes. (Perhaps it was all that Mexican pottery they bought during their stay.) In the end, they were faced with leaving many of their favorite things behind or paying astronomical rates to ship things home. The moral here is to pack light on the front end to save room for all those inevitable treasures you'll acquire along the way.

Another reason to limit what you bring along is that you can't really be sure what your housing situation will provide until you get there. If you rent a furnished place you might very well have access to a television, VCR, and other "luxuries." And keep in mind that many countries have electrical standards and transmission and broadcast systems different from those at home, which will render your electronics useless unless you are prepared with the necessary converters, transformers, and adapters. So check the country's electrical requirements first. (See *Chapter 9: Is Anyone Out There?* for more specifics.) It might make more sense just to wait and buy what you need after you arrive.

Tip: If you decide to wait and purchase items abroad, departing expats can be excellent sources for those appliances, electronics, and other large or bulky items that are difficult to travel with. Most expats are glad to hand off these things at a very reasonable cost. Other good places to check for used appliances and equipment include classified ads in local papers, university and coffee shop bulletin boards, and bulletin boards in supermarkets and bus and train stations.

Bargaining Power

If you plan to buy appliances and electronics abroad, you might be able to use your purchases as negotiating opportunities with potential landlords. The first house we lived in had a washing machine but no dryer. This was fine since there was a convenient roof deck with a laundry line and sun all day long to dry everything. The second house we moved into didn't have either a washing machine or a clothes dryer. Our new landlord told us that his renters usually just sent their laundry to the dry cleaners. This wasn't an affordable or practical solution for our family with two young children and very few clothes in our suitcases. So we offered to buy a washing machine for the house if our landlord agreed to split the cost of it and pay for the plumbing hook-up. We would use it while we lived there and he would own it once we moved out. He loved the idea. He knew he could charge more in rent in the future if he had a washing machine available to his renters and, unlike him, we had the cash to buy the washing machine up front.

Mexico is a cash-only society. There's little buying on credit, which makes purchasing larger items very difficult for many Mexicans. By paying for the cost of the washing machine up front, we ended up helping our landlord in the long run and saving ourselves a ton of money and hassle in the short run. We worked a number of similar deals in that second house and our landlord immediately recognized every opportunity as the win-win situation that it was. We split the cost of having the neighborhood ironmonger make and install beautiful stairway railings in the rather dangerous three-story stairwell that existed when we arrived. The house was a safer place during our stay and a more attractive place when we left.

Tip: By looking for creative opportunities when it comes to housing and creature comforts, it's possible to save yourselves some cash, provide some "luxuries" during your sabbatical, and provide lasting benefits to friends and acquaintances. For example, we bought a cheap used refrigerator to augment the tiny apartment-sized one in our second house. At the end of our stay, we gave it away to a friend whose only responsibility was to come and get it. Another win-win. We didn't have to worry about getting rid of it and our friend got a free refrigerator in reasonable condition.

San Miguel sits in the arid highlands of Mexico at 6,300 feet above sea level. Most houses lack insulation or heat in the winter and are without fans or another cooling source during the brief but hot and windy months of April and May. During our 18 months there, we bought a few small comfort items including a fan and an electric blanket. At the end of our stay, we gave these and a few other things to our maid, Josephina, who had very little in the way of money or comfort in her life. Josephina cried when we gave her our gifts and with much emotion told us that, in her whole life, she'd never owned a fan, an electric blanket, or even an electric coffeemaker. These items, rather small and inconsequential for us, made enormous differences in the lives of our Mexican friends in San Miguel.

Moving Around vs. Staying Put

I've already mentioned that staying in one place for your sabbatical makes sense financially because you don't incur all the travel costs related to moving around and you can almost always work a better deal on a long-term lease. But let's say your family intends to live in several different cities or regions during your sabbatical. You're not planning to live the nomadic life exactly but you want to experience the rhythms of life abroad in a variety of locales, six months here and six months somewhere else.

That's exactly what we'd originally planned for our sabbatical. We anticipated living in San Miguel for six months and then moving to the nearby university town of Guanajuato for our remaining year abroad. Every bit of pre-trip research we did was based on that plan, and we lived for several months in San Miguel with that intention. However, about six weeks before our six-month lease was due to expire, we found ourselves rethinking our plan drastically, based on everything we'd learned about our family, our goals, and life with kids abroad. Some of our initial priorities had shifted and some had dropped off the map entirely.

Going into this adventure, moving around seemed to make sense and was a source of great excitement to us. But one of our central priorities was writing. As our projects progressed, our desire to pick up and move to a completely new city waned in intensity. We had also underestimated how long it would take our family to settle into a new home and city. We now understood that a move would mean serious disruption to our writing schedule. We'd have to get to know a new city all over again from the ground up, and just getting to know the schools, playgrounds (if there were any), and grocery stores, would take a lot of time away from our main objective, writing.

We had also begun to meet interesting people and our kids had started to develop some bonds with teachers and friends. We wanted to let their newfound sense of independence in a new culture and language continue to grow without forcing them to start over again in a different city. We'd finally gotten a good sense of the schools and had made plans to switch our kids to different schools for the upcoming school year. Many of the expats we met were, like us, staying for only a short time — six months or a year. We had said quite a few hellos and goodbyes during our first few months in San Miguel, but some expats we met were staying longer and we'd started building some promising friendships. We weren't excited by the idea of rushing off and letting them languish.

So we decided to stay in San Miguel but to move outside of the downtown area, which, to our way of thinking, had too many tourists and too many opportunities to speak English. We moved to a very Mexican neighborhood about a 15-minute walk from the central square. By doing this we accomplished several important things. We were surrounded by Spanish-speakers, so we had to speak Spanish more often. The rents were significantly cheaper, so we cut our monthly rent payment nearly in half. Most significantly, we had a whole new area of the city to explore. We'd almost forgotten, just in that short six-month period, how exciting that sense of newness is. By simply plopping ourselves down in a different area of town, we were able to experience it all over again. It wasn't, of course, the same as arriving in a completely new city with that magical daylong sense of discovery. But it was enough to reenergize us and open our eyes to a completely different area of the city and the people who live there.

The Best Laid Plans Change

Your family's overall plan and goals may be completely different from ours, but you will undoubtedly encounter moments when you question your original plans about where to live or what to do next. You may wonder if exploring a particular region or country is more important than digging into a community and establishing more serious relationships with the people around you. You'll also have to gauge how well your family adapts to change. How did everyone do with the initial move? What kind of adventure is everyone hungry for at the moment? Does the notion of searching out new schools and grocery stores sound exciting or appalling? Are your kids finally feeling settled and establishing some bonds with the locals (or other expats)? Or have they had enough of where you are and want to try someplace new? Maybe you've met people with a beach house they're willing to rent. Maybe you've heard about someplace wonderful just down the road that you'd like to try. Or maybe you've struck up a friendship with another family and you're ready to head off together to parts unknown. The point is to remain as open as possible during your time away to changes in "plan."

We were surprised that we chose to stay in the same city for the bulk of our adventure. But it made sense given our key objectives.

Having a relatively clear sense of what your goals are as a family makes an enormous difference in everyone's level of satisfaction. But your goals may change during your adventure. Be open to that. Maybe what you thought was the most important thing becomes the least important. One family we know came to San Miguel determined to learn Spanish. They put the kids in Mexican schools and the parents spent their time in intensive language classes. After six months, they decided they were missing out on too much of everything else in Mexico. They took out a short-term loan over the Internet, pulled the kids out of school, and spent the next three months touring the beach communities in the south. They didn't regret it for an instant.

By all means make a plan and take it seriously, but don't close the door to opportunities that may await you. Plans inevitably change, and really, the only plan worth taking seriously is one that embraces the changes that are bound to happen.

5. GET READY, GET SET . . . YOUR SABBATICAL COUNTDOWN TIMETABLE

"The kids, at times, feel deprived of specific things but they also seem to have a greater overall sense of contentment with what they have. Cleome talks a lot about missing her Beanie babies and, in retrospect, we should have pressured her to bring along a few more toys to populate her room and imaginary worlds. She contents herself reading or playing Zoo Tycoon on the computer. Asher fashions his necessary guns, swords, and arrows from found objects, including sticks, tools, and even pieces of toast on occasion. They both watch an occasional video. I suspect that once we return, unpacking those boxes of toys in the basement will truly feel like discovering buried treasure." El Grito #5

Getting ready for your sabbatical can be enormously exciting and fun if you're organized and can start preparations early enough to remain calm during the inevitable snafus that are part of the process. Preparations include readying yourselves psychologically by setting family goals, reading everything you can find about traveling abroad in the destination you've chosen, and imagining the best — and worst — of what awaits you. Preparing financially is obviously very important and is discussed in detail in the following chapter, *The Money Thing*. But perhaps the most exciting (and overwhelming) aspect of preparing for your sabbatical is sitting down with a list of all the concrete tasks you need to accomplish and figuring out how you're going to get everything done before you go.

The *Sabbatical Countdown Timetable*, below, will help you to research, organize, and complete these myriad tasks. Beginning a year in advance, it will help you count down to that fateful day when you finally hit the road. The list covers everything from how to obtain the necessary legal documents for your family and deciding what to do with your house, your pets, and your belongings to the best way to pack your bags for the adventure that lies ahead. There's a lot to do but every step you take brings you one step closer to your grand exit. So take a deep breath and get ready, get set . . . go!

Sabbatical Countdown Timetable

One Year to Six Months Before Departure

Research and Obtain the Necessary Legal Documentation

• *Check that passports are up to date; submit applications if necessary.*
The first thing to do is to make sure everyone in your family has a valid passport. Be aware that there is no such thing as a family passport in the U.S. Everyone, even the baby, needs a passport to travel abroad. Travel regulations adopted by the U.S. government in the wake of 9/11 require that all air travelers have a valid passport, even if their destination is the Caribbean, Bermuda, Panama, Canada, or Mexico, and all who travel by land or sea to these countries may need a passport as early as January 2008. This is a change from the past when a passport wasn't necessary to travel to or from these countries, whatever your mode of transportation.

Getting a passport is a very straightforward process. You need the application forms, proof of citizenship, passport photos, and the application fee. U.S. citizens can download application forms from the U.S. State Department's site on the Internet (http://travel.state.gov) or get them by mail or at many branch post offices.

All of the information you need to meet the requirements can be found on the site, along with a list of passport agencies, post offices where you can apply for passports (sorted by zip code), and specifics about what you'll need to prove citizenship. In the U.S., that's generally an original birth certificate or an official copy (with watermark) for each person in your family. You'll also need two 2x2-inch passport photos of each applicant taken within six months of your application.

Note: Get a supply of passport-size photos to take with you. You can have passport photos taken at copy shops, drugstores, photo studios, and even some post offices. Get more copies than you think you'll need — six or eight per person is a good number. You'll need these unflattering little photos not only for passports but also for visas and the smattering of official documents you'll inevitably end up needing once you reach your location (think library cards, school IDs, and so on). Passport photos can be pricey, so it pays to call around and compare prices.

• *Applying for a passport.* A person applying for a U.S. passport for the first time, no matter what age, must apply in person. Parents or guardians of minor children must apply in person, with their children present. One parent or guardian will also need to sign the child's passport. To do this properly, print the child's name and then sign his or her name in the appropriate spaces. In parentheses, write (mother), (father), or (guardian) next to the child's name so the passport officials know who signed for the child.

Note: There are special travel requirements for children under the age of 14. American kids under age 14 need the legal consent of both parents and/or guardians to apply for a passport and to travel across U.S. borders. If your child will be traveling with only one parent or legal guardian, check to see whether you will need specific documentation authorizing that person to take the child across the U.S. border. Typically a notarized letter signed by each parent or guardian giving the other permission to take the child out of the country, along with the child's birth certificate, satisfies the requirements.

Tip: Err on the conservative side and apply for your passports about six months before your scheduled departure, especially if you will also be applying for a visa. It can take six to eight weeks to receive a passport, and you can't apply for a visa until you have the passport in your possession. Getting a visa (see below) can take an additional six to eight weeks.

If you already have a valid passport, check its expiration date. Renew it before your departure if it will expire during or soon after your sabbatical. Some countries won't admit foreigners whose passports are set to expire within six months of entry.

Tip: Wherever you're located, use the Internet to research visas, passports, and border crossing requirements. The necessary documents can usually be downloaded to your computer using Adobe Acrobat (free online). Canadians will find information and downloadable forms at www.ppt.gc.ca.

• *Apply for any necessary visas or work permits.* A visa is a document issued by the consulate or embassy of a country giving you permission to visit for a specified purpose and period of time. Depending on the length and destination of your sabbatical, your family may require a long-term visa. Check on this immediately. Most countries require a visa if you will be staying longer than 90 days. Some countries, like Portugal, require a visa for visits longer than 60 days. Most countries require you to get your visa before leaving your home country.

Contact the embassy or consulate of the country you will be visiting to request specific information about its visa requirements. Most foreign embassies and consulates have several locations in the U.S. and Canada and can be accessed online using the search term "Consulate General of [name of country]" or "foreign embassies in [country]." Make sure the consulate or embassy you are dealing with has jurisdiction over your state or province of residence. For example, consulates located in Chicago typically have jurisdiction over states located in the Midwest.

Note: Be forewarned that applying for a visa can be incredibly time-consuming. If you go into it expecting a problem or two, the whole process may feel less painful. (You may not have any problems at all if you're very lucky, but don't count on it.)

Visa applications typically require you to assemble a variety of documents, which you then need to send along with a fee, more passport-sized photos, the application forms, and your passports, to be processed by the consulate. Depending on the type of visa you apply for (see below), additional documents may be required. These can include: notarized statements from the police regarding your criminal record (or lack thereof); a notarized letter from your doctor stating that no one in your family has a communicable disease; proof of immunizations; and bank statements and/or a notarized letter from your banker stating that you have a specific amount of money available to support yourselves during your stay. These documents are relatively easy and inexpensive to obtain. You make a phone call or two to find the right office, make the formal request for the document, and then go to the records department of the central police station, your doctor's office, and/or your bank to pay for and retrieve the notarized documents. Just make sure you emphasize beforehand, when you make your formal request, that the documents must be notarized. Some offices have notaries available only during certain hours or on certain days.

In addition to paying the fees for these documents and the cost of the visa itself (which varies by country but averaged roughly $125 per person as we were going to press), some foreign consulates also require that your documents be translated into the country's native language before they will grant your visas. As we discovered when we did some research on spending our sabbatical in Portugal, translations can be astonishingly expensive. They can also take a long time to complete. Depending on the country, it's also possible that you will have to apply for your visas in person. Following the terrorist attacks in Spain in March 2004, for example, the Spanish government began requiring that all applicants for residence, work, and business visas apply and pick up their visas in person. If you live close to the appropriate consulate, this requirement won't feel too onerous. If, however, you need to travel some distance to the consulate that has jurisdiction over your state or province of residence, you may well start to wonder whose stupid idea this family sabbatical thing was in the first place. I'm not trying to scare you. I'm just giving you fair warning that applying for visas may well be the most frustrating bit of red tape you'll encounter during your sabbatical. That's why it's so important to get an early start on the application process.

> *"I remember writing down a list of things we would need to take care of, and it seemed like the whole idea went from a wonderful dream to a very long 'to do' list in a short period of time. The day I started researching the visa requirements was a real turning point. It seemed that it was quite complex, took a lot of legwork to get the needed paperwork, and there was nobody who would give you a straight answer! Did all of us have to appear at the consulate in Chicago or could one of us go to deliver the papers? Stuff like that. Everything they told us in Chicago from the Spanish consulate was completely dismissed by the immigration authorities once we arrived in Spain; so then we had to re-create all the documentation once we were there. This was clearly the nightmare of the trip — particularly ironic since while legally you need to do all this, on a practical basis, we could have done our year there without any special papers."*
>
> — Frances

• *Types of visas.* There are several different types of visas available depending on your reason for being in a particular country. The type you need will likely come down to how long you plan to stay in the country and whether or not you plan to work there (legally). Tourist visas are generally issued by customs officials at a country's border (and stamped in your passport). Typically, they allow you to remain in the country legally for 90 days or less. Student visas, work visas, and short-term business visas allow you to remain in the country for a longer specified period of time to follow a course of study or engage in legal employment abroad. These visas all require signatures and documents from foreign officials. You have to apply for them ahead of time and then carry them into the country with you. If you are confused about which visa you need or whether you'll even need a visa for your sabbatical trip, email the appropriate consulate for more information.

If you intend to work abroad, bear in mind that applying for and getting an official work visa is a guaranteed headache. The process can take a long time and the visa itself may never materialize. I don't profess to know the legal ins and outs of employment abroad but if you decide to go this route, it's advisable to find employment with a U.S. firm that is already doing business in your sabbatical country. If you will essentially be self-employed, you may be able to skirt the work visa issue if your income is made outside your sabbatical country. Have a good long chat with a tax advisor before you leave to discuss this issue.

If you're not planning to work during your sabbatical, you'll most likely need a general visitor visa, sometimes called a retirement or residence visa. This allows you to live in a country for an extended period of time but does not confer the legal right to work, vote, or receive the majority of financial and medical benefits available to legal citizens. Residence visas generally allow you to remain in a country for one year, at which point you must leave, apply for an extension to your existing visa, or go through the application process again to secure another year-long visa.

Mexican officials issue tourist visas (FM-Ts) at the border that allow you to remain in the country for 90 days if you're traveling by air and 180 days if you're crossing the border by car. All other Mexican visas are best applied for prior to leaving the U.S. (although it is possible to apply for visa extensions while abroad). For our sabbatical, we applied for the FM-3 *visitante rentista* ("retired person") visa that allows visitors to remain in the country for one year without working if they can provide various documents and meet specific income requirements (explained below). This visa also allows the holder to bring in specific household goods and vehicles tax-free. A year is the longest a nonresident can legally remain in Mexico on a "retirement" visa. Since we were staying for a total of 18 months, we knew we would have to revisit the visa issue after our initial year was up.

To apply for the FM-3 visa, we had to get a variety of notarized documents from the police department and our doctors. The stickiest issue by far was that it required us to prove we had $60,000 in income available to us during the one-year visa period. The visa application instructions read: "Applicant must show proof of monthly income equal to $2,000 USD for head of household and an amount equal to half that figure for wife and each of his other dependents." (Welcome to Mexico where all wives are assumed to be dependents.)

Note: Current Mexican FM-3 visa requirements are less onerous, requiring a minimum monthly income of $1,000 for head of household and $500 for each dependent.

Proof of financial solvency is a common requirement for long-term visas. In Spain, for example, you need to provide proof of $75,000 in annual income plus $15,000 per additional person in the family to qualify for a one-year visa.

Since we couldn't legally work under the terms of the FM-3 visa (and didn't plan to), our challenge was to prove a monthly income equal to $5,000 for the first year of our sabbatical. We decided to show that we met the requirement by providing copies of our monthly bank and brokerage statements. We figured that Mexican officials wouldn't look closely at the types of accounts . . . just the total figures. How were they to know that much of that $60,000 was locked away in our IRA accounts?

> *"We flew to Chicago to visit the Italian Consulate to try to get the appropriate visas. The more documents you provided them, the more they wanted, with no end in sight. We finally just gave up!"* — Channing

• *Do you really need visas?* By now you may be wondering just how important visas really are. Is it worth going through the hassle to cross all your t's and dot all your i's to be "legal" visitors to another country? Or could you avoid all that red tape by just entering the country on a tourist visa and hope for the best? I guess the best response I can give is, it depends. It depends on your level of personal comfort with risk. It depends on what your pre-trip research turns up regarding a specific country's entry, exit, and residence requirements. And it depends on the country you'll be living in and what kinds of activities you'll be involved in once you're there.

It's quite possible that your visas will never once be checked during your entire sabbatical abroad. The vast majority of people we know who went to the trouble of getting visas and/or renewing them abroad rarely, if ever, used them or needed to show them to anyone. We only needed our visas once and that was to register our address abroad with the local authorities immediately after we arrived in San Miguel. Did we need to do this? Legally, yes. But no one was the wiser when we switched addresses six months later and didn't bother to reregister.

That said, it's also possible that you'll need to show your visas any number of times — to cross borders without incurring financial or legal penalties, for example, or to enroll your children in school. You may also be required to register your visas with local authorities when you arrive. And it's possible that officials will want to check your visas if you're the victim of a crime, if someone in your family has a serious health issue and needs to be airlifted out, or if some kind of political turmoil occurs while you're living abroad.

It's hard to know whether the hassles and costs of obtaining visas on the front end are more or less costly or onerous than the financial or legal consequences for getting caught without them. We know of a family that didn't bother to get visas for their year-long stay in Ecuador who, just prior to their return, had U.S. relatives scrambling to help them assemble last-minute visa documents so they could leave Ecuador without incurring significant financial penalties.

In our own case, when our Mexican visas were due to expire after the first year, we seriously considered not renewing them and just taking our chances at the border six months down the line. But no one could tell us what the specific penalties were for crossing and getting caught with expired visas other than that we risked a fine and/or jail time. In the end, we chose to renew. We took a bus to San Antonio, spent a weekend stocking up on basic necessities, and then crossed back into Mexico and received new 180-day tourist visas to see us through our remaining six months.

Was it worth the 16-hour bus ride each way with two young children? I don't know. No one ever checked our documents. Even when we left Mexico for good six months later, no border official looked at our tourist visas or passports or seemed to give a fig for where we'd been or for how long. We have since found out that this rather lax attitude regarding legal documents is especially true when you cross the Mexican border on a bus. But how could we have known that ahead of time? And that may change as border security continues to tighten in this post 9/11 world. As I mentioned, it comes down to your personal comfort level with risk. We didn't want to spend the last leg of our sabbatical running "what-if" scenarios involving Mexican police officers and Mexican jails. And besides, we'd been in Mexico for a year and needed to replenish some of our supplies anyway.

If I had it to do over again, I'd probably do the same thing. For me, certain risks just aren't worth it. But your family might make a different choice based on your comfort level and all that you learn about your sabbatical destination's laws and border requirements. I'm sorry that I can't give any more concrete answers about what to do, but I can at least offer a bit of advice. If, after researching the visa issue for your particular destination, you decide not to get the legally required visas before leaving home, I suggest you bring along all the necessary notarized documents just in case you eventually find you need them.

• **_Check pet entry requirements._** If you have pets and have decided to bring them along, it's time to recheck your destination's pet entry requirements. These vary by country. Some countries welcome pets with open arms. Others are much more restrictive. So be sure you check the entry, vaccination, health certificate, and quarantine requirements well in advance by contacting the consulate or embassy of your sabbatical destination. Also, use online bulletin boards to query expats living in your sabbatical destination about their experiences bringing animals over the border and living abroad with their pets. (Some travelers have reported having to pay an unofficial "customs tax" to get their pets through customs.)

Whatever the official requirements, plan to bring along a copy of your pet's vaccination record, and ask your home vet if he or she will be a resource for you while you live overseas. Then don't hesitate to use the Internet to research general health concerns regarding your pet while you're living out of the country. (For an excellent discussion about how to prepare your pet for overseas travel, pet supplies to bring along, and living with pets overseas, consult Melissa Brayer Hess and Patricia Linderman's book, *The Expert Expatriate*, Chapter Six; see *Resources*.)

Tip: If you decide to leave your pet behind, start looking early for somewhere it can stay while you're gone. It's usually best to get your children used to the idea of being without the family pet by moving it to its new home several weeks before your own move.

Decide What to Do with Your Home

Deciding what to do with your house while you're gone is a big issue, emotionally and financially. I'll talk about finances in the following chapter, *The Money Thing*. For now let's look at your options. If you are currently renting, it's easy: just check the lease and give the appropriate notice. If you own your home, it's more complicated; you can leave it empty, rent it, or sell it.

Renting your house can help finance your sabbatical. We did it and it suited us. But renting is a significant commitment and, quite frankly, it's not for the faint of heart. If you're a person who worries about the least little thing or has an expectation that after leasing your house to a stranger for a period of time, it will look exactly the same as you left it when you return, don't lease it. Even the most responsible renter won't care for your place the same way you do.

Finding someone to rent your house is a leap of faith that the person to whom you're renting will pay you an agreed upon sum each month and will take relatively good care of your house in your absence. But a signed contract is no guarantee of anything. All you can do is make your best effort to find good renters, offer them a reasonable contract, provide a good property manager, and hope for the best. (I'll talk more about renters, contracts, and managers in the following chapter.)

• *Start making (or contract for) necessary repairs if you plan to lease your house.* Making sure your house is in excellent condition before you leave will set a standard of care for your renter as well as help get you the most rent possible for your house. Undoubtedly this will mean making some long needed repairs before you leave. Although you may have adjusted to the "funny" hot water tap in the shower, your renter will most likely prefer something a little less hilarious. And if the garage door sticks a little now and again, fix it. Attempting to solve a problem back home when you're living abroad can easily make that tiny molehill resemble the proverbial mountain.

Note: Your overall goal, once you've left for your sabbatical, is to be able to limit communication with your renters to once a month — to thank them for depositing their full rent check in your bank account. With this in mind, accept the reality that whether you're renting your home furnished or unfurnished, it's probably going to take a bit of work to get it ready for someone else to move in. And you have to build in time to do that work.

Six Months Before Departure
Begin Basic Research on Flights, Schools, Housing

• Make your flight and ground transportation arrangements if you're going on a pre-trip visit to your sabbatical destination.
• Begin researching transportation to your destination (flights, maps for driving, trailers to haul luggage, etc.).
• Make arrangements for the transportation of your unaccompanied personal effects.
• Make arrangements for the transportation of your pets if they will be traveling separately.
• Begin researching housing options in your destination (see *Chapter 4: Finding a Home Away From Home* for more on this).
• Inform your child's current school of your sabbatical plans. (See *Chapter 7: School Daze Part One.*)
• Begin researching schooling requirements in your destination. (See *Chapter 8: School Daze Part Two*).

House Matters

• *If you intend to sell your home:*
  - Choose a reputable real estate agent to market the property for you.
  - Employ an attorney.
  - Organize a Power of Attorney in case the sale is not finalized before your departure.

• *If you intend to rent your home:*
  - Market the property yourself through advertisements in newspapers, bulletin boards, and by word of mouth. Or choose a reputable rental agent to market the property for you.
  - Hire an attorney to study the tenancy agreement. Or draw up your own agreement. It's easy to find sample rental agreements at bookstores or online (see "Other Useful Internet Sites: Legal Forms" in *Resources*).
  - Decide who will manage your property in your absence. Ask a friend, neighbor, or relative; or hire a professional management agent.
  - Get consents for the rental from your mortgage company and insurers and make sure your renter has renter's insurance if necessary.

  Again, expect the renters to put some wear and tear on your house while you're away. (See *Chapter 6: The Money Thing* for more on the pros and cons of leasing your house.)

TWELVE TO EIGHT WEEKS BEFORE DEPARTURE

• Make a reconnaissance trip to your sabbatical location if possible. While there, you might choose your house, a bank, and/or schools(s) for your children.

School Matters

• Notify your children's school of your departure if you have not yet done so.
• Get copies of all pertinent school records (See *Chapter 7: School Daze Part One*).

TWELVE TO EIGHT WEEKS BEFORE DEPARTURE, CONT'D.

House Matters

• Remove your name from junk mail lists (this can take up to three months to kick in).

• *If you intend to leave your house empty:*
  - Check your insurance coverage.
  - Advise your mortgage lender.
  - Make security arrangements for your home.
  - Arrange for cleaning, gardening, snow shoveling, grass cutting, and other maintenance as necessary.
  - Arrange for someone to check the property on a regular basis. (See the following chapter, *The Money Thing*, for more on this.)

Health Matters

To protect your health while overseas:

• Arrange medical and dental check-ups before you go.

• Go over vaccination records with your doctor and arrange extra shots, if required. If your doctor or HMO offers "travel clinic" services, be sure to take advantage of them. Such clinics specialize in helping travelers prepare for trips to other countries by offering vaccinations, immunization shots, and helpful, up-to-date recommendations about medical services, food, water, and other health concerns in countries around the world. (See also *Chapter 13: Getting Sick*.)

• Arrange for an AIDS test if your host country requires it.

• If you take prescription medication, make arrangements with your doctor for obtaining a supply, and ask the doctor to write a letter documenting your need for them.

• If you or a member of your family has any special medical conditions, ask your doctor for a copy of the pertinent medical records for use by your doctor abroad.

• Consult with your doctor about whether you will need any preventative medications, such as quinine, where you will be living. Make arrangements to acquire these if needed.

• Consider taking along a supply of eczema cream, nebulizer/allergy medications, and other medical supplies your family may need that might be difficult to locate abroad. How do you know if it will be hard to find? Ask your doctor and pharmacist and check the message boards. Generally speaking, the more important a medication is to your family, the more important it is to bring along a supply. Also make a point of having someone back home prepared to send you more of particular items if you can't find them abroad. We had a hard time finding dental floss, of all things, and more importantly, hydrocortisone cream.

• Apply for International Health Insurance if necessary (see *Chapter 13: Getting Sick* for more on this topic).

• Put together or purchase a family first-aid kit (see page 73).

"I'm originally from the UK and I arrived in the U.S. with a backpack and a bicycle. I had previously lived and traveled in Australia, Puerto Rico, and Holland and my medical kit typically consisted of a bottle of tea-tree oil. But now with two children, we had a suitcase of medical supplies to cover everything from a dose of the trots to acute asthma." — Sarah

Financial Matters

Begin your financial preparations (see also *Chapter 6: The Money Thing*):

• Contact mortgage brokers, stock advisors, etc. and ensure that you have online access to all your accounts. Also, change all statements to online notification if you no longer want hard copies mailed to you.

• Notify your banks. Ensure that you have online access for all accounts. Arrange for automatic payments, deposits, and withdrawals as necessary. Get the name of an employee, his or her local telephone number, and both the 800 and local numbers for each of your financial institutions. (You may not be able to access the 800 numbers back home from your sabbatical destination.)

TWELVE TO EIGHT WEEKS BEFORE DEPARTURE, CONT'D.

Financial Matters, cont'd.

• Set up electronic "bill pay" accounts for all anticipated payments including mortgage, utilities, and insurance.

• Prepay utilities, insurance, and the like if automatic payments are not possible.

• If you receive government benefits (for example, Social Security or Veterans benefits), make arrangements to have your money sent to your new location.

• Review your will to ensure it still reflects your wishes. Arrange to meet with your attorney to make any desired changes or to make a will if you don't have one yet. You can create a simple will very economically using do-it-yourself software. (See "Other Internet Sites: Legal Forms" in *Resources* for programs.)

• Arrange for Power of Attorney, if required.

• Advise any insurance companies with which you have policies that you are moving to live overseas temporarily. (Companies have been known to refuse to pay out when they have not been so advised.)

• Draw up a preliminary overseas budget and begin calculating your monthly expenses at home and abroad. Begin strategizing how you can economize on anticipated expenses.

Packing and Storage Matters

• Decide what to do with your car(s). Arrange for storage or sale if necessary.

• Start packing up your house and disposing of unneeded items (see "Packing Up Your House" below).

• Consider whether you want to put some things in storage, and make any necessary arrangements.

• Arrange for moving companies to carry out a pre-move survey if you will be moving your belongings into storage.

TAKE A FAMILY FIRST-AID KIT FOR YOUR HOME ABROAD

You can purchase ready-made first-aid kits from any camping or medical supplier online. A cheaper option is to buy a soft-sided multi-zippered storage bag and put one together yourself. Include:

- Sterile gauze pads.
- Bandages/Band-Aids in a variety of sizes.
- Adhesive tape.
- Sterile cotton balls.
- Antibacterial hand wipes.
- Small jar of Vaseline.
- Scissors, tweezers, safety pins, Swiss Army knife.
- Digital thermometer.
- Small cold pack.
- Anti-itch cream such as hydrocortisone or calamine.
- Antibiotic cream or ointment.
- Syrup of ipecac.
- Aspirin, Tylenol, ibuprofen (adults' and children's).
- Cold tablets.
- Cough syrup, throat lozenges (adults' and children's).
- Antihistamine (Benadryl oral and ointment).
- Diarrhea medicine (adults' and children's).
- Sunscreen, lip balm, insect repellent.
- Vaginal cream for infections.
- Spoon/oral syringe to administer kids' doses.
- Moleskin for blisters.
- Inhalers, special medications, etc.
- Any other specific over-the-counter medication that your doctor or pharmacist recommends for your sabbatical destination.
- Emergency medical reference book.

Optional:

- Antibiotics such as amoxicyllin.
- Louse treatment.
- Pinworm treatment.
- Rehydration mixture.
- Lotrimin (or other clotrimazole- or miconazole-based) anti-fungal.

Tip: Do not pack your first-aid kit in your carry-on luggage if you fly. Airports keep changing their carry-on restrictions, and you might not be able to take it aboard.

SIX TO FOUR WEEKS BEFORE DEPARTURE

- Arrange any needed flight tickets, hotels, and either a car for hire or an airport shuttle to get you to your flights. If friends or relatives have a large enough car, they may be able to chauffer you.
- Consider the need for independent tax/financial advice on your status as an expatriate and see your tax advisor prior to leaving (see also *Chapter 6: The Money Thing*).
- Arrange with the post office for your mail to be forwarded (see *Chapter 9: Is Anyone Out There?* for details).
- Send out change-of-address cards, and make arrangements for staying in touch with friends and relatives.
- Renew your driver's license if necessary so it won't expire while you're gone.
- Cancel subscriptions to book clubs, magazines, home Internet service, and cable.
- Notify credit card companies and cancel cards, if necessary.
- Make a detailed inventory of the contents of your home including value and age. (You may want to take photos for insurance purposes.)
- Get a safe deposit box in which to store important documents and valuables while you are away.
- Make final decisions about what things to take with you overseas and what things to leave behind.
- Hold a garage sale and give household items that don't sell to charities and friends to minimize storage needs and make some extra cash.
- Make final arrangements for moving day with your moving company (if you're using one).
- Collect copies of legal documents such as marriage, birth, adoption, and divorce certificates to take with you. Make two copies of each document. Put the originals in your safe deposit box.
- Collect copies of additional documents you may need to take with you (insurance certificates, medical records, optical and/or medical prescriptions, school records, references).

• Deplete food in your kitchen cupboards and freezer.
• Deplete stocks of alcohol. (Plan to throw a big party before you leave!)
• Contact your local election or voter registration office if necessary to register as an overseas voter.

Two to One Week(s) Before Departure

• Complete any house repairs and home maintenance tasks that need doing, such as draining the fuel from the lawn mower.
• Make sure that gutters, air conditioner, garbage disposal, etc. are all in good working order.
• Compile a master address/email/phone list.
• Cancel milk and newspaper deliveries.
• Advise utility companies of your turn-off date for gas, electricity, water, and telephone.
• Dispose of houseplants.
• Pack the possessions you are taking with you.
• Sort out those items you will need to keep with you when you travel.
• Double-check that important paperwork is available and collected in one folder to be hand-carried and not sent in luggage.

Departure Day

• Be sure your important paperwork and valuables (see above) are safely stowed in your carry-on luggage.
• If you plan to leave your home empty:
    - Drain down water.
    - Disconnect the gas.
    - Turn off all the lights.
    - Lock the doors and windows.

Items to Hand-Carry

- Passports.
- Visas.
- Work permits and employment documents (if necessary).
- Plane tickets.
- Money.
- Traveler's checks.
- Currency.
- Credit cards.
- Driver's license(s).
- Essential medication.
- Health and vaccination records and certificates.
- Extra passport-sized photos for legal documents abroad.
- Certified birth certificates for every family member.
- Adoption papers.
- Marriage/divorce certificate(s) — copies are fine.
- Mortgage and property management information.
- Financial information, including:
    - Credit card numbers and contact information for each card.
    - Investment information.
    - Bank account information.
    - Insurance forms for house, car, life, and medical.
    - Power-of-attorney forms.
    - Copies of recent tax returns.
- Drug and eyeglass/contact lens prescriptions.
- Dental records.
- School records.
- Address books.
- Jewelry.
- Things for children to do on the flight or car ride.
- At least one change of clothes if you're flying, in case your suitcases don't arrive with you.

Packing Up Your House

Let's step back a bit in time to twelve to eight weeks before departure. O.K. You've got your document applications underway. Your bedside is littered with books and brochures about traveling in your highly anticipated new home. You've told everyone where you're going and when you're leaving. You've decided to keep, sell, or drive your car and you know by now whether you're renting or selling your house or just leaving it empty while you're gone. It's finally time to start packing up. But where do you begin? It can seem pretty overwhelming.

The first thing to do is whittle down your inventory. Start by getting rid of what you're not using right now. What's in those mystery boxes down in the basement and out in the garage? What's up in the rafters? How long has it been since you've looked in those high kitchen cabinets and behind the coats in your closets? Take a good hard look around and start getting rid of stuff. Our rule of thumb was if we hadn't used it in a year, it was either time to get rid of it or to at least ask ourselves if we really needed it. The point is to lighten your load any way you can.

The fifty percent rule

Our family's goal was to get rid of half of everything we owned. That may sound drastic but once you start culling through all the stuff you own, you may be surprised at how good it feels to start sending things out the door. Selling furniture you don't like or rarely use is not only money in your pocket, it's less money spent on storing useless stuff while you're gone. Donating items to charity is a good deed and a tax write-off as well. Think about it as recycling. The less stuff you're paying to store, the better, and psychologically it feels great to cleanse ourselves of the flotsam and jetsam of our stuff-driven lives.

"We had to rent our house out. This was a big ordeal because we had lived in the same house for twelve years. Twelve years of accumulation! We had to get rid of most of our

stuff and had lots of garage sales, made trips to the Goodwill, trips to the dump, called for Salvation Army pick-ups, and so on." — Rob

Books, toys, clothes

Start by filling a box or two with books to sell back to the used book-store. And then another. And another. Have the kids go through their toys and decide which they absolutely want to come back to and which they're either done with or simply want to give away for someone else to play with. Help them cull through their favorites by limiting the number of toys they can bring along on your sabbatical. Then have an empty box available for things they want to hang onto. Donate the rest of the usable toys to charitable organizations, along with all the clothes your kids won't fit into when you return.

Go through your own closets and get rid of any items you haven't worn in the past year. Do the same with linens, Tupperware, pots and pans, you name it. Things you've kept around thinking you'd use them some day — bye bye. Ski gear you hope the kids will grow into someday — bye bye. Pick it up used when you need it instead of storing it and waiting to see if it might still be usable five years from now (which, of course, it won't). Think light. And then think even lighter.

You're not going to want to come back to the same old knick-knacks. You'll have new ones to set on the shelves from your wonderful adventure. Get rid of that framed wedding gift you never liked; you've paid your dues and had it on the wall long enough. That old futon mattress from college up in the attic — sell it; it's not good for your back now anyway. Have that garage sale and stock it with things you haven't used in years. Once that's done, you'll really be ready to start packing up the house.

Tip: Pack the things you will need immediately upon your return somewhere accessible. Label the boxes and write a note to yourself about where you packed what. You may believe that you will remember where things are, but you won't. Those last few days before leaving are crazy with way too many things to think about. Six months or one year later, everything that happened in the last few weeks before you left on your adventure will be a blur.

> *"We underestimated greatly the time and effort it takes to put your life on hold and arrange for finances, care of property, etc. for a sabbatical of seven months. The six-apartment building that we had bought and were still in the process of renovating had to be jobbed out to one of our workers to complete. We hired our realtor to rent out the apartments while we were gone. We did not find a renter for our house until three weeks before our departure at a rate much lower than what our realtor thought we could get. But it was still a great way to subsidize our trip. I had to thoroughly clean, organize, and pack away a lot of our personal items. Luckily, it was just a couple renting so we just had to pack up two bedrooms. Our house never looked so good! Then it was the job of what to bring with us. Andy decided to buy a small trailer so we could bring two computers, a printer, bicycles, scooters, two extra chairs, an extra reading light, and lots of clothes and kids' books to donate to the schools in our sabbatical destination."* — Kim

Choosing What to Bring Along

It may be easier to decide what to get rid of than what to bring along. Deciding what to bring depends largely on where you're going. If you're traveling to a place where most things are readily available, your list is going to be significantly different from the list you'll make if you're traveling to a place where locating supplies will be a challenge. Do your research ahead of time. Use the Internet to ask specific questions of other expats and tourist agencies.

You may also be limited by your method of travel. Traveling by car may or may not allow you more leeway than an airline baggage allowance; it will depend on your vehicle's size and how many of you are traveling. We traveled by airplane and were each allowed two suitcases per person as well as one carry-on apiece plus our laptop computers. There were four of us so that equaled eight pieces of luggage and four carry-ons.

For an 18-month trip, we obviously couldn't bring everything we wanted to bring or everything we thought we might need. Also, we were interested in traveling as light as possible to keep the airport/transit situation simple. So we committed to packing extremely light, trusting that we would either find what we needed or make do with what we could find in our destination. For Michael and me, we invested in two roomy, high-quality rolling suitcase/backpacks with zip-off daypacks (which we used as carry-ons). We got a smaller version of the same for Cleome. At seven years old, she needed to take charge of her own luggage, we agreed, since Michael and I would have our hands full with Asher and the rest of our belongings. In addition to those three suitcase/backpacks, Michael had a guitar, and he and I each had a laptop. We also had one large box of books and a very large rolling zip-up duffle that contained everything else. That was actually less than our legal baggage allowance but it was certainly the maximum we could handle. The whole airport/customs/transportation thing gets crazy fast, so we were glad we limited it to those items.

When making your own luggage decisions, consider not only your mode of transportation to your destination, but also your transportation needs during your stay. Will you be traveling by bus or train? Will you need tough and durable luggage that can suffer some abuse? Will you need versatile luggage that can serve more than one purpose, such as being both a backpack and a suitcase? Will your luggage need a handle and sturdy wheels to let you roll it over cobblestones? Will you need to carry it any distance? In our experience, less is more, especially when it comes to luggage.

> *"Find out what things won't be available where you are going and then prioritize what you really need to have with you. In China, English books were almost nonexistent so it was essential for us to bring many. Stanley needed picture books (we got really sick of the ones we brought too!) and Isaiah was a beginning reader so I had to bring a whole range of books. There were a few food things that I brought for special times and homesick moments — like chocolate chips and things like baking powder and vanilla, which could not be found where we were in China. It made a huge difference that we had them."*
> — Rachel

"Personally, I like to travel light but I realized that my children would find security and pleasure in the familiar, so we brought along as many toys and books as our airline baggage allowance would bear." — Sarah

The three most important things

To help you focus on what to bring along and to narrow your packing list, you might ask each person in your family to make a list of the "three most important things" they want to have with them. These are comfort items for those first few weeks abroad, when isolation and the sense of "foreignness" are most extreme. They can include things like a personal CD player and some favorite CDs, an iPod, favorite framed pictures or photograph albums, a favorite mug or cup, toys, stuffed animals, a blanket, computer games, a favorite pillowcase or sheets and towels, DVDs, and nonperishable foods.

"We brought lots of games that were small, interesting, and time intensive — like cards, chess, and Mancala. Our five-year-old learned to play chess so well that he regularly kicks butt against Kaya's friends when they come over now, to his extreme delight. And our family, in assorted pairs, will often pull out a chessboard now as a way to connect and to slow down. It has become more than a game; it's an emotional comfort brain food reminding us of our special time together. I also recommend lots and lots of books for the kids. Kaya ran out, but we had visitors replenish." — Julie

Baby and toddler equipment

The amount of equipment a tiny human being requires each day for survival is stupefying. I won't go through the list of what you could bring along if you had all the space and money in the universe. I'll just assume that space is at a premium because you are either flying to your sabbatical destination with baby in arms or you're driving. If you'll have a car during your time abroad, you will obviously need a car seat/carrier for your baby or toddler and a booster seat for your older children (up to 80 pounds is the current recommendation). Beyond that, your equipment needs are largely determined by your budget, luggage allowance, and your sabbatical destination.

We brought along a stroller for Asher, our then two-year-old. It was helpful in the airports, but we didn't use it even once in San Miguel. The streets were cobbled and much too rough for a stroller to be any use. We decided not to bring a toddler backpack because Asher was getting too big for one and it was too cumbersome to pack. In Mexico, he either walked (complaining the whole time) or rode on Michael's shoulders. It seemed to work out fine.

Note: If your child is used to riding in a backpack and you can fit it in your allotted luggage allowance, by all means bring it. But be aware that if you use it, you will stand out like an American sore thumb. Even to us, and we're used to them, seeing American tourists carrying their kids in these brightly colored carriers against the muted 400-year-old stonework was quite jarring. Also, in a hot climate backpacks can be very uncomfortable and unhealthy for the kids. They get the double-whammy of direct heat from above and being enclosed in a stifling nylon straightjacket. Toddler backpacks are doubtless more helpful in temperate locations.

You can probably get along without much else in terms of large, cumbersome equipment. If you can fit a portable crib/playpen, go for it, especially if you'll be doing any traveling in the country itself; the hotels you'll be staying in may not have any reasonably safe cribs to offer. Leave the baby swings, bouncy seats, and the like at home. They're bulky, short-lived in terms of usefulness, and undoubtedly you'll find other ways to keep your baby happy while abroad. A hammock swaying gently beneath a shady tree beats the mechanical hum of a baby swing anytime.

"Our kids are voracious readers. We worried about managing to find enough English-language reading materials for them. But there were just enough bookstores, libraries, and other expats willing to circulate books that it worked out okay. Someone suggested that we bring along a few holiday things from home and this did feel nice around Christmas." — Frances

"We brought lots of games like Scrabble and backgammon. Kids play with them more abroad since they don't have the built-in friends they do back home. We also brought lots of Lego and K'nex which were great for our 9- and 11-year-old sons to play with together."   — Kim

My Suggested General Packing List

• Adapters, currency converters, surge protectors, or any other equipment you'll need to use your electrical appliances and computer in your destination. Check electricity requirements online to see what you'll need. (See *Chapter 9: Is Anyone Out There?* for more on computer hardware and software.)

• VCR/DVD player and tapes/DVDs. Double-check that your VCR is an international model that can play tapes in another format if necessary. NTSC, PAL, and SECAM are formats used in different parts of the world. (NTSC is the U.S. standard.)

• Comfortable, sturdy shoes/sandals for everyone.

• Versatile toys and art supplies including small plastic animals and people, inflatable pool and beach ball, kids' software, and family games.

• Books. Bring as many books as possible. That includes language books, bilingual picture books, dictionaries, cookbooks, storybooks, novels, coloring books, activity books — anything you can think of. Books become much more valuable abroad than at home. It's not only because books written in English are expensive and in short supply overseas. It's also because there's suddenly so much more time for reading once you've left your busy lives behind; the number of hours in the day seems to increase exponentially when you leave the States. Books will help fill those hours and are also valuable as trading currency with other families.

Tip: Be sure to include an English-language cookbook or two with recipes that use local ingredients.

• Kid-sized cups, plates, bowls, and silverware.

• A favorite bath toy for each child.

• A nightlight (if the voltage is compatible).

• A supply of your kids' favorite foods that may be difficult to obtain such as peanut butter, cereal, baby formula, and snacks. Make sure you get items that won't spoil.

• Small, lightweight sports equipment such as balls, Frisbees, and rackets.

• Holiday decorations if you'll be away during an important holiday.

• Swimsuits, goggles, and beach towels.

• Clothes for two seasons.

• First-Aid kit with all medicines you'll need for the first month, including Tylenol, cough medicine, bandages, and prescription antibiotics. (See page 73 for a more comprehensive list of items to include in your first-aid kit.)

• Digital camera, batteries, and cables that will allow you to download your photos to your computer.

• Permanent marking pens, zippered plastic storage bags, toilet paper, antibacterial wipes.

• Blow-up mattress for guests.

• Baby/toddler safety items such as outlet plugs and drawer stops.

• Travel alarm.

• Flashlight with batteries.

• Coffee, tea bags, small coffeemaker (see *Chapter 10: We're Here!*).

• Bottled water for flight and first day. If you are flying to your sabbatical destination, wait and purchase it after you clear security. Or pack a few bottles in your checked baggage.

• Sunblock, tampons, diapers, wipes, and baby formula. These are typically very expensive in other countries, so bring a good supply.

CREATE A FAMILY HARDWARE KIT FOR YOUR HOME ABROAD

A soft-sided zippered storage bag works great. Be sure to include the following in your kit:

- Flashlight.
- Candles.
- Can opener/bottle opener/wine opener.
- Small screwdriver kit for repairing eyeglasses, etc.
- Swiss army knife.
- Batteries (in a variety of sizes).
- Binoculars.
- String.
- Small stapler and extra staples.
- Childproofing supplies (if necessary).
- Matches.
- Twist-ties.
- Various sizes of "zipper" plastic storage bags.
- Small sewing kit.
- Duct tape/black electrical tape/cellophane tape.
- Measuring tape (inches/metric).

Tip: You can pick up tricky little multi-function contraptions online that offer screwdrivers, scissors, knife, stapler, etc. all in one handy tool as a substitute for some of the items listed above.

6. THE MONEY THING
HOW TO FINANCE
YOUR SABBATICAL

"We do, at times, wish we had more money so we could travel and take advantage of the concerts and restaurants this city offers in abundance. But even more often I think about how lovely it is to boil life down to this tiny box of money, thoughts, activities, and belongings. I suppose that's actually the most Mexican of anything we're doing. I feel like we're slowly reducing our sense of entitlement and acquisition — those American habits of assessing each situation based on what there is to take, buy, or own." El Grito #5

At first glance, coming up with enough money to fund your family sabbatical may seem like an impossible dream. But it's really not that hard to come up with the dough. Don't scoff. If we can do it, you can too. It's not magic and it's not impossible. It simply requires sacrifice and preparation along with a little grit and imagination. If you want to do this wonderful thing with your family, you can. And here's how:

• Pay off your debts.
• Start living more cheaply at home.
• Put anything extra into your sabbatical savings account.

If you're willing to start cutting out "luxuries" today, you'll be surprised at how quickly tomorrow turns into the first day of your sabbatical. By luxuries I'm talking about vacations, new cars, new furniture, new clothes, dinners out, and the like. Sure, these are pretty much all the things you reward yourselves with for toiling so hard at "the daily grind." So giving them up may initially sound like too much sacrifice for your family. But if you can keep reminding each other that by not eating pizza out tonight, you'll be helping save for a big pizza dinner in Italy next year — well, the whole thing becomes a lot more palatable.

Next, consider the various ways you can make extra cash while you're living abroad. If you can count on income from investments or wealthy relatives, it will obviously help enormously. But even if you can't, there are other ways to make passive income during your sabbatical. Leasing out your house and using the monthly rent to offset expenses abroad is one of the easiest and most important because undoubtedly you'll be able to find something cheaper to rent in your destination. What about selling your cars and furniture? How about taking out a short-term loan? Ultimately, if you want to embark on this adventure but you don't have enough in your savings account and guaranteed income while you're away to cover the entire cost, you can always fudge a bit on the sabbatical idea and cobble together enough work at home or abroad to cover the difference during your time away.

Consider working over the Internet or starting a small business abroad. You could offer a private service such as teaching English or consulting. You could garden or work in construction. You could try your hand at writing travel articles or a book like this. One family we know moved to Spain for a year. The father, a professor, taught an online course for a university back in the States and his students never even knew he was out of the country. How tough can correcting tests be when you're holding a glass of Spanish vino in one hand? The possibilities are really limited only by your desire and determination.

A number of families we know are financing their lives abroad by having one parent work back in the States and commute abroad regularly to spend time with the family. This works especially well in families where one or the other parent has employment with a fairly flexible schedule. Another family uses the Internet to oversee their real estate investments back in the States and they're able to live abroad easily with only an occasional jaunt back home to deal with the inevitable problems that arise. In yet another family, the parents tag-team in six-month increments so that one works while the other takes time off. This is possible for them because each has a fairly portable career (one works in construction and the other is a graphic artist). Such situations require both flexibility and sacrifice. They also typically mean the adults are more interested in continuing their family adventure than in serious career advancement. But for these families, the value of living abroad outweighs other considerations. And while none of these situations might feel right for your family, the point is there are numerous ways to finance your sabbatical abroad. All it requires is a certain level of resolve and the creativity to make it happen.

> *"Orin was looking for work and found a one-year position in China that he thought he had a chance of getting. When he got it, it was perfect because the job paid for most of our travel costs and gave us a place to live and support for making arrangements, which in China are especially difficult if not impossible to do on your own."*
> — Rachel

How We Did It: Our Three-Year Plan

We funded our 18-month-long sabbatical on a total budget of $54,000 (see details below). We financed it completely through a combination of rental income and savings (and a surprise mid-sabbatical $5,000 gift from a sympathetic grandfather). That $54,000 figure included our transportation, a two-week beach vacation, all our rather luxurious living expenses in Mexico, the maintenance costs of our home back in Minnesota, two years of health insurance, monthly life insurance premiums, private schools for both kids, and paying off two different loans. We were easily able to save enough for our sabbatical over a three-year period despite the fact that I worked only part-time and a significant portion of our monthly income went to quality part-time daycare for our toddler. The way we did it may sound radical but it actually wasn't difficult. And although it took us three years to reach our goal, we could have cut this time in half had I been working fulltime.

We started saving for our sabbatical in 1998 by depositing $3,684.58 in a money market fund with our broker. This wasn't IRA money or college funds. Tapping into either is risky business and you should think hard before using these sources to fund your adventure. The money in our savings account was "extra;" something we'd vaguely been referring to as "the new car fund." Once we decided to take a family sabbatical, the "new car fund" instantly transformed into our "family sabbatical savings account" and we were on our way. Over a three-year period we cut out the majority of extras in our lives and deposited everything left over each month into our savings account. It really started to add up and surprisingly, except during rare moments, we barely felt the pinch. For three years we consciously engineered our lives to live much more simply and cheaply. We gave up vacations, used only one car (Michael took the bus to work), rarely ate out, cut down on the number of "enrichment" classes for the kids, and didn't make any large new purchases that weren't related to our trip. And during that three-year period, we paid off nearly all of our debts and put away $35,000. We didn't have to starve ourselves or give up fun during those three years. We just made sure our fun was closer to home and we did a lot more cooking in our own kitchen rather than going out.

Living simply and living well: Drawing up a preliminary budget

Simplifying our lifestyle at home was excellent preparation for our lives abroad. The simpler you can live, the more comfortable you'll be anywhere you go. And of course, you'll also need much less to live on. Keep in mind that the rest of the world doesn't typically share the American obsession with stuff. People make do with much less. By adopting the "less is more" lifestyle and making careful decisions, you can live in relative luxury overseas on much less than you might initially imagine. But you must also be willing to compromise comfort in some areas to achieve comfort in others. As an example, by choosing to live in Mexico, we were able to live in homes several times larger than ours in the States with a maid, gardener, and many extras. But we also had to be willing to drink bottled water, cope with erratic power outages, and rustle the occasional scorpion. Choosing to live without a car also saved us an enormous amount of money, not to mention numerous headaches. We initially thought that living without a car might be difficult, but it was actually the opposite. Most cities of the world offer quality mass transit that's equal or superior to the mass transit options available in the U.S. Becoming a zero-car family overseas can positively impact your overall sabbatical experience as well as your budget's bottom line.

The first step in figuring out how much money you'll actually need to finance your sabbatical is to draw up a preliminary budget. Obviously there are numerous factors that will affect your budget's bottom line. These include: how long you'll be gone; where you're going to live; what kind of housing you're going to want; whether or not you'll be traveling from place to place (with all the attendant transportation, lodging, and meal costs), and the cost of schools and utilities, among many other things. All you really need to start with is a general idea of how long your sabbatical will be and where you're going (see *Chapter 2: Where to Go and For How Long?*).

There are a variety of online and library resources that will give you good general figures for what it costs to live in various cities around the world. The U.S. State Department puts out the *Indexes of Living Costs Abroad* (check your library) that shows comparative costs in a variety of categories for the U.S. and cities abroad. The United Nations also offers cost of living information for its employees living overseas. You can access the data by requesting it online. Travel books can also be good resources. Rosanne Knorr's *The Grown-Up's Guide to Running Away* (see *Resources*) compares the daily living costs in cities throughout Europe and Central America and gives excellent suggestions for cutting costs while living abroad.

To help get you started on your preliminary budget, I've included the budget for our own sabbatical. You can download a blank sample budget with representative categories from my website: www.familysabbatical.com

OUR 18-MONTH BUDGET

Monthly Expenses in Minnesota

Mortgage (includes taxes and insurance)	$ 425
Utilities as agreed by contract with our renter	$ 85
(She paid gas, electric, and phone. We paid garbage, water, and house maintenance – shoveling, grass cutting, etc.)	
Life insurance premiums	$ 40
Student loan payments	$ 190
International catastrophic health family insurance premium	$ 160
(See below for more on this.)	
Car insurance (for our stored car)	$ 15
Car loan	$ 55
Total Monthly Expenses Back Home	**$ 970**

Monthly Expenses In Mexico

First Six Months (The Splurge Phase)

Rent	$ 800
Maid/Gardener	$ 220
Telephone	$ 35
Internet	$ 0
(Typically you'll pay $25 to $60 per month depending on the type of connection you have, but we got lucky. We signed a six-month contract for Internet service with a local provider in San Miguel and were never charged even though the service continued for the entire 18 months we lived in Mexico. See *Chapter 9: Is Anyone Out There?* for more about connections and costs.)	
Gas	$ 35
Electric	$ 50
Water	$ 10
School/Daycare/Uniform/"Inscription" (averaged out)	$ 180
("Inscription" is the initial registration fee we paid to enroll our daughter in her school.)	
Food/Liquor/Household supplies	$ 400
Entertainment/Babysitting	$ 100
Miscellaneous (Includes one-time out-of-pocket medical payments and weekend travel.)	$ 150
Total Monthly Mexico Expenses First Six Months	**$1,980**

Note: We figured correctly that for the first few months (as we learned the ropes of the new place we'd moved to) we would spend more and then decrease that spending in relation to our learning curve. We also chose to spend more on our initial six-month rental knowing that we would then be required to find something significantly cheaper for the last twelve months.)

Our Total Monthly Expenses First Six Months   **$2,950**

Monthly Expenses In Mexico
Last 12 Months (Living Within Our Budget Phase)

Rent	$ 600
(Includes water and maid; we didn't need a gardener here. We got this rate by paying in advance in cash.)	
Telephone	$ 30
Internet	$ 0
(Still free, amazingly enough, but a representative figure would be $40.)	
Gas	$ 40
Electric	$ 25
School/Daycare (averaged out)	$ 235
(Includes inscription, uniforms, supplies, transportation.)	
Food/Liquor/Household supplies	$ 400
Entertainment/Babysitting	$ 100
Miscellaneous	$ 150
(Includes classes, tutors, books, doctor and dentist visits, shoes, movie rentals, etc.)	

Total Monthly Mexico Expenses Last 12 Months (approx.)   **$1,580**

Our Total Monthly Expenses Last 12 Months   **$2,550**

**Our Approximate Monthly Total Expenses Averaged
Over 18 Months**   **$2,700**
(Not including one-time payments for travel, visas, etc.)

Note: If you plan to have a car, you will need to budget a realistic monthly amount for insurance, gas, and maintenance. This can add significantly to the cost of your sabbatical depending on where you move, parts availability, import taxes, etc.

Income vs. Expenses (18 months)

Available Monthly Income

Rent from St. Paul house	$ 900
Savings	$ 1,500
Earnings abroad and unexpected gifts	$ 600
Total Available Monthly Income	**$ 3,000**

Total Income Available for 18 Months	**$54,000**
Monthly expenses for 18 months	$ 48,600
One-time payments and set-up fees	
(Including transportation, visas, etc.)	$ 4,805
Total Expenses for 18 Months	**$53,405**

The goal here, obviously, is to match your expenses and income as closely as possible with a bit left over for emergencies. As you can see, we matched it VERY closely but we did fine and, thanks to some unexpected gifts, we arrived back in the States with enough left over to float us for a few months until we found a reasonable source of income.

The 20% cushion

With any luck, your sabbatical will be nothing but blue sky and sunny days. But in the event that something catastrophic occurs or your family happens upon some marvelous and previously unimagined opportunity that's going to take a bit of extra dough, it's important to have some money squirreled away to cover the unexpected expense. In the middle of our sabbatical, our insurance company raised our homeowners' insurance rates. At the same time, our school costs increased significantly during the second half of our sabbatical when we discovered a much higher quality (and more expensive) preschool for our toddler. Then we decided to go to the beach for two weeks over Christmas. And my dental bridge broke and I was facing $1,000 worth of dental work . . . You get the picture.

You need to have a cushion somewhere, somehow, that allows you financial wiggle room in a fluid and largely unknown and uncontrollable situation. The amount will depend on your own personal comfort zone. Is an additional $5,000 stashed away somewhere enough? Can you borrow money easily in a pinch without jeopardizing a friendship (or a familial relationship)? Can you find work over the Internet or in your sabbatical destination relatively quickly if need be? What if there's a medical emergency back home and you need to buy a roundtrip ticket quick? Can you afford it without throwing your sabbatical plans out the window? Make sure you've got some bucks stuffed under a mattress somewhere and include the amount in the fine print of your trip budget. Don't plan on using it, but make sure it's available if you need it. In our case, while we didn't formally include it in our budget, we always knew there was a particular bit of stock we could sell off if we hit dire financial straits.

"The value of the dollar plummeted while we were in Italy. If only we had moved all our money into Euros rather than living off dollars and using our U.S. bank cash card!" — Channing

The rule of thumb is to calculate your budget and then pad it by 20%. It's like planning any large construction project, except in this case you're building an adventure. If you live simply and cheaply most of the time, any extra money can be saved for unexpected emergencies or even better, unexpected enrichment opportunities that arise during the course of your stay.

Making Money During Your Sabbatical

The biggest and most obvious source of passive income for your sabbatical is renting your home. You will most likely be able to charge a renter more for your house back home than you will pay to rent a house abroad. If not, look around for cheaper digs abroad because the difference between what you receive and what you pay is critical income. We used the income we received from our renter's monthly payment to cover our mortgage, taxes, and insurance; house maintenance costs (shoveling, garbage hauling, grass cutting, water, etc.); Michael's student loan payment; life insurance payments; monthly medical insurance premiums; car storage insurance, and our annual income taxes. That meant we could apply every bit of our savings and any other income we picked up during our sabbatical to the cost of the sabbatical itself.

Rent out your house

The upside of renting your house is obvious. You can make money doing it. The downside is the potential headaches that come with being a landlord. And be forewarned, there will be headaches. Despite that, everyone we spoke with agreed that the assorted minor hassles they encountered were a small price to pay for having a renter to keep their family's adventure afloat.

I don't want to gloss over the fact that being a landlord, even temporarily, can be a real drag. Even if things go smoothly, there are going to be a few (or more) things that need your attention, and it's not easy dealing with them when you're thousands of miles away. That's why it's critical to (a) leave your house in as near flawless condition as possible; see *Chapter 5: Get Ready, Get Set . . .* , (b) find a responsible renter, and (c) engage someone to manage your property or at least to watch over your house while you're away.

> *"We had a lot of repairs to do to our house to get it ready to rent. Then we had to find renters we were comfortable leaving our house with. We also asked a friend to act as our property manager — collect the rent and check in from time to time to make sure things were OK."* — Rob

I wish I could tell you the secret to finding a responsible renter but I think it might just come down to plain dumb luck. Start the process by doing everything you can to get the word out about your place. Place an ad in the paper, tack up notices on supermarket and university bulletin boards, and spread the word among your neighbors, friends, and colleagues that you're looking for someone to rent your place during the period that you'll be gone. You can also use rental managers or agencies. For a significant fee, they will help you locate renters and take over the management of your property while you're gone. If money is no object, this might be a good way to go. We have friends who had very good experiences paying someone else to take charge of the entire matter and who felt that, overall, they received more in rent and encountered fewer headaches by leaving the whole thing to professionals. However, we also know a number of families who felt they paid way too much to property managers who got them less in rent than promised, found less than desirable renters, and ultimately provided poor management services or at least services that weren't worth the price. Obviously it comes down to your individual financial circumstances and the types of services available in your particular area. It can't hurt to call around and see what professional property managers and rental agents charge for their services. Do, however, read the contract carefully so that if you decide to go this route, you'll understand exactly what services you're paying for, how much say you'll have over the rental amount and the identity of the renters, and what recourse you'll have if the property management company doesn't perform to your expectations.

To get an idea of how much rent you can get for your place, check out your local newspapers for the cost of equivalent rentals in your area. You can also try calling a few realtors to get their suggestions. You want to walk the line between getting enough to help finance your sabbatical without pricing yourself out of the market. You may also want to charge a bit less than the market rate in exchange for some flexibility on the part of your renters. For example, you may want to reduce the rent a bit in exchange for storing your car and belongings in the garage while you're gone. What you lose in rent in this case might net you significant savings in storage costs. Another example: We have friends who own a very large house in Chicago. They chose to rent out only two of the five available bedrooms in order to store their belongings in the other three for the duration of their sabbatical. They received less in rent than they might have, but they also saved significantly on storage costs and general hassle.

Decide early on whether to rent your house furnished or unfurnished. This is completely dependent on your individual circumstances, the norms of rentals in your community, and your personal comfort level concerning your belongings. If your house will be rented to college students who typically have little in the way of furnishings, you might get significantly more each month by renting it furnished. You will, of course, want to remove your most precious belongings and also ask for a significant damage deposit. Another possibility is to rent your house semi-furnished so that you don't have to mess with moving out large items such as beds, storage units, and washer/dryers.

Start the rental process early enough so that you don't end up feeling desperate. Four to six months ahead of your departure is not too early to start placing ads and getting the word out. Take recommendations from friends, and interview everyone who expresses an interest. Ask all prospective renters for references and follow up on them before making any promises or signing anything. Despite all your hard work and careful interviewing, there are no guarantees that you're going to find the perfect renter. It may just come down to your gut feeling, timing, and that old leap of faith. We found our renter through a friend, and after we did a bit of socializing with her, we felt extremely comfortable leaving our house in her hands.

> *"We did not have a lot of people interested in renting our house, which made us a bit nervous. However, we ended up with a tenant who took really good care of our home. We put all our belongings in storage and hired a management company to oversee the house."* — Channing

> *"Our economic situation required us to rent our house while we were gone, which we thought would be no big deal because we live near campus in a college town. It turned out to be much harder than we expected and we didn't get anywhere near enough rent*

to cover our mortgage, which is what we had hoped for, though otherwise the rental situation worked out very well for us." — Julie

Who's minding your house?

It's important to find someone trustworthy to manage your property. At the very least, you need someone your renter can contact in case of an emergency and who can make minor repairs. Although we elected not to formally hire someone to manage our property, we met others who did and I can't say their ride was any more or less smooth than ours. It all depends on the problems that arise while you're gone. In our case, we paid for basic house maintenance such as snow shoveling, garbage pick-up, watering, and grass cutting because we wanted to make sure those things happened predictably in our absence. We also asked my brother to be the on-call guy for our house, which was only a mile or so from where he lived. He graciously agreed to do a minimal number of seasonal chores and, most importantly, to gather our mail on a monthly basis. (We handled the majority of our finances and other communications electronically.)

It went along fine for a few months — until he and his wife had their first child. I bet you can guess what happened after that. That's right. Nothing. He was so overwhelmed by the responsibilities of fatherhood that he was lucky to remember his name half the time, much less remember to go over to our place and help our renter change a light bulb.

We were lucky. Despite the benign neglect of my poor overwhelmed brother, our renter had few problems and thus, so did we. We were also fortunate to have neighbors across the street who pitched in and changed some light bulbs, moved an air conditioner, and offered their help to our renter at a few critical moments. My father grabbed the mail every couple of months, and all in all things went pretty smoothly.

The majority of problems we did encounter basically came down to a lack of communication. When the "flapper" in the toilet malfunctioned and our renter called a plumber to replace it (at a cost of $131), we had no say in her decision. Ditto on the garbage disposal that she had fixed to the tune of $350. Obviously those repairs could have been made by someone other than a plumber (or a different plumber) for a quarter of the cost. But despite her initial assurances that she would inform us as problems came up, our renter just went ahead and had the repairs done without notifying us and then deducted the cost from the next month's rent. We were thousands of miles away and she did what was most convenient. As a renter in a similar situation, I'd probably do the same.

My advice is to write everything you can think of into the rental contract so that your renter and/or property manager understands how involved you want to be in dealing with repairs and other problems. If you want to be notified about necessary repairs before they happen, state that clearly. In our case, even if that had been written into the contract, I don't think it would have made any difference to our renter. She wasn't paying for it and she didn't give a fig about the cost. I can't say I really blame her. The bottom line is that your renter has you over a barrel. Our experience points out how critical it is to find a trustworthy renter and someone reliable (not an expectant first-time parent) to keep tabs on your house while you're gone.

> *"Having a rich uncle Bob in the background who'll pull your cha-chas out of the fire if you need help is very handy. Many of our extended family members and friends took on the work of overseeing our fortunes here in the U.S. for the duration of our trip."*
> — Toni

Drawing up the lease

Once you've met the twin challenges of finding a trustworthy renter and someone to manage the place, the next step is to write a rental contract you and your renter can both agree to. You can involve an attorney in writing up a rental agreement or you can do it yourself. We did it ourselves using a lease template from the Minnesota Multi Housing Association. However, you can easily find lease templates at bookstores that specialize in business forms, as well as online (see "Other Useful Internet Sites: Legal Forms" in *Resources* for some sites). All the standard information is there and you're free to write in any other items that seem appropriate.

Itemize everything that is included in the renter's monthly payment such as garbage services, water, sewer, and yard maintenance. Also list your tenants' responsibilities in terms of the utilities they will pay and any agreements you have regarding your tenants performing routine maintenance on your property. If you choose to rent your house furnished, accept the fact that things will suffer general wear and tear in your absence. But be sure to specify in the lease what constitutes "damage" (which the renter is liable for) versus "normal wear and tear." (And do purchase appropriate insurance coverage just in case.)

It's fairly standard these days to ask for the first and last month's rent plus a security deposit equal to one month's rent. That way you'll recoup some of your losses if your renter moves out early (as ours did) or leaves you with property damage or any outstanding bills. One thing I wish we'd written into our contract is some sort of financial incentive for on-time rent payments. Our renter continually paid her rent 10 days to two weeks late and sometimes even later. We never resolved this particular issue but she did eventually pay her rent each month and that was the most important thing.

If you decide to rent out your house

• Make a list of things that need to be repaired at least six months before you leave. Leave things as maintenance- and problem-free as possible.

• Leave your renter with a "User Manual" for your house that details its idiosyncrasies as well as necessary details about maintenance, emergency numbers, names of neighbors, and so forth. (This manual was also helpful to us upon our return when we couldn't remember basic household facts such as when the garbage and recycling pick-ups were scheduled.)

• Sell or give away 50% of your stuff. If you can get rid of even more, do it. You'll raise funds for your trip, help someone else out who needs that stuff more than you do, have less to store, have less to worry about in general, and have less to mess with when you return. You'll be very surprised by how little you've learned to live with when you get back.

Work during your sabbatical

The notion of working during your sabbatical is a bit of an oxymoron, isn't it? The dictionary definition of sabbatical is "bringing a period of rest," as in Sabbath — no work. And really, taking time off and not working during your sabbatical can have a profound impact on your entire family. If there's any way you can take a true family sabbatical where nobody works at a paying job, I urge you to do it! You might not have this opportunity again until you retire and by then, your kids will probably be long gone.

But what if you want to work a little while you're gone? Or, and this is the more likely scenario, what if earning a little bit of cash during your sabbatical is the difference between being able to swing it financially or not going at all? Then by all means, work.

As I've already mentioned, there are numerous things you can do to bring in a few bucks while you're living abroad. Thanks to the wonders of the Internet, Michael designed a house addition for clients back home during the first few months of our stay and that was a nice little chunk to add to our bank account. Halfway through our sabbatical, I taught a six-week creative writing class to some visiting U.S. high school students and that, along with a strange little writing gig that fell into my lap, put close to $2,000 in our pockets. The amount seems rather trivial now, but $2,000 goes a long way in Mexico. Even more importantly, I was able to claim some legitimate self-employment income that allowed me to write off many travel expenses on our taxes. (The irony is that we made so little during that period we didn't need the write-off. But it's something to keep in mind for your own tax situation.)

Making money abroad legally

If you do decide to work abroad, make sure you check thoroughly into the legality of your endeavors. Depending on where you are living, it can be extremely difficult to legally find work with a foreign firm unless you can provide a skill that the locals lack (computer expertise, for example). It may ultimately be easier to work for yourself by providing a skill or service that's in demand. Can you build furniture? Repair computers? Teach writing? Teach English or another language? What about waitressing or bartending? Perhaps you're an artist and can teach painting or even knitting. The Internet can also provide you with excellent opportunities to work on projects from afar. Keep in mind that you're not looking for a regular weekly paycheck. You just need something to cover the difference between what you've saved and/or can get in rent or other passive income, and what you need to live in relative comfort during your sabbatical.

Handling Money Abroad

Years ago traveler's checks were the preferred way to carry money abroad. But times have definitely changed. These days it's much harder to find places to cash traveler's checks other than a bank, which requires standing in long lines and often offers less than stellar exchange rates. While stores and restaurants in major cities may accept traveler's checks, most others won't.

We found that ATM cards are a better way to go. Simply use your ATM card to make weekly or biweekly withdrawals of cash in the local currency from your bank or brokerage account at home. You'll receive excellent exchange rates at a minimal cost. There are no lines to speak of and you go when it's convenient for you rather than when it's convenient for the bank.

You'll find ATM machines nearly everywhere now. We used the ATM card for our Smith Barney FMA account (see below) and were charged $1.50 for each withdrawal. We typically got a few hundred bucks out each time at the best exchange rate of the moment. We had no problems whatsoever using cash for everything. Mexico, generally speaking, is a cash-only culture, which is the case in many countries around the world. We didn't write a single check for 18 months, and while we each brought along a credit card for emergencies, we never used either one.

Tip: Be sure to have at least two different ATM cards with you in case one gets lost or eaten by the machine (as happened to Michael's one day).

"ATM machines were great for getting cash and we used them much more than the bank account we set up in San Miguel." — Kim

Foreign bank accounts

We decided not to open a Mexican bank account because getting cash from the ATM worked fine for us. But if you're running a business or living in a large city, you might need a local checking or other bank account to cash checks or prove residency.

If you decide to open a bank account abroad, be advised that you will typically need several different forms of ID, among them your passport and a utility bill or other official bit of mail addressed to you at your foreign address. This can be a bit sticky since you may be renting and the bills may come to your address in your landlord's name. You can try using your rental agreement or just fudge things a bit. When we were applying for a "resident visa" in San Miguel we got around this by simply writing in our name above our landlord's on one of our water bills. The visa official didn't really care as long as he had the necessary information to complete the paperwork. The same thing goes for officials at banks, police stations, or anywhere else there are specific forms to be filled out. All the blanks on the forms need to be filled in whether you have the information or not. Often, you're asked to give the names and phone numbers of three residents who can vouch for you. Well, if you've just moved in and you know almost no one, what do you do? The common practice in San Miguel, and I suspect many other places throughout the world, is simply to make them up. So long as you provide three likely sounding gringo names and three different local phone numbers, nobody really cares if you're making it all up.

The official can fill in the blanks and you can get your documents or open your bank account or get your video rental card or whatever it is you're trying to accomplish. Everyone gets their job done and goes home happy.

Paying bills abroad

In Mexico and many other countries, paying bills is something you do in person or through a bank. You don't use the mail because you can never be sure if or when the payment will actually arrive at its destination. If you open a local bank account, you can sometimes have bills automatically paid through your account, and some of the larger utility companies offer electronic payment services or payments via a credit card. But in many towns, you still have to walk to the electric or telephone company building and stand in line to pay the bill. I liked this aspect of life abroad, although it infuriated a lot of the other gringos I met. It isn't efficient. It isn't necessarily fun. But it forces you to slow down and do nothing but smile at everyone around you, practice your foreign language skills, and be reminded once again that you're definitely living somewhere else in the world.

Walking around with money

We never had a problem with pickpockets or theft while we traveled but we were always cautious about flashing money around. Part of living abroad safely is being sensitive to the culture you're visiting and not acting the part of the ugly tourist. If you're wearing expensive clothes and jewelry, and you're loudly trying to line up some locals to take their picture with that really nice looking camera you've got slung about your neck, I'd try to rip you off too.

Cultural courtesy ensures your own safety. Don't flaunt your relative privilege in a world filled with desperately poor people, and don't walk around with a purse or wallet full of large bills. Keep the bulk of your money hidden in a passport holder or money belt and have only a few small bills available in your pocket, backpack, or small purse. You should generally walk around with only enough money to fill a beggar's outstretched hand, buy some fresh produce, and bite the bullet and order yet another ice cream cone for the kids.

If you're specifically out on a buying spree and you're carrying around a large amount of money, look around before you take out your money to pay for an item. If someone you don't know seems a bit too interested in your wallet, tell the vendor you'll return later. Or ask if there's a more private place to handle the transaction. The vendor will undoubtedly hustle away anyone lurking nearby if not doing so means the possible loss of your business.

Observe sensible precautions. When you're withdrawing money from your bank account electronically, use an ATM in a populated area in broad daylight or one that you know quite well. Better yet, use an ATM machine located inside a bank. By all means, avoid using ATMs at night. Be wary, too, of using any isolated ATM machine in unfamiliar surroundings. There are numerous ATM scams at work. A common one involves the use of sophisticated equipment that attaches a false front to an ATM machine. The altered machine performs exactly like a normal ATM except that after you insert your card and type in your password, you get nothing back except an enormous headache after you realize your card and password have been stolen.

If your ATM card is ever lost or stolen or you're a victim of ATM fraud, it's critical that you report it immediately to the issuer of the card so your account can be cancelled.

> *"Do as much electronically as possible. Get direct dial numbers for credit cards or other institutions back home before you leave because the 800 numbers they list often cannot be accessed outside the U.S. or Canada. Give someone back home power of attorney, and get a local post office box with U.S. mail forwarding. It was great the first few months to get magazines forwarded to us, along with all our mail."*
>
> — Kim

Taking Care of Business Back Home

The easiest and most reliable way to pay all your bills back home is to set up monthly, quarterly, or one-time electronic payments through what's called a "bill pay" account. Bill pay accounts are like regular bank accounts with some enhanced options that can be very helpful when you're overseas. Once you fill out the appropriate paperwork to open one up, you can transfer funds into it from regular bank accounts; write checks towards it; have funds deposited into it from nearly anywhere; use debit, credit, and ATM cards associated with it, and set it up to pay nearly any bill including sewer and water, insurance, rental and loan payments, and credit card charges. These accounts are completely flexible and can be changed at any time using a password and an Internet connection.

We arranged to pay all of our bills electronically and automatically through a central brokerage account at Salomon Smith Barney (now a subsidiary of Citibank and simply Smith Barney) called a Financial Management Account, or FMA. But you can find something similar at nearly every brokerage or bank around the country. Brokerages typically charge a minimal annual fee to set up the account ($50 for our FMA at the time) and give you numerous options for how to use it.

Tip: Be aware that some banks charge a fee for every bill paid electronically from your account. We found that brokerages generally offered a better deal by charging an annual fee rather than a per use charge. We transferred the majority of our sabbatical savings to this account and used our ATM cards to access our funds from overseas. Our renter deposited her monthly payments into this same account using pre-addressed deposit slips and pre-stamped envelopes. This is a great way to centralize and organize your business dealings. Make sure you set up your account so that you can negotiate any bank transfers via fax, telephone, and email as well as in writing since there are times you may have to transfer funds in a hurry.

Tip: It's prudent to set up your bill pay account several months before you leave so you're sure that everything's working smoothly. By paying at least a few months of bills electronically while you're still at home, you can work out any bugs that might occur on the front end. As long as you have consistent Internet access to monitor your account, it's a relatively painless way to manage things while you're away.

> *"We managed our money over the Internet, paying our bills online and keeping track of our bank accounts. I even arranged a short-term loan toward the end of our trip completely online. Then, to get cash, we used our Tyme (ATM) card. This system worked very well for us. We didn't need a bank account in Mexico and we brought very little money in traveler's checks."* — Julie

Make sure to read all the limitations and requirements associated with your bill pay account carefully. Some banks allow these accounts to go dormant after a specific period (usually a year) if no deposits or checking activity is associated with the account. Be aware that electronic payments are not considered checking activity. We found that out the hard way with the garbage bill, and we were lucky a family member back home could deal with it in person for us. Bottom line: have someone back home available to deal with emergencies. Also, get the direct dial telephone number and a personal email address from somebody at each bank, brokerage, insurance company, utility, etc. that you'll be dealing with while you're gone.

> *"Before you leave, it's very important to make a face-to-face or some other direct contact with a person at your bank or any other institution that you'll need to do business with back home. Get their phone number and a personal email. Rob managed to do that with one person at our bank and it made a world of difference. Dealing with other agencies (to resolve a glitch in our house insurance and reinstate our car and health insurance) was a huge and costly headache. We could only get their 800 numbers and 800 numbers don't work abroad. So, make a contact, let them know who you are and what you're doing, and get their email address."* — Marline

Tip: It's not a bad idea at all to give someone back home power of attorney so that they have the authority to handle any financial and legal matters that may come up unexpectedly while you're gone.

"We gave my mother power of attorney over our checking account, so she could sign checks – she paid a few monthly things for us, like our mortgage and our credit card. We didn't have any problems."   — Rachel

The Long Arm of the IRS

The tax man cometh, even overseas. All of the information you need regarding filing from overseas is readily available on the IRS website. The rules are not complicated and depending on how long you're planning to be gone, if you're out of the country on April 15, you'll have several months beyond the official filing date to file your taxes without penalty. Do confer with your tax consultant prior to leaving, particularly if you plan to earn any money during your sabbatical.

There are specific reporting requirements for money earned overseas (although in many cases you needn't report it on your U.S. tax return if it's less than $80,000). Paying foreign taxes, however, is a different ball of wax altogether. If you've been working (legally) for a foreign company and are required to file taxes in another country, consult a tax advisor there and be prepared to take a fairly significant tax hit.

If you will be self-employed while overseas, ask your U.S. tax advisor about writing off big-ticket items such as airplane tickets, luggage, laptop computers, and such. Some states will also allow you to deduct a portion of the educational costs for schooling your children abroad, including tutoring, books, and supplies.

It's not difficult or complex to deal with your taxes while you're away. Just make sure you consult a tax advisor before your sabbatical to clarify all the income reporting requirements, write-offs, and deductions you may be entitled to during your time away. Do the research and preparation before you leave, and you'll be fine.

Note: If you do your own taxes, then you already know how to get to the necessary software to fill out your tax forms and file electronically. If not, you may want to look into this before you leave.

7. School Daze Part One: Working with Schools at Home

"Asher attends a jardín de niños (daycare) for a half day at the same place Cleome goes to school. Cleome wears a uniform each day (our little Mexican/Jewish/Catholic schoolgirl) and winds around the cobbled streets downhill to her school, about a 15-minute walk from home. The school is a bilingual private elementary school with perhaps 40 students. There are three other students who are also norteamericanos. Later in the day, it's a much harder 30-minute walk uphill — dodging cars, elderly Indian women, and the ubiquitous dog poop. All with Asher nodding off and drooling on your shoulder."
El Grito #2

How do you find the right school abroad and how will your current school react to your plans? And what about coming back? Will your child be ready academically to rejoin his or her classmates at home?

Schooling is such an important issue that I devote two chapters to it. In the balance of this one, I'll outline some of the concrete steps you can take to ensure a smooth departure from and reentry into your child's school at home. In the next, I'll focus on finding the right school abroad for your child and your family.

Plan for Your Child's Smooth Departure and Reentry

It may seem odd, but a good way to start preparing your child for attending school abroad is by laying the groundwork for your child's return to his or her current school before you leave. Obviously, a lot can change during your time away and you may ultimately decide not to return your child to the same school. But your children (and you) will feel much more comfortable with the idea of leaving teachers, friends, and school administrators behind if they know they have a place waiting for them when they return.

Don't be surprised if school administrators aren't exactly thrilled by the idea of you taking your kids out of school for a family sabbatical. Some school districts even have policies that prohibit or discourage parents from removing their children from school for longer than prescribed vacation periods. The reasons are partly financial and partly academic. Schools receive money for students who are present. In tight financial times, you may be told that you risk losing your child's spot at the school or are jeopardizing his or her academic career by taking your child out for an extended period of time. The child's age will likely make a difference. If you plan to take a sabbatical with older children, be prepared to "make up" your child's time away by doing special projects, tracking your child's class through assignments and tests, and/or by providing specific documentation of your child's academic progress abroad. While these measures are not usually required for children in the lower grades, they're not necessarily unheard of in competitive school districts or popular schools.

The priorities of educational administrators are often more administrative than educational and because your situation may not fall neatly into anyone's area of responsibility, you may worry that your child's future placement will fall into one of those deep, mysterious "cracks" in the system. Try the steps outlined below. Then, if you still find your school officials "unable" to work with you in this area, keep your anxiety to a minimum and continue to work quietly behind the scenes to ensure your child's reentry on your return. No one I've spoken with has had a child turned away by their school after returning from a family sabbatical.

A word of caution when dealing with school officials. Don't burn any bridges that you may need to cross upon your return. While some people may be inspired by your plans, there will likewise be those who are threatened by this type of adventure. They may be envious, scared, or just downright confused by your desire to step outside their safe and tidy world. Humor them. There's a good chance your child will be welcomed back even though it may seem uncertain or even unlikely when you leave.

Do Your Homework Early On

Talk to your child's principal as soon as you know you'll be leaving and find out if there's an existing school or district policy regarding long-term absence from school and eventual readmittance. As I mentioned in *Chapter 1*, taking your children out of school is easiest when they're young and gets progressively more difficult the older they are. If there is no official district policy regarding long-term absences, your school principal is likely to be the one in charge of managing the comings and goings of individual students. If you're lucky enough to have a school principal who is sympathetic to your family's adventure, congratulations, because your battle is largely won. If, on the other hand, you find your principal reluctant or disinterested in your sabbatical plans, there are things you can do to gain his or her support:

• *Enlist help on the ground.* Find a teacher, a staff member, or an administrator at your child's school who is sympathetic to your family's adventure and who is willing to advocate on your behalf — preferably someone who has a personal relationship with your child. This is the most important thing you can do to maintain a surrogate presence and ensure minimal friction upon your child's departure and return. We were extremely lucky that Cleome's second grade teacher was a bundle of enthusiasm and wished us nothing but the best on our adventure. She made suggestions about how to best approach the principal, gave us books to take with us so that Cleome could stay on a par with her classmates academically, and even threw Cleome a going away party on her last day at school. She also paved the way for Cleome's return to fourth grade. (See *Chapter 20: Going Back* for school reentry suggestions.)

• *Petition the principal (or school district) by letter.* First, find out who makes the final decision regarding a child's enrollment status. Then write that person a letter outlining your request to remove your child from school for a specific period of time. Include your projected departure and return dates, and describe:

- How you will keep your child academically on a par with his or her classmates while you are on sabbatical.

- Why you think this is a valuable educational experience for your family.

- How your family will use this experience to help the school community upon your return. For example, you might offer to bring back cultural studies materials such as foreign language books, movies, and games, or to do a school-wide slideshow and lecture when you come back.

It may also help to mention some concrete things you will contribute to the school while you are gone, things like an online journal for classmates and digital pictures of your destination.

Ask your principal (or appropriate district official) to sign off on your letter and request that it be added to your child's official school file.

Caution: If your school principal is the one who makes the final decision regarding your child's enrollment status, do not involve the school district unless absolutely necessary. It will only complicate matters and anger your child's principal. Principals run their schools like fiefdoms and districts rarely intervene on behalf of families who want the rules bent on their behalf.

Ultimately, whether or not your efforts to ensure a smooth, officially sanctioned departure are acknowledged, you will at least have left a paper trail that may carry weight with administrators upon your return.

"Both the elementary and the middle school were VERY supportive. They suggested home schooling in math and making sure our kids continued to read a lot and to try and encourage writing. They said the kids wouldn't miss much and if they did, they could pick it up when they returned, like kids who are transferred in. Kyle had just started middle school in Hinsdale and there was a lot of stress and high expectations on homework and tests. Going to Mexico was going back to a small class environment that was more nurturing. When he started seventh grade when we returned, I could tell he was a lot more mentally prepared for it than when he was in sixth grade."

— Kim and Andy

Tip: Find out if your child's current school will require any documentation from your child's school abroad to be readmitted when you return. If the answer is yes, put it on your calendar as something to think about once you're living abroad.

• ***Get involved with your child's school before you leave.*** Make yourself an important part of the school's success and you have a much greater chance that they'll bend over backwards (or at least give you the time of day) when you return. It's a good idea in any case. Host the second grade dinner. Volunteer for field trips. Be a class reader. Find out if there are teachers (or classes) who might benefit from having a contact on the ground in the place you'll be going. Offer to create a website for the school while you're gone as part of a class research project. Mention that you'll be bringing back information and class resources for the school when you return. This may not help your cause, but it can't hurt. You want to be as much of a helpful presence as possible up to your departure date so the school community will remember you fondly while you're away.

Consult With Your Child's Teacher

Schedule a time to sit down with your child's current teacher to discuss what supplemental homework and areas of study might be necessary to keep your child's skill level on a par with his or her peers'. Ask the school for workbooks and texts you can take with you to supplement your child's education abroad. Or at least get the names of the books your child would have been reading and working in during the time you'll be gone and purchase the books yourself. You can often buy textbooks directly from the publisher online or through educational booksellers.

Tip: Discount bookstores (and others) often carry a good selection of workbooks (aimed at homeschoolers) for every grade level and subject. Look online for excellent booklists by grade level and reading ability as well as for organizations that offer support to parents interested in homeschooling or in helping their kids with any type of study program at home. You'll find some of these organizations listed in "Other Useful Internet Sites: Homeschooling" in *Resources*.

Don't worry that your child will fall behind while you're away. It's just as likely that your child will return with a bit of an advantage over classmates who stayed at home.

> *"The kids were very excited about returning to school (except the youngest). We did find, however, that the high school education in Mexico for my oldest pushed her ahead here in the States. Math was much more advanced in Mexico and she is thoroughly bored in Level I Spanish here, which she must take regardless of her experience. The same with my youngest daughter, whom I moved up a grade in Mexico. She is thriving here in second grade. My son is cruising through the same here as in Mexico."*
>
> — Karen

Plan for a Smooth Reentry

Be prepared for a snafu or two when you return, but do all you can on the front end to make your child's reentry problem-free. Ask a friend, a classmate's parent, or a family member to fill out any necessary school applications or "Intent to Return" forms during your absence. If you have any trouble, email your special advocate at the school to pinch-hit for you one more time. (And remember to bring him or her back an especially nice thank-you gift!)

SCHOOLS AND RED TAPE

As you gather important documents to bring along with you on your sabbatical, make sure you include the previous year's transcripts from your children's U.S. schools. They may not be necessary, but if they are, having them with you will save you an enormous amount of time and any number of headaches. Also, as I mentioned in *Chapter 5*, bring along the original (with watermark) birth certificate for each member of your family. Every major and minor official wants to see this, even if they can't read it.

Caution: Don't let anyone keep the originals. Hand out copies like water but guard the originals with your life.

Find out from your children's U.S. schools what type of documentation will be necessary to demonstrate their attendance at their foreign schools upon their return. Nothing may be required. But since it can take a long time to get things from overseas schools, you will need to ask for these documents well in advance if they will be needed when you return home. Bureaucracy anywhere is seldom efficient and in most places in the world it moves at a snail's pace or not at all. Save yourself some headaches and request copies of any documents you think might even vaguely come in handy.

8. School Daze Part Two: Finding the Right School Abroad

"The kids have settled in well to their new schools. Cleome, in particular, has turned out to be nothing less than amazing. Her best friend now is a girl from her class (a Mexicana) and it's thrilling to hear them whisper secrets in Spanish all night long during sleepovers. The results from Cleome's recent batch of tests came home yesterday (get ready for some parental bragging) and she scored such high marks that her picture was posted in the 'Quadra de Honor'" — the 'Square of Honor' on the school courtyard wall. Remember, everything (even English) is in Spanish. We were astounded and she was pretty proud of herself as well. Asher, cute and spunky as ever, is potty-trained (ecstatic cheers) and is thriving in his school. We stumbled upon a Spanish Montessori program that appears to be on a par with, or even better than, anything we've found in St. Paul, with real educational facilities (as opposed to a collection of motley, abused daycare toys), an excellent director, and best of all — grass!"   El Grito #5

Education abroad is a complex topic and probably one of the greatest concerns for parents dragging their kids halfway around the world. Getting advance information about schools in the place you'll be heading is often difficult if you can't visit beforehand, which is usually the case if you're on a limited budget. Moreover, schools offer your family some of the best and most natural opportunities to meet neighbors, make new friends, and bridge the language and culture gap abroad. Keep in mind that attending school abroad is a very different experience from attending at home. Taking a family sabbatical is an enormous learning experience in itself and the most "educational" aspect of attending school in another country is *being* in another country. That goes double if you're planning to do it all in another language. For all those reasons, finding the *best* school in a particular city is a lot less important than finding the *right* school given your family's particular set of circumstances.

Finding the right school for your child depends largely on three things: your child's individual learning style, your family's sabbatical goals, and the academic options available to you in your sabbatical destination. Rest assured, wherever you spend your sabbatical, going to school abroad will be a very different experience for your child from going to school back home. Even if the school offers a primarily English-language environment, you'll undoubtedly encounter a variety of cultural, social, and educational challenges. And if your child's school day is conducted in a language other than English, those challenges will expand dramatically. The more relaxed and flexible you and your children can be on the front end regarding academics, the better overall academic experience your family will have during your time away.

> *"The logistics of getting our children ready to attend school were much harder than we expected. We had to get uniforms made and travel to a larger city over an hour away to purchase books."* — Julie

> *"The kids had to have three uniforms: white sailor dresses for the girls on Mondays (white pants, blue suit jacket, and ties for the boys), red sweaters and plaid skirts the other days (red sweaters and blue pants for the boys), and navy sweat suits for both girls and boys on the P.E. days. They assigned a lot of copying which I found very strange and I didn't ask the kids to do it. One night, Chloe's homework was to copy a whole story from her reading book, and to write the numbers and their written names from one to three hundred. That would have taken even a Spanish-speaking seven-year-old child at least four hours, so I'm not quite sure what that was about."*
> — Leah, with Gabe (9) and Chloe (7), who lived in
> San Miguel de Allende for six months

It's helpful to think of your search for schools abroad as an exploration as opposed to an effort to find the right fit immediately. You may be surprised to discover that the right school for your child abroad is very different from your child's school back home. It might not be prestigious, or have a small teacher-pupil ratio, or even be that academically rigorous, and yet still fill the bill.

Note: There's necessarily a lot of give and take between schools abroad and visiting families. It will be much more pleasant for everyone if you can resist the urge to control every aspect of the experience at the beginning. Oftentimes, you'll end up cobbling two or more schooling options together to come up with something that works for your family and your kids. Don't be surprised if you finally hit upon something that works only after trying one or two things that don't.

Decide on Your Academic Goals for Each Child

Before you start exploring schooling options, it's important to discuss the relative importance of the various academic goals of your sabbatical for your children. Is fluency in another language a top priority? Do your kids need to keep up with their studies at home? Are there specific subjects or topic areas you want to them to concentrate on? Is socialization with the local population a priority, or is meeting other kids from around the world more important? What about their English studies? Will you bring work from back home for them to complete each day alongside the homework from their new schools? Will you need language tutors for your kids on a daily basis? How will your kids complete their homework in an unfamiliar language? Many schools abroad are run by religious organizations. Do you have a religious or pedagogical preference?

If your primary education goals for your kids are learning to speak the language of your sabbatical destination and interacting with its culture, the biggest decision you'll face regarding schooling abroad is whether to go the full immersion route and put your kids in schools taught completely in another language, or whether a bilingual approach (where some subjects are taught in English and others in the native language) might be more appropriate. Other options may include private "American" schools (where classes are taught in English with the option of taking classes in the local language), homeschooling, and a variety of language classes, private tutors, and tiny private schools willing to educate your children any way you see fit. Often, there are so many choices that it's hard to know where to begin (see "Shopping for Schools," page 138).

Taking the Immersion Route

If you want your kids to achieve fluency in another language, the immersion route is a good way to go. But, and this is a big but, immersion commonly backfires for two reasons. First, the kids are ill prepared for the experience, and second, they don't spend enough time in the school to move beyond an initial transition period to actual language learning. If the reason you are choosing an immersion experience for your children is to help them achieve fluency in another language, I urge you not to do it unless your kids are going to stay in the school for more than six months and preferably for a year or two. Two years is probably perfect to have your children reach any sort of true fluency.

Why you need six months plus

At six months, your kids will most likely just be starting to really learn the language. During the first two months of an immersion experience your children will learn a great deal about school uniforms and schoolbooks. They'll become experts in such things as the myriad requirements regarding book covers, page designations, pen and pencil colors, and acceptable styles of handwriting. The entire family will become familiar with the multitude of rules and regulations that foreign schools have regarding parental involvement (parents are typically NOT welcome in or even near the classroom in many schools abroad), along with the holidays, gym days, lunch behavior, classroom comportment, and rigorous and sometimes confusing (and archaic) homework demands.

Your kids will meet all their new teachers and classmates and go through a period of suspicion, possibly a bit of taunting or teasing, before finally gaining some level of acceptance (which can often lead to downright friendship if you're there long enough). So actual language learning takes a back seat initially while everything else takes precedence. Eventually, by month three or four, when you've finally got the hang of things, you and your kids start realizing that, by golly, they're actually starting to speak the language. Hooray! Now if they've only got another month or so to go before it's time to return home, you can see how discouraging the whole experience might feel.

"It was hard not being able to understand the kids (or people in general) in the beginning of the year. I thought everybody was making fun of me. Sometimes the differences in cultures made things very hard for me, too, like the way the kids interact at school." — Anthony, age 11

"Schools were really challenging the first year. Both Isaiah and Stanley went to Chinese schools — Stanley went to a daycare and was younger so even though he didn't speak, it was not such a problem. For Isaiah (9) there were many challenges. The main one was that we were unrealistic about how quickly he would pick up the language. Another was that it is highly unusual for an American child to go to a Chinese school — and they had no idea how to help him adapt. He actually became a bit of a troublemaker because he couldn't understand what was going on and would talk to people and sometimes bother them when they were trying to work. The teacher was afraid to communicate this to us because she was worried it would reflect badly on her as a teacher. The problem continued until it got a lot worse and we finally found out about it. If he had been a Chinese boy, Isaiah would have been hit, but the teacher knew not to hit him as we had made that clear. It was very complicated." — Rachel

Help your kids over the rough spots

If your family is willing to commit the time and energy necessary to making the immersion education experience a successful one, there are a number of things you can do to help your kids early on:

• *Start before you leave.* Early and ongoing exposure to the language and culture of the country you'll be visiting can make an enormous difference. Language classes, tutors, camps, CDs, DVDs, bilingual books, movies, restaurants — whatever you can find — will give your kids some idea of where they're headed and what they may encounter. This will help a lot. Even a few months of after-school or weekend language classes can give kids a few phrases to begin with and, perhaps more importantly, start to develop their ear for the language they'll be hearing all around them in the months to come. If you can afford it, consider moving to your sabbatical destination a month or so before the school year begins both to acclimate your kids to their new home and to find a private language tutor or to enroll them in language classes. Depending on your children's ages and learning styles, a mixture of language classes back home or abroad before school starts, and then one-on-one tutoring once school begins, can help keep your child's interest and confidence level high.

> *"A big thing would have been to come one to two months earlier in the summer to put our kids in language classes (at least two to three hours a day) before they started school. If a family can only come for one semester, try to make it fall. That way you might be able to come earlier to take language classes and get oriented. Also, kids are just gelling socially in their classes in September. Both kids agreed that a month of intensive language class would have helped them so much. Some families we met had their child do three hours of language a day for a month before starting school. That really, really helped them."* — Marline

• *Make a commitment as a family to learning the language — parents as well as children.* Not that everyone needs to achieve fluency, but it's extremely helpful if every member of the family is engaged in language learning at some basic level. Often, the success or failure of an immersion language experience simply comes down to one thing: practice. (For more information on language learning for adults, see *Chapter 15: Bridging the Great Divide.*)

• *Be honest with your kids about the challenges.* Don't sugarcoat the immersion experience when you discuss it with your kids. Let them know that it will be tough going at the beginning. Have clear-cut non-academic goals for them to achieve initially: make one new friend in their class; learn the names of two people who sit nearby; find out if the school has a soccer or volleyball team they can join. Make sure your kids understand that you will be there to help them any way you can and that you have confidence in their abilities to meet the challenges they're inevitably going to encounter. The immersion experience can be spectacularly unsuccessful if not approached with a great deal of flexibility and an appreciation for how difficult it is to learn a second language and to adjust to a new culture.

> "I'd tell parents not to worry too much about their kids having some rough patches at school. Even though it was terribly hard for Lilly in the first one to two months, it got better and she really enjoyed it. There was something important about her learning that things can be very, very rough and then get better." — Marline

> "Some of the children in my daughter's school were not very nice to her at times and she felt isolated. The flip side to this, though, is that she will probably be much more empathetic in the future to newcomers in her school here in the U.S. It also took our children longer to learn Spanish than we had expected." — Julie

• *Do your research.* A little front-end research into your child's school options and the reality of the school day in your intended sabbatical destination can go a long way to preparing your entire family for the challenges ahead. Knowing what to expect will help lower the stress levels and keep everyone on a more even keel.

> "I would have really tried to find out more about people who had tried to put their children in Chinese schools. I had never spoken to anyone and didn't know anyone who had tried to do that. It might have helped me prepare better." — Rachel

"For my eighth grader there were no bilingual programs that I could find since most of the bilingual programs go from first to sixth grade. Vasconselos seemed like a well-respected private school that had a very strong bilingual program until the sixth grade, so we figured Drew's classmates would be able to speak English. What I didn't realize was that most of his teachers would NOT speak English. The teachers who could speak English taught in the grades that had the bilingual program! Even though Drew had three and a half years of Spanish, it did not prepare him to study geography, chemistry, and physics in Spanish. After four months, it became apparent that he was not getting very much from the academic program — although he was becoming conversant in Spanish." — Kim

Be sensitive to what your child is going through

Expect that initially, immersion learning will be difficult for your child and he or she may feel afraid, grumpy, or out of sorts. Be patient and empathetic. Celebrate the tiny successes. You learned the name of a classmate? Hurray! You understood the homework assignment? Fantastic! What they are doing is hard and it will take time for them to feel OK. Try to offer help wherever you can but don't push too hard. Your child may already feel like a square peg in a round hole. Being pushy and intrusive with their teacher or with school officials (who may not speak any English) will only make them feel more uncomfortable. Ask gently what you can do to help. You may be surprised at what sorts of creative options are possible.

"As a parent, be a helpful advocate, not a demanding one. We suggested that we could help our daughter (age 11) if we could sit next to her for a couple of weeks. The director of the school allowed us (Rob and I taking turns) to sit in for a couple of weeks. We sat right next to our daughter and whispered key words and directions into her ear. Just that two weeks helped her enormously to have the confidence to continue. The other kids didn't mind at all having a parent there (unlike in the U.S. — these kids are accustomed to multi-generation mixing). For our eighth grader it wasn't so difficult. By that age there are enough Mexican kids who know rudimentary English to help out a foreign student." — Marline

If it doesn't feel right, try something different

Above all, it's important to remain flexible. Try to keep in mind that the immersion experience may not work for your child at a particular time or at a particular school. Decide as a family how much time everyone is willing to commit to a specific school experience. If it doesn't appear to be working out, try something else.

"We chose to have our children in totally Spanish-speaking schools. It was good for both their language development and developing a sensitivity to those in their classes at home who just don't 'get it.' The children went to three different schools. The boys, ages 9 and 11, went to a private military academy that a friend of ours, a captain in the army, got them into. In many ways it was the 'best' school of the three. Kira (16) chose to go to an all-girls high school. It was considered the best public high school in the country. Ellen (13) didn't want to go the all-girls route and picked a high school that was co-ed. It was not a real 'hot' school academically."   — Tani

"We had arranged for our children to attend a nearby elementary school in which only Spanish was spoken. Both kids were the only non-Mexican children in their classes. The first several weeks went well, but it then became increasingly difficult for our daughter. Her teacher had an unrealistic expectation about how fast she should be learning Spanish (I say this as a language major myself in college). I think Kaya might actually have learned more Spanish if she had been in a bilingual school with formal instruction because she often ended up in classes with a lecture-type format that she was at a loss to understand. In retrospect, I would have found a place that had a bilingual or an English-speaking school for my daughter (age 7). Although immersion worked for the five-year-old, it was too hard for my daughter, especially because there were no English-speaking kids in her life outside of school either unless we traveled." — Julie

Immersion school pluses

Despite the difficulties of the immersion experience, it is certainly one of the best ways for your children to become fluent in another language as well as to experience the richness and complexity of another culture. If you can give them enough time and if they stick it out, they will ultimately be welcomed into a foreign school community and allowed to cross cultural boundaries that are simply closed to outsiders. They will make potentially lifelong friendships with their classmates and teachers. And they will learn more about themselves and their strengths than they ever imagined possible.

> *"It was a tremendous growth experience for both girls. The schools they attended were small — one class per grade level. The girls claimed there were no cliques and the kids were extremely inclusive of everyone. Our eighth grade daughter said the boys and girls interacted very naturally without the rumors of boyfriend/girlfriend if you talked to each other. Both girls said they could be more outgoing and natural, and both said they talked more and said and did things they'd be too self-conscious to do at home in their rather large middle school. Our older daughter said it was nice because the kids were 'just normal, not fast like in the U.S.' In general, we felt the content of classes was more academically rigorous than in the U.S. We were especially impressed with science and history education. We were also quite impressed with the textbooks. In fact, in comparison, some of the texts our sixth grader has here at home look like fluff compared to the Mexican texts she had."* — Marline

The bottom line for successful immersion learning

• Prepare your children with early and ongoing tutoring in their new language.

• Give your kids enough time to achieve fluency. A year or more is best. Six months is the absolute minimum.

• Be prepared for an initial transition period that can be frustrating for both kids and parents.

• Believe that it will get better.

• If your child remains consistently unhappy after several months, consider switching schools or trying something different.

SOME ADVICE ABOUT IMMERSION LEARNING FROM KIDS, FOR KIDS

Emory (age 13) and Lilly (age 10) offer this advice for making the immersion experience more successful:

1. Get there at least a month before school starts and take language classes.

2. Have your parents help you find a friend/buddy before the first day of school. We had buddies and it really helped. Your parents can find them by contacting your school's director for names of families who might live close to you and have kids in the same grade or parents who know some English.

3. Expect that the first day and maybe even the first week will be really, really hard and scary. After the first day or two it gets better. Don't think it will stay that hard the whole time.

4. Don't try to tell your classmates all about your ways and your country; be interested in learning about their ways. It's fun.

5. At school, just do things their way. In Mexico, you have to take notes in a certain way. You have to write all capitals in red, then change pencils to continue the word in blue. You have to cover your notebooks a certain way. Don't complain. Just do it. Besides, you learn some good habits from their ways.

Bilingual Schools

Bilingual schools are a good option if you want your kids to be exposed to a new language and culture and you aren't going to be living in a particular city for longer than six months. They can also be used as a springboard to an immersion experience if you are going to be in a city for longer than six months and your child has no previous exposure to the language. Starting with the bilingual experience in such cases can give your child the necessary foundation in the new language and the self-confidence necessary to make an immersion experience truly successful. It can also help socially. In the bilingual school, you'll meet both foreign and native kids and parents and give yourselves a good leg up in the area of socialization. This is what we did with our daughter Cleome and for her, it proved very successful.

Bilingual schools in Europe, Mexico, and other parts of Central and South America tend to be private institutions, sometimes with religious affiliations. They are typically geared toward teaching English to native kids. The teachers might be native speakers with some English language ability or foreign-born ESL (English as a Second Language) teachers hired to teach English to local students.

Typically, half the day is taught in English and the other half in the native language of the country. In Mexico, we found that "English class" really comprised several subject areas that were taught in English. Math and science were taught in Spanish. We found that the "English" subject areas were one or two grade levels below those back home, but that the other subjects were either on a par with or more advanced than what was being taught back home, especially in the elementary grades.

Limitations of bilingual schools abroad

A bilingual school can improve your child's ear for learning a new language and teach basic classroom language skills. It can introduce cultural differences and help your child develop socialization skills gradually and all within the familiar framework of English. But it's important to keep in mind the limitations of a bilingual school. Many parents of English-speaking children feel disappointed at the end of a bilingual school experience because they failed to understand that the school's primary goal is teaching English to speakers of another language rather than teaching another language to English-speakers. This is a critical difference and it's why English-speaking children who go to bilingual schools abroad typically do not achieve fluency in another language. If both English and another language are being spoken in your child's classroom, which language do you think your child will choose to speak? Whichever is easier. If there are gringos and foreign language speakers (natives) in your child's classroom, whom will your children gravitate towards on the playground? Do you see where I'm heading? Who can blame kids for wanting to hang out with people who speak their language and share their customs and beliefs? If this is fine with you and you don't mind that your children will only slowly pick up phrases and words in another language, then this is a good option for your kids. They'll have fun meeting other kids from around the world; they'll learn the basics in another language; and they will continue to keep pace academically (*más o menos*) with their peers back home.

Tip: Use language tutors regularly to supplement the bilingual education and your child's language skills will improve over several months.

> *"I finally decided to move my kids to a bilingual school here in town. It had a great reputation and was the only school with Spanish as a Second Language (SSL) classes, which of course meant more gringos. It was what I was trying to avoid, but you can never predict how your children will react to different things. And it wasn't just the immersion thing that was bothering them, it was the quality of education they were getting. This was a private school. (Can you imagine what the public schools are like?) Anyway, what did I expect for $45 a month? I paid $280 a month per child at the bilingual school. It was normally $180 but I had to pay extra for the SSL teacher/class. Oh well, I was already spending about 40 bucks a week on tutoring for them."*
>
> — Leah

Immersion vs. Bilingual: Some Pros and Cons

I'm not convinced one route is necessarily better than the other *if* you have a significant period of time (a year or more) to spend in a city. If your sabbatical is shorter, I strongly suggest going the bilingual route (see above).

Unrealistic expectations

This is an area where unrealistic expectations are very common. We've met many families who naively (and with the best of intentions) committed their children to one or the other type of schooling with unfortunate results. Yes, children are more receptive to acquiring a foreign language than are adults. And given the right environment they'll learn it much faster than you (and torture you with their superior skills). But it's still a difficult process, and sink or swim doesn't work for everyone. Adjusting to a new school and social environment is challenging even at home. If in addition the culture is unfamiliar and your child's school day is conducted in a language other than English, those challenges expand dramatically.

Be especially thoughtful in your decision making if your child already speaks the language of your sabbatical destination. Immersion would seem to be a natural choice in such a case. But beware of making assumptions regarding your child's likelihood of success based solely on his or her ability to speak the language. Remember, it's not just the language of instruction that will be different for your child in an immersion experience; it's everything. One family we know put their 13-year-old son and 10-year-old daughter in a Mexican public school because both had grown up speaking Spanish in their home back in New York. It became apparent after a short time that despite the kids' ability to speak the language, the cultural and pedagogical differences in the school made it very difficult for them to learn effectively or to make friends with their peers. The family ultimately looked for other schooling options.

Going both routes

Given that our sabbatical was 18 months long, we had the luxury of trying out both the bilingual and immersion routes. We enrolled our then seven-year-old in a bilingual school for the first six months and then moved her to an immersion situation for the remaining year of our sabbatical. For our family and our daughter, that worked out very well. The six months of bilingual instruction gave Cleome (and the rest of our family) a gentle introduction to the language and culture. It also gave us time to learn about the immersion schools in San Miguel so we could choose the best one for our daughter when the time came.

I suspect Cleome would have learned Spanish more quickly had we gone the full immersion route right away. On the other hand, the adjustment to leaving home and living in a different country might have been much more difficult, and it would have required a lot more energy on our part to make her happy enough to learn another language. An unhappy child, no matter how bright or motivated, won't learn a new language whatever route you choose.

Good friends who moved with their four-year-old son and eight-year-old daughter to Guanajuato City, about an hour and a half from San Miguel, immersed both kids immediately in a Mexican school. Their son did fine but their daughter had a very difficult adjustment period for the first two months of their six-month stay. She was profoundly sad and felt completely isolated from her peers. As a result, she drove the rest of the family so nuts, they very nearly moved to San Miguel, where bilingual options were available. Another family we know who had a total of six months for their sabbatical adventure elected to go the full immersion route with their second and fourth graders. They got off to an incredibly bumpy start and, after a month, switched to a bilingual school and spent more time with private tutors.

How immersion worked for our daughter

We were lucky because we had the luxury of time on our side. After six months in a bilingual school, our daughter finished second grade and seemed (finally!) truly interested in speaking Spanish and motivated to *habla español*. It was obvious to us that an immersion experience was the only way Cleome would learn to speak more or less fluent Spanish in the year that remained of our sabbatical. We chose a private *mexicano* school and filled out the application for third grade. By then, all the required uniforms, book-covering, plastic wrapping, and so on was old hat. What wasn't old hat was being the only *gringa* in a school of 500 students and in particular, the only *gringa* in her third grade class of 47 *mexicano* strangers. Can you imagine? Her classroom back home had 20 kids in it and they all spoke her language.

We already knew that Mexican schools had heavy homework loads and, of course, that homework would now be completely in Spanish. We told Cleome right from the start that we would help her all we could and that we didn't care how she did academically. The priority was language learning; if she failed every subject, we didn't care. And we truly didn't. Our family's academic goals for the kids were learning about Mexican culture and learning Spanish. Everything else was secondary. Miss Paula, our tutor, helped Cleome with homework three times a week for an hour after school but the rest really was up to Cleome.

Frankly, we were extremely nervous about our decision to enroll her in this school, but Cleome loved it. Not that there weren't a few hurdles and awkward moments. But she thrived there. She made great friends, loved her teacher, and by the third month at her new school (nine months after we arrived in Mexico) she was on her way to serious fluency and was scoring at the top of her class on exams in every subject. Academically, we were pleased with the overall level of difficulty, the topics covered, and the teaching methods used. There was more rote memorization than in her classroom back home and we continued to have her do an hour of American homework each day to track her U.S. classmates, but she never seemed to find it too onerous.

"You might consider asking your children which subjects they enjoy most or which subjects are taught by friendly teachers who are clear in their teaching style. Then consider dropping one or two classes (taught by other teachers) and substitute a basic language class for them, taught if possible by one of the teachers they like. Often teachers are willing to pick up extra money by tutoring in language. Or the director of the school may know of someone. One of our daughters chose to focus on Civics and Spanish Literature not because they are necessarily her favorite subjects, but because these teachers were unusually clear, well organized, and wrote frameworks clearly on the board. In short, our daughter could follow them better."

— Marline

Deciding which route to take

Given our daughter's personality, age, the length of our sabbatical, and our family's overall sabbatical goals, an immersion experience right off the bat would have been terribly unfair to Cleome and quite probably would have been unsuccessful. That first six months of bilingual education was critical for boosting her self-confidence and providing an introduction to Mexican school culture, one that was quite different from her school culture back home. However, your child may thrive in a different sort of educational environment. One family we know who also spent 18 months in Mexico immediately enrolled their three children, ages 8, 10, and 12, in a private Mexican school. The two younger children had very good results with the immersion experience (after the bumps and lumps of the first few transition months). It was unfortunately much more difficult for their 12-year-old, who ended up hating his time there.

> *"There are no resources to help a foreign child integrate unless you choose a bilingual school. Our youngest daughter had little to no Spanish. We actually put her back a year into fifth grade in Mexico to make it easier and because the sixth grade class was much larger. Kids tried to help her but her inability to understand their intentions or to respond overwhelmed her. I was called to school many times to find a sobbing and shaking child. She was convinced they were taunting her, which really wasn't the case."* — Marline

Exploring Other Schooling Options

Immersion and bilingual programs are by no means your only schooling choices for your kids abroad. Many locations offer a wide variety of options, and if none of them suits you, you can homeschool.

Homeschooling

There is a great deal of information available on this topic online and in libraries and bookstores. If you are not currently homeschooling, I urge you to do some serious research before undertaking this with your child abroad. It requires considerable commitment from a parent or hired tutor and it can limit your family's exposure to the local culture rather drastically.

We had originally planned to homeschool Cleome in Mexico for the first six months and brought along a number of books and workbooks with that in mind. But after only three days of homeschooling our plans changed radically. We realized that (a) Cleome needed a friend right away and school was the easiest place to make that happen and (b) homeschooling was a huge commitment and we resented the amount of time and energy it took away from our own creative activities.

We did not abandon every aspect of our homeschooling plan. For the duration of our sabbatical we continued to supplement Cleome's Mexican education with the workbooks that we had brought from home. She continued to track her U.S. classmates in math, and we also worked on English spelling, grammar, and writing using a homeschooling workbook designed to keep these skills exercised. This extra tutoring amounted to between a half-hour and an hour of additional homework each day depending on her daily homework load. Overall, this small bit of supplemental tutoring was enough to keep her academic skills on a par with her classmates at home.

Tip: Consider adding supplemental academic (as opposed to language) tutoring by either you or a private tutor if your children will need to return home with a specific set of academic skills.

A homeschooling caution. If you're already homeschooling your children, you know vastly more than I do about this topic and I can only salute you for your commitment to your child's education. If you intend to continue homeschooling your children during your sabbatical abroad, I suggest that you think very carefully about the impact of that decision on your family's overall experience. As foreigners, you will most likely already feel a sense of isolation from the world around you. And schools abroad, even more so than back home (where there are usually other places to meet families in your area), are invaluable places to meet both local and other expat families — something that's critical for experiencing the richness of the culture around you.

Alternative schools

Depending on your sabbatical destination, you may be surprised at what is or is not available in terms of alternative schooling options. In some places, public schools or private religious schools are the only options. In other locations, the choices can be as varied (and mind-boggling) as they are in the U.S. We were surprised at the variety of educational philosophies and programs available in San Miguel (pop. 65,000) in addition to the many public and private schools (the majority of them Catholic, with varying degrees of emphasis on religious doctrine). While the options thinned notably in middle school and beyond, in the elementary grades there was a Waldorf school, a United Nations school, a Montessori program, military academies, language schools, and a significant number of other small private schools with a variety of educational philosophies, most of them attempting a bilingual program with varying degrees of success. Really, it seemed like a new school popped up every few months or so. There was also an "American" school that was reputed to be extremely rigorous academically. The subject matter there was personalized to each student and taught completely in English. A few families we know moved their kids to this program when neither the bilingual nor immersion routes worked out for them.

Most of the private bilingual options were twice or three times the cost of the local private schools (the monthly tuition at Cleome's bilingual school was the equivalent of $135 a month, three times the price of her immersion school, and the "American" school was even pricier). We did hear scattered reports both in Mexico and elsewhere of families paying significant tuition for average to poor quality education for their kids. However, generally speaking, as with most things, you get what you pay for. Of course, the costs of private schools abroad are relative to the local economy. Depending on where you go, the private school tuition may be significantly cheaper than a similar program back home.

Shopping for Schools Before You Move

The Internet can be an excellent way to gather information about local schools from other parents who are living in the city you'll be moving to. Many expat parents participate in message boards online and are happy to share their knowledge and experiences about sending their kids to schools in cities around the world. If you can afford it, of course, a pre-sabbatical visit to your destination may give you some idea of the different schools available to your children. But don't worry if this isn't an option for you. A quick look at a school rarely gives you an accurate sense of how your child might do there. So even though you may feel uneasy about not having something set up beforehand, it's often better just to wait until you arrive and get the lay of the land before committing to a specific school. Once you're on the ground, you can start visiting the local schools and talking to other expat families around you before making any decisions.

"The Internet really helped with finding schools. We were able to get info on a couple of possibilities and then rolled the dice and applied, basing the decision mostly on location, reputation, and how much vacation they gave. We figured for a year, it wouldn't matter too much if it were less than ideal. We were extremely lucky that the school happened to have openings for both our kids, as it was fairly small. That could have been tricky otherwise." — Frances

Note: The tuition cost will undoubtedly impact the make-up of the student body and whether (and which economic segment of) the local population will be represented. Keep that in mind as you shop the local schools.

Note, too: Class size varies a great deal in schools abroad and it isn't necessarily an accurate indicator of anything. Cleome attended a bilingual school for six months with a total of seven students in the combined second, third, and fourth grades. The following fall she moved to a large, private, Mexican Catholic school and was the only *gringa* in a class of 47 students. She enjoyed both of them and did very well at each one.

Enrolling Your Kids Abroad May Be Harder Than You Expect

As excited as you may be to enroll your dear, sweet child in a local school abroad, you may find school officials a bit cool to the idea initially. In some areas of the world, American children have the reputation of being a handful. Classrooms abroad are often quieter, more subdued places than their American counterparts. Teachers wield their authority differently and frown on pupils questioning their superior experience and knowledge. Our daughter was ultimately accepted but only after she took a lengthy examination and we completed a series of difficult interviews with the director.

Tip: Plan on several weeks of very hands-on involvement in arranging your children's school lives after you touch down, whether or not you have something prearranged.

Stay Flexible

Don't be afraid to try a variety of different schools and/or programs until you find something that feels right. Many families we know (including ours) started at one place and after a few months, depending on how their children were doing or what they'd heard from other parents, moved the kids to a different school until they were happy. That's a difference between schooling choices at home and abroad. In the States, it's important to find the right place for your children at the start of the school year and then keep them there to enhance stability and allow them to develop relationships with their peers and teachers. But in a foreign country, particularly if the language is new, the situation is more fluid. Everything's new and relatively temporary. No one's going to be hurt or offended if you try several different options. The most important thing is to find something that works for your children and your family as a whole. Remember, the experience should be fun. If it's not, and you and your kids are unhappy, *no vale la pena* (it's not worth the trouble).

If this whole process feels a bit hit and miss, that's because it is. There are no right or wrong ways to do it. All you can do is consider your child's interests, motivation, and ability to learn another language, the length of your sabbatical, and the various options available to you in your sabbatical destination. Then pick something and go for it. If you aren't happy with it, change it. One of the best things about living abroad is that the whole experience is about education in one form or another. A specific school or academic experience is just one out of the many learning experiences your child will have during his or her time abroad. So if after trying a certain school or a specific tutor for a few months, your child's interest or skill level changes — or you discover a potentially better fit someplace else — make the change. Staying flexible and keeping things in perspective will help you eventually find the school or educational situation that feels right for your child and your family. Ultimately, you can never know for sure how the whole thing will turn out until you try it.

Get A Tutor If You Can

Once you're abroad, language tutors can make the difference between fluency and failure. Tutors can not only help you and your children learn a new language and work through homework assignments, but also help you navigate the potentially rocky terrain of a new school culture. Your child may come home from school the first day and tell you that she needs to wrap each of her 15 notebooks in a certain colored paper and then in a specific kind of plastic. Your child cannot remember the exact color of the paper nor recall the word for plastic in the native language and you, of course, have no idea where to buy either but . . . it's all got to be done by tomorrow. Your child is already frantic because he or she is the only one in the class who doesn't have this done yet and it must be done because she doesn't want to feel any more like an outsider than she already does. Who can you ask about this? Your tutor.

And how about that school uniform? Why does your child need a certain uniform for Monday that's different from the uniform for the rest of the week? And why is there yet another uniform for sports day? And why does the capital letter of each sentence have to be written in red pen? And what's that thing that your child has to write across each piece of paper before she even starts the homework? Don't go nuts. Ask your tutor.

And ask her where to buy school supplies. And clean meat. And where does she or he get the laundry done? And how do you take the bus to . . . ? A language tutor can become an invaluable ally for your family, a friend to your kids, and someone who eventually invites you into her own life as well. Our daughter's tutor, Miss Paula, became an important person to all of us and enriched our family's sabbatical experience enormously.

How to find your tutor. You can find language tutors abroad by word of mouth, by looking at ads in newspapers and on bulletin boards around town and at the local high schools and universities, and through teachers at your child's school. Ask other expat families for suggestions and check the Internet as well. Don't be afraid to try different tutors, different hours, and different approaches. Not every tutor is a good teacher and certain tutors will have personalities and styles that mesh better with those of your children. Language classes and camps both here and abroad can be located in a similar fashion.

9. Is Anyone Out There? Communicating With the Folks Back Home

"These last few months have passed about as quickly as the first couple weeks had passed slowly and, as you can see, our website has languished a bit along the way, waning in priority as our life here has gently but firmly come to supplant our life "not there." In retrospect we can see that the first couple months here were spent just arriving: getting adjusted and finding our way around, building new routines like sandcastles out of the seemingly endless beach of days, taking up the easy slack in a new language — every new dumb word an accomplishment, everyone we met a new friend."   El Grito #4

Nearly every city of any size offers an opportunity to be as connected to the world as you care to be. That's either good or bad news depending on your point of view. What will vary a great deal are the cost, types, and dependability of the available mail, telephone, and computer-related communication services.

Dealing With Your Mail

Before contemplating electronic communications abroad, it's important to set up an efficient system for handling your snail mail back home. Life will continue there while you're away on sabbatical. Dealing effectively with your mail back home will help you prevent problems and keep you abreast of both the routine and unexpected — anything from an unanticipated bill to news of births, deaths, and marriages.

Handling the incoming mail back home

If you know your permanent address abroad before you leave home and you're fairly sure you'll be staying put awhile, the easiest thing to do is to fill out a change of address form at your local post office (or online) and list your new address abroad. You can also use pre-printed postcards provided by the post office to notify friends, relatives, and business contacts of your new address abroad. If you forget to notify someone, the U.S. postal service will forward your first class mail to your new address for one year and second class mail (magazines and such) for 60 days. It will not forward bulk mail or packages (third class mail). Simply informing all your correspondents of your new address is the cheapest and most reliable way to go, assuming you know where you'll be and that home mail-delivery service is available and dependable in your sabbatical destination. Canada Post will forward nondutiable mail for as long as you like for a fee. Rosanne Knorr's *The Grown-Up's Guide to Running Away from Home* has an excellent change of address checklist that will help ensure that you don't forget anyone who should know of your new address, from your tax service to your veterinarian (see *Resources*).

Forwarding your mail to your home abroad. If your housing plans are more fluid and you plan to stay someplace temporarily until you get your bearings, you'll need to have your mail forwarded to you. There are a variety of ways to have this done. And even if you have your permanent address before you go, you may want to consider having your mail held and forwarded to you later if you're concerned at all about the reliability of mail service to your foreign home address. The U.S. Post Office will hold your mail for up to one month and then forward it overseas, but you'll be responsible for the extra international postage charges when it arrives at your new address. This gets very expensive and also you won't get anything on time, which is a problem if you're paying bills by mail. (See *Chapter 6: The Money Thing* for information about paying bills online.) Moreover, you'll be paying to have all your mail forwarded, including the junk.

A less expensive option is to have your mail forwarded to a postal box or another address back home, such as a friend's or relative's house. You can then make additional plans to have it forwarded to you abroad, ideally after someone has culled through it to make sure you're not going to be paying international postage on the last five grocery store circulars. The U.S. Post Office will forward first class mail to an address within the U.S. for up to one year free of charge. This can be an excellent way to go if someone is willing to shoulder the responsibility of grabbing the mail at your P.O. Box or their own address, and then packing it up once or twice a month and mailing it to you. If this is the method you choose, I suggest you leave some money with this good-hearted soul to cover postage and also have them keep track of mailing costs so you can reimburse them at the end of your sabbatical for any additional postage you might owe. Also, it's not a bad idea to toss in a bit extra on the front end so they can take themselves out to dinner a couple of times at your expense. You're asking someone to do you a pretty nice favor here. Everyone will feel better if you can find some way to express your appreciation. At the very least, plan to bring them back a nice gift from wherever your adventure takes you. Better yet, do both!

Time-sensitive mail. Most time-sensitive material can be sent to you online if you request it. This includes bills, monthly bank and investment statements, insurance and mortgage documents, tax forms, utility statements, and most other important communications. Moving to online communication allows you to cancel the mailing of paper copies. That's not only more environmentally friendly but also helps you save on international postage because you can have your mail sent to you less frequently and in greatly diminished volume.

Leave very explicit instructions with whoever is handling your mail about how often you want your mail sent and what you do and do not want mailed. Sending a package of mail internationally can get pricey since you're charged by the ounce. Decide if all those kitchen and electronics catalogs are really worth the cost and, if not, ask your buddy to recycle them. Even better, cancel those catalogs before you go.

Periodicals and catalogs. Frankly, I would suggest you cancel all your magazine, catalog, and newspaper subscriptions for the duration of your sabbatical. Why? For two reasons. First, forwarding periodicals abroad can be very expensive. Second and more important, periodicals are one more way we distract ourselves and chop our days up into tiny discrete increments. Magazine articles are getting shorter and shorter to accommodate the typical reader's lack of time and ability to concentrate. Go cold turkey during your sabbatical as much as possible by leaving behind all your usual distractions — the media in particular. You'll be surprised at how much difference it will make in your ability to concentrate on more important projects (or at the very least to read more *books*). If there are certain periodicals or specialty catalogs that you simply can't do without, make sure you inform the circulation departments of your new address several months before you leave. It can take weeks for change of address notifications to take effect.

Tip: However you decide to handle your subscriptions, cancel all bulk and nuisance mailings before you go by sending a note to the Mail Preference Service, Direct Marketing Association, P.O. Box 643, Carmel, NY 15012-0643. Include your full name, address, zip code, and your request for them to "activate preference service." You'll still get any catalogs that you've specifically requested.

How we handled incoming mail

During our sabbatical, our renter graciously consented to let us continue receiving mail at our home address. She tossed it into a bag and passed it along to one of my relatives whenever they remembered to come and retrieve it. Then they "couriered" it to us — that is, whoever was next visiting us, simply hauled it along. We had enough visitors during our 18 months abroad that whenever someone visited, they brought along with them all of our accumulated mail. We didn't need to have any of it sent to us on a regular basis because we handled all of our most important and time-sensitive communications online. That meant less mail coming for us in general, less mail for our relatives to cull through, and less mail being transported in someone's suitcase. That said, we were still surprised at the amount of junk that got through our filter. Whenever a guest showed up and handed us a bulging folder with three months' accumulation of mail inside, the vast majority of it immediately went into the recycle bin (or would have if San Miguel had a recycling program).

The only time we had a problem with this system was during the first few months, before a visitor (my mom) showed up with our first mail call. Unbeknownst to us, one of our credit card companies had turned a charge over to a collection agency for nonpayment. It was the charge for our one-way car rental from Minneapolis to Chicago to catch our flight to Mexico. We'd actually paid the entire car rental bill in cash but had used a credit card number for the required security deposit. The company hadn't recorded the cash transaction and had billed our credit card. Because we'd paid off that credit card before leaving the U.S. (and weren't using it in Mexico) we never checked our records online. Luckily, we still had the car rental receipt (hang on to things like that!!!) and sent a copy of it back with my mom, who did battle with the car rental agency once she returned. Overseas, the 800 numbers you use to call about matters like this at home either don't work or cost you if they do. So we were grateful we didn't have to wage the battle from Mexico. It all worked out fine and our credit record wasn't affected but it does point out how careful you have to be in your financial transactions if you're going to be leaving the country for any period of time.

Caution: Be sure someone trustworthy is checking your mail regularly if you won't be doing it yourself. And do remember to bring along direct contact phone numbers (not the 800 numbers) for your bank, credit card companies, and the like.

Explore private mailing/package services. Companies that specialize in mailing and delivery services are available in many cities throughout the U.S. and Canada and around the world. These include companies like Mailboxes Etc. and Pack 'n' Mail. You rent a private mailbox for a monthly or yearly fee (longer is cheaper) that can be paid by check or charged to a credit card and paid online. Unless you're absolutely certain that a private U.S. postal box is the way to go for your entire sabbatical, I would recommend retaining the flexibility of a monthly contract. It's a bit more expensive but the built-in flexibility may offset any additional cost. The private mailing service will follow your instructions regarding receiving and forwarding your mail. If you use a service here in the U.S. or in Canada, be sure it can accept and forward parcels and that you can contact it easily if your forwarding instructions change.

How we handled outgoing mail

We occasionally used a private mailing service located in San Miguel that charged us fifty cents to mail a letter and a flat rate based on weight to mail a package. The mail was sent in bulk from San Miguel to a central clearinghouse in Laredo, Texas, which mailed the letter or package to the specific address back home. This same service was available in reverse for receiving letters and packages from the U.S. This proved to be much cheaper for us than using an equivalent service in the States because the Mexican service did not assess a monthly (or annual) box rental fee plus a service fee each time mail was forwarded. We simply paid the flat fee and that was that. Our San Miguel mailing service also offered private mailboxes for a monthly fee of about $15, fax services, computer services, daily Express Mail service, packing and shipping, and myriad other services. Such services can be found all over the globe but they do cost money. If you'll be using them often, budget accordingly.

Mailing and receiving packages abroad

Receiving packages by mail from back home can be breathtakingly expensive depending on the customs charges of the country you're living in and what's being sent. We paid $15 in Mexican customs fees for a single computer game we ordered from Amazon.com. I don't think the software itself cost that much. Books are one of the cheapest things to receive across the Mexican border and computer items one of the most expensive. One solution we found was to ask visitors to bring these items along with our mail and take back things to mail, distribute, or store. No one ever balked and we figured it was just part of the rent for coming to stay with us. Of course, that didn't eliminate the need to send and receive shipments directly, especially when it came to holidays and birthdays. A cost saver for such occasions was using the private mailing service in San Miguel that had the clearinghouse in Laredo, Texas. Friends could send letters and packages to us at the Laredo address, which were then carried overland to the mailing service storefront in San Miguel. All we had to do was show up and ask if there was any mail for us. Thus, we didn't have to pay for a private postal box.

Build in some flexibility. I encourage you to build flexibility into your mailing and package-handling plans because you will most likely discover relatively inexpensive and dependable ways to send and receive mail and packages once you arrive in your destination. Often a local bank, an international brokerage, or the local American Express office can provide a variety of these services if you open an account or do business with them. My suggestion is to have a preliminary strategy in place when you depart and be prepared to tweak or change it after you have settled into your life abroad.

Tip: When friends and relatives send packages to you, have them mark the packages "GIFTS." In some countries, this may significantly reduce (though not eliminate) the customs charges you will have pay to receive packages from back home.

Postal delivery services in your destination

Overland and airmail service is available almost everywhere in the world. But the speed at which your letter or package is delivered can be remarkably slow and the reliability rather hit and miss depending on where you're living. Mail delivery was extremely dependable when Michael and I lived in various European countries some years ago. The same goes for the year we spent in Israel. But our experience with the Mexican postal service was a bit different. A letter sent from the U.S. and delivered via the Mexican postal service might arrive as early as a week later or as late as a month after it was mailed. There was no way to predict. Packages were definitely opened by customs, and a number of people we met complained of specific items never reaching their intended destination. I think we received everything sent to us except for one gift sent by my sister to our kids at Christmas time, and that was probably OK since paying the custom taxes on gifts sent from the U.S. can cost more than the gift itself (see above).

It's always a good idea to introduce yourself to the local mail carrier, if there is one, and to locate the nearest post office soon after you arrive. Some post offices offer General Delivery or *Post Restante* service, where they receive and hold mail for you for daily or weekly pickup. Some post offices have a daily General Delivery list that you can check to see if your name appears. If it does, there's mail waiting for you. Now, whether they can actually locate your mail at the very moment you ask for it is never certain, at least not in San Miguel. You might be required to return later "when Señor Armando is available." At our local post office (the only one in town) we often wondered what everyone else did since Señor Armando seemed to be the only one who could actually help us.

Tip: If you absolutely need assurances that whatever you send or have sent to you will arrive on time and intact, and you have the least bit of doubt regarding the reliability of the local postal delivery service, use a private mailing/package delivery service instead.

Telephone Services

There's a reason that everyone uses cell phones overseas. Local phone service (like the local utilities) can be expensive, unreliable, or nonexistent (or simply expensive *and* unreliable). Service via land lines may or may not be available in your area, and if available, it's often hit or miss. Companies in countries from Italy to Mexico are notorious for providing slow, lousy phone and utilities services. Therefore, when you agree to rent a home abroad, double-check that telephone service (if it's supposed to be provided) is actually available and functioning at the time you sign the lease. Despite the promises of even the most honest and well-meaning landlord, if there's no telephone service currently available in the home, it may well be months before the phone company gets around to installing (or fixing) it.

Cell phones are a convenient alternative. Just be aware that companies abroad may bill very differently from those you're used to dealing with at home. Check the terms carefully before signing the agreement.

> *"Job number one was to buy a cell phone, as the whole world here has one, and since we were looking for an apartment, we knew we would need to be in contact with realtors."* — Frances

Pay phones

You'll need a phone card to use most pay phones abroad. The cards come in different denominations. Simply insert the card and dial the phone number. The amount of the call is automatically deducted from the card. You can purchase the cards at many convenient locations, including pharmacies, corner stores, banks, and airports.

Long distance service

Obviously you can make long distance telephone calls from just about anywhere in the world — and often pay through the nose for the pleasure of it. Whether you're calling from a phone booth, a long distance telephone office in town, or from your home or cell phone, do some serious comparison shopping when it comes to long distance phone costs. Rates in Mexico using TelMex, the national long distance phone company, averaged $2 a minute to call the U.S., including calls to 800 numbers! Obviously a few chats at those rates could break the bank pretty quickly. Luckily there are lots of competitors out there offering much cheaper rates. Long distance phone companies, callback services, and computer calling services are all vying for your business and can be used from a variety of locations around the world.

Long distance calling cards and plans. Some U.S. companies offer prepaid calling cards. These can be a good deal if you buy them on sale. Before you buy, make sure they can be used from your destination country and find out if you can add additional time to them from abroad. You'll find some of the cheapest long distance prepaid calling cards at large warehouse outlets such as Sam's Club and Costco. In contrast, most of the direct-billed calling plans (charged to your credit card) offered by U.S. telephone companies, such as AT&T's USA Direct, are relatively expensive. Check into these carefully if you plan to use them while you're abroad. Make sure you won't be charged astronomical fees for calling your Aunt Esther on her birthday.

> *"For long distance calls we found the cheapest was buying an AT&T calling card at Sam's Warehouse before we left. It had very low rates and was easy to use, and we could use it when we traveled within Mexico."* — Kim

Callback services. These are a good option for calls to your home country. When you sign up, you're given a specific U.S. (or Canadian) number to dial when you want to make a long distance call from anywhere in the world. After it rings once, you hang up and within a few seconds a computer rings you back. You are then free to dial any number you want to call. You can sign up for the service in person or online. You give the provider a credit card number and pay a minimal initial fee. Your credit card is charged for the calls you make.

When we were in Mexico a number of companies were offering callback service, Alliance Callback and WorldLink among them. Check out the *New York Times* travel section for a good list of providers. The call rates are reasonable. We used one that charged 23 cents a minute until we found an even cheaper deal.

Computer and Internet phone services. VoIP (Voice over Internet Protocol) is well worth looking into if you will be hooked up to an Internet Service Provider (ISP) in your home abroad and you expect to be making a lot of long distance calls. VoIP is a method for taking analog audio signals, like those in a telephone call, and turning them into digital data that can be transmitted over the Net. VoIP taps cable or DSL Internet broadband connections to let you make and receive an unlimited number of calls for an average, as we go to press, of $30 a month.

There are three basic ways to use VoIP. The most common is to use a device called an ATA (analog telephone adapter) that is provided by your VoIP service provider (often bundled free with the service). It allows you to connect a standard telephone to your computer or your Internet connection. You plug the cable from your phone into the ATA (instead of a wall socket), and you're ready to make VoIP calls. The second method is to use a specialized "IP" telephone, which looks like a normal phone but contains an Ethernet connector that connects directly to your computer's router. The third and easiest way to use VoIP is called computer-to-computer service. You don't even pay long distance charges with this system. All you need is the appropriate software (available free or at very low cost on the Internet from a number of companies), a microphone, speakers, a sound card, and a cable or DSL Internet connection. If you're interested in trying it, check out some of the free VoIP software. It takes just a few minutes to download and set up. Have a friend or relative download the software, too, and you can chat together on VoIP to get a feel for how it works.

This is very cool stuff but before signing up for one of these services (assuming they are available from your sabbatical location) read the contract terms carefully as there can sometimes be hefty activation and cancellation fees. Also, the sound quality of VoIP services depends on the quality of your Internet connection. Occasionally we got a bad line and it felt like we were talking from Russia circa 1940, but for the most part it worked out well. VoIP service suppliers include AT&T CallVantage, Verizon VoiceWing, Vonage, Skype, and net2phone.com, among others (see *Resources* for URLs).

Using Computers Abroad

Computers make living abroad and remaining in close communication unbelievably easy (too easy if you're the obsessive type). We communicated almost exclusively via email and the computer. We read the *New York Times* online and perused message boards to learn more about Mexico and to get kid-friendly travel tips. The kids surfed the Web for homework and research projects. We also took care of nearly all of our business and personal communications over the Web. It was a breeze.

You may be surprised to find how many out-of-the-way places are wired — either right to the house (using either cable hook-ups or dial-up service) or through Internet cafés. Internet cafés are literally everywhere, sometimes on every corner, and the going rate ranges anywhere from $2 to $6 an hour. Many people we know regularly park themselves inside an Internet café during the hottest part of the day and log on to take care of business, check email, and catch up on the news while sipping something cool.

Note: If there are only a couple of Internet cafés in town, there may be a significant wait since, in our experience, most have only two or three computer stations active at any one time. But we were continually surprised at the way Internet cafés seemed to sprout up overnight in the most improbable locations.

> *"We used email and got a cable Internet hook-up. It was our best purchase of the year! We were all able to look up information on topics we were studying like Spanish, math, reading, cultural assignments (geography, social studies), everything! We even used it to download a school application for my son's junior high school (back in the States) and submit it on time."* — Rob

> *"Thanks to our landlord, who bullied her way through the red tape, we were able to get Internet access at home."* — Channing

Depending on where you end up, you may have a broad selection of Internet Service Providers (ISPs) or just one or two. You may even find both dial-up and high-speed cable modem services available. Most ISPs allow you to sign up on a monthly or annual basis and pay for either unlimited hours or a specific number of hours per month. Typically you get a better deal by signing up for a longer period, but it all depends on your needs. Ask around before you sign up as there may be significant differences among suppliers in both price and dependability.

> *"We had a few computers with us. My husband worked for an Internet company for a while when we first got there. He also volunteered his expertise to friends opening an Internet café, as well as to a hospital and a boys home. We used the Internet to maintain contact with the U.S. through emails and even through phone calls placed through the Net. I also wrote a couple of novels using the computers."* — Tani

The all-important online master contact list

If you don't already have a well-organized online address book, now is the time to get going. Before you leave home, email everyone your new address abroad. This will help you begin compiling a complete online contact list, which will become invaluable during your time away. Include everyone that you will need to keep in contact with, from business associates to neighbors — your doctors, brokers, bankers, friends, teachers, school administrators, attorneys — you name it. Be sure to include their street addresses and telephone numbers as well as their email addresses. If you need to contact people while you're gone, email is usually the most inexpensive and efficient way to do it.

> *"We did have a computer with us and I used email a lot – for me it was essential for just connecting emotionally with people other than my husband, and some of my friendships were strengthened. The kids didn't use email much then (that's really changed in the last two years) but they did play computer games sometimes."* — Rachel

> *"I would die without my computer and email. Being able to email friends and family makes a difference. And my husband has to use it for business. Otherwise he wouldn't be able to be here. We really couldn't do without it."* — Jody

Adapting to the local electrical system

I'm nearly one hundred percent sure you know more about your specific computer requirements than I do, but you will also need to consider the electrical requirements in your sabbatical destination. As you doubtless know, electrical systems differ in different parts of the world. The voltage may be 110, 120, 220, 260, or something else. The frequency may be 50 or 60 hertz. And wall sockets come in various configurations. All of which means you may not be able to simply plug in and use your appliances and electronics in your sabbatical destination. Unless your computer, appliances, and other equipment are designed to operate on both 110 and 220 voltage, you'll need a converter (for small appliances) and/or transformer (for computers and electronic devices) to solve the voltage incompatibility and adapters to let you plug in to the local sockets. Carefully research the requirements of your destination to be sure you know what you'll need. You'll find detailed information on a number of web sites, among them www.walkabouttravelgear.com.

Tip: Be aware that while you can use transformers with both electrical and electronic equipment, converters work only with electrical appliances. You must have a transformer to operate computers and other electronic equipment on foreign voltage.

I have a few general suggestions for additional items you may want to bring along to ensure that everything runs smoothly:

- A long telephone cord.
- A modular telephone adapter.
- Plugs that provide both two- and three-prong adapters.
- A 3-to-1 power plug for plugging in a printer and/or external modem along with your computer.
- An extra electrical extension cord.
- High-quality surge protectors for the voltage in your destination.

Tip: Always protect your computer(s) and other sensitive electronic equipment from power failures by using the best surge protectors you can find. This is one of the most important things you can do to safeguard your equipment abroad. It's also wise to unhook your modem and power cords during storms to protect against surges during lightning strikes. (See *Resources* for websites that offer more specific information regarding electrical requirements overseas.)

Software

Bring along whatever you think you might need to conduct your business and/or to use for word processing and your children's schoolwork. Repair, cleaning, and rebooting disks are probably well worth dragging along as well.

A word here about pirated software: You will undoubtedly run into pirated computer software in every conceivable language and for every computer setup, even in the farthest and most remote areas of the world. My husband was astonished to find expensive English-language architectural 3-D modeling software being sold in a tiny Mexican flea market at a quarter of what it costs in the U.S. We also found an amazing selection of DVDs, VCRs, music CDs, computer games — you name it. Were they worth buying? That depends on how you feel about buying pirated software. Do you have ethical concerns about ripping off the rightful owners of their hard-earned profits? Or do you consider it a simple matter of economics and entrepreneurial chutzpah? Whatever your views, be aware that quality-wise, it's hit and miss. Sometimes pirated programs, movies, music, and games are excellent; other times they aren't even playable. You never know until you get them home and try them out. Bottom line, if you buy pirated materials, be aware that they are illegal and it's a roll of the dice whether the five bucks you hand over for that "$30 computer game" will actually buy you a bargain or just get you another bit of trash to toss into the garbage.

And speaking of computer software . . . you have an opportunity during your sabbatical to rethink decisions about everything because everything is new. If the amount of time your kids spend on the computer or their choice of games is a concern, this may be an excellent opportunity to address both issues. Choose the computer games and software that you're going to bring along carefully since there will be more pressure for your kids to lobby for additional screen time — in the early months in particular before new friends and activities really kick in. You can take advantage of their interest by investing in some high quality educational software that will actually enhance their language, math, and geography skills. There are many excellent language tutorials available for kids that really can help make language learning fun. And if your kids are science nuts or are really into cooking, why not indulge their passions and get them software that will challenge their brains and expand their knowledge base while at the same time deepening their appreciation for their new home? Look for educational software that relates to the history, food, and culture of the area you'll be living in.

Tip: If your kids beg to bring along certain games or activities you're not all that fond of, by all means let them pack one or two. The point is not to torture your children. Keep in mind that they'll already be doing without quite a lot of what they're used to. Think of those obnoxious computer games as little bargaining chips. "Sure honey, you can play 'Rock'em Sock'em Robots.' Right after you finish your French homework and write that email to Grandpa Glynn."

> *"The international language of video games certainly got the kids connected with kids there before their language skills kicked in. What has been nice since we've been home is that they can log on and play games in real time with their Spanish friends."*
> — Frances

Finding computer repair services abroad

Wherever there are computers, there are bound to be computer problems. Having a software or hardware problem abroad is definitely no fun, and we had both. But rest assured that you'll be able to find quality computer services abroad just as you can back home. A good way to find a reputable computer repair service is to talk with expats who are running businesses abroad, because they are likely to have had more experience with using computers abroad in general. You can also find quality repair services through your local ISP as well as through the owners of Internet cafés. In our case, when my computer came down with a virus thanks to an infected floppy disk, and Michael was unable to access his files after his expensive new computer broke down, we got a recomendation from the owner of the private mailing service we were using. The guy she suggested was excellent, a fellow expat subsidizing his life abroad by repairing computers.

Note: The importance of finding a good computer repair person abroad cannot be overstated, particularly if computers will play an important role in your life abroad. Be sure to ask around for recommendations soon after you arrive and treat your equipment kindly. The likelihood that something will go wrong with your computer seems directly correlated to how great a role it plays in your lives.

Establish a Family Website or Blog ("El Grito" is born)

The idea of creating a family website for the duration of our trip was born out of all the inquiries we received from friends, colleagues, and family about why we were going on this crazy adventure and what kinds of things we'd encounter while away. Also, Michael's an artistic fellow who loves taking digital pictures and dinking around obsessively on the computer. And of course we're both writers. A family website or blog is a great way to document your sabbatical for friends back home and a great resource for yourselves after all is said and done. We were continually surprised by the number of people who checked out our site and contacted us with comments. It became an important way for them to keep us present in their lives and helped them visualize the sorts of things our family was experiencing abroad.

Note: Creating and maintaining a family website or blog takes as much or as little effort as your skill and expectations require. If blogging had been around when we were in San Miguel, we'd have established a blog instead of a website because it's even easier.

WHY WON'T MY BEST FRIEND WRITE BACK?

Despite your best efforts to keep the folks back home updated on your lives abroad, don't be surprised if the people you regularly communicate with when you're at home (via email, letter, telephone, or face-to-face) never once even email you while you're away. This, despite numerous pleas for just a single email, anything.

It's a mystery why some people feel compelled, interested, or at least motivated to stay in touch and others simply do not. Perhaps some just don't feel comfortable with email or wonder whether their letters will actually arrive. Others may feel relieved that one less person is around demanding their attention. Yet these same people will be genuinely overjoyed to see you back months or years later and pick up right where you left off.

Many of our friends abroad had similar experiences with a 'best friend' who never, not once, emailed or sent a letter while they were away. In our case, I think it had a lot to do with how busy everyone is in the States. Days, weeks, and months go by and your best intentions to write that email or make that phone call just get lost in the day-to-day rush of getting through your day until you can finally collapse into bed.

Perhaps even more surprising than those who didn't write were those who did. People who in a million years we never thought we'd hear from suddenly contacted us. Something about our trip or something mentioned on our website captured their imagination and compelled them to get in touch. It was so great to hear from these relative strangers now and again. There were also one or two regular communicators who seemed to love being able to chat over so much distance with so much ease. These regular chatty updates from home were lifesavers. Little nuggets of nourishment from the old home soil.

10. WE'RE HERE!
ARRIVING IN . . . PARADISE?

"We appeared to be here but were substantially still very much there, or rather not there: we were not working, not huddling half-frozen huffing into cupped hands, not hermetically sealed indoors looking out, not driving maniacally everywhere and nowhere, not traipsing the aisles of Target and Rainbow dutifully every weekend. Being not there was the spice that made this strange new dish not merely interesting, but truly damn tasty." El Grito #4

Congratulations, you've done it! You've said goodbye to what's known and hello to what isn't. You've left behind those stressful weeks back home filled with last-minute snags, unanticipated packing details, and too many goodbye dinners with friends and relatives. You've flown, or driven, long hours to a country that's not yours, to a completely different language and culture, and to a town where you may not know a soul. The flight or drive itself was bound to have been difficult at times. The kids were undoubtedly restless, hungry, and too excited (or bored) to sit still. Your family might also be dealing with a time change and the resulting jet lag. Everybody is tense, grumpy, and hard to satisfy, and normal conversation has been replaced by snipes, whines, and occasional snarls. As you drag your heavy luggage and weary selves into some strange house, hotel, or apartment, you might well be wondering, what in hell are we doing here?

I don't mean to scare you, but it's quite possible that the first few days of your sabbatical will be the most physically and psychologically challenging of the entire trip. It's also possible (although highly unlikely) that everything will go without a hitch. The kids might behave like perfect angels, customs officials might smile broadly and wave you through with your luggage intact, and everyone might arrive in your new home feeling happy, energetic, and raring to go. If that happens feel especially blessed because miracles are rare. It's much more likely that you'll arrive with a dull headache and whiny children. If you can anticipate a slightly bumpy arrival in paradise and have some immediate strategies for how to cope, it will undoubtedly make for a smoother landing for everyone.

Let me suggest that the very first thing you do in your new home (once you pay off the taxi, get all your luggage inside, and shut the door) is take a long, slow breath. Then take another. And one more. If anyone in your family knows a good joke, this is an excellent time to tell it. It's also the perfect moment for a big, squashy family hug. You don't do group hugs? We didn't either until we landed in Mexico. Try it. It's a great way to feel like a team; like it's your family against this big, new world around you. Feeling better? Not quite? Read on. You will.

Traveling Styles

If you've done a lot of traveling with your spouse and children, then you already know how differently different people travel. Especially when it comes to arriving in a new place. Michael likes to stash his luggage in a train station (bus station, airport) locker, and step outside to wander off in whatever direction looks promising. He's not especially particular about sleeping conditions or restaurant locations. He rolls with the punches and is content to move from one unplanned event to the next.

I, on the other hand, am much less flexible. I feel disoriented when I arrive in a new place and I immediately like to go to the place we'll be staying that night, stash my luggage, and take a shower. I want the place to have hot water (at least some of the time), be reasonably clean (but not immaculate), and be located in a neighborhood where I won't feel uncomfortable wandering down the street alone during the day. Once these basic necessities are met, I'm perfectly content to spend the day wandering around just as Michael does. Overall, our general traveling style is the same. We're not guidebook or tour-bus people. We're lounge in a café, read books in our hotel room, and kick around the market people.

OK, so what does all this have to do with our family's trip to Mexico? Everything. Not only do Michael and I like to settle in differently, but we also had the untried and unknown traveling styles of two young and very demanding humans to contend with. The more you can understand about how each of you likes to greet a new place, the calmer and more open you're going to be to what's around you in those first few days and weeks. And since your kids will take their cues from Mom and Dad, if you're not shouting at each other your first morning or first week or first month abroad, your kids will probably be more relaxed at the start of your big adventure too.

To get started, help your children learn about their own travel styles and talk in detail, as a family, about each of your expectations upon arrival in your new place. Have a conversation about exactly how you will be traveling to your new destination. Help the kids imagine the process of leaving your home. Are you flying or driving or traveling by train? What do your children need to pack? What food will you eat along the way? Will you need to sleep in a car or airplane? How long will the journey take? What will happen once the airplane lands? And imagine finally arriving in your destination. Talk about waking up in your new home and what that first day might entail.

Tip: Whatever your own travel styles, be prepared to make some adjustments once your trip is underway, because your children's travel styles (probably largely unknown when you embark) will need to be taken into account as well. It's also a good idea to discuss everyone's bottom line needs for the first 24 hours after you arrive in your new home.

In retrospect, I would have stashed the medicines in the luggage and brought coffee, filters, and a mini coffeepot in my carry-on instead. If morning coffee is a necessity, bring it. Either a tiny coffeepot or instant. Whatever gets you by. If you can't function without that first cuppa' Joe, don't make everyone wish you'd missed the flight from home by going without that first morning. Kids wake up starving? Bring peanut butter sandwiches and breakfast cereal from home. If you can't find milk nearby, let them eat it dry.

Surviving The First Few Days

Bring a few comforts from home for that first day because everyone's going to feel out of sorts (and jetlagged) waking up to, say, roosters, no toilet paper (bring a roll if you're not sure), no clean water, or whatever surprises greet you that first morning. You won't immediately know where to get coffee, money, or food, and dragging your tired, freaked out children through unfamiliar streets to an unfamiliar restaurant to eat unfamiliar food won't be fun. We know. We did it. Remember those three most important things each family member brought along (see *Chapter 5*)? Get them out immediately after you arrive. These are the things you and your kids will turn to early on when you're feeling confused or anxious.

> *"When we first arrived in China the lack of language ability was profound. By the end of the experience, we had better language ability and had become much more comfortable with not having a common language and having strategies that we could use to get needs met like food and a bathroom or a hotel. But when we first arrived everything was so incredibly unlike anything we had ever experienced that it was magical and overpowering. The lack of clean green spaces for the kids to play in was a constant difficulty, as was the staring. Stanley was three years old when we first arrived and bore the brunt of being different – he was touched constantly and while he tried to be understanding, it was hard on him."*
>
> — Rachel

"There is the infamous story of our drive down to San Miguel with the nine-hour detour because I couldn't find a map of Mexico at any gas stations and I took the wrong highway south. We ended up driving at night across a treacherous mountain road with 54 roadside crosses for all the people who had died driving it. We arrived in San Miguel after 11 p.m. and couldn't find the house because most of the roads were one way and I was used to finding my way around by walking. We had not received the key in advance and so had to find our property manager's house to pick up the key."

— Kim

On our first morning in San Miguel we stepped gingerly along the cobbled streets and headed to a restaurant right off the central square. We ordered so-so food, watched the kids eat almost nothing, drank mediocre coffee, stared at each other dully across the table — and paid more for that breakfast than for any other during our entire trip. Let's just say it was not exactly how I'd envisioned my first morning in paradise. After that experience, we always made sure we traveled with a coffeepot and coffee, a box of breakfast cereal, and a liter carton of milk.

Tip: In most countries outside of the U.S., milk comes in liter cartons that don't need to be refrigerated, and you can buy them by the dozen.

After that underwhelming breakfast, I wanted to spend a good chunk of that first day outfitting ourselves with necessary groceries and housekeeping items. Michael thought I was nuts. He wanted to start exploring immediately. We had a sleep-deprived fight in the central square where we snarled at each other like bulldogs, completely oblivious to the burros, crumbling facades of 500-year-old buildings, and the little old Indian women milling around us. We finally reached a compromise. We would kick around the open-air markets and stock up on fruits and vegetables. We plunged into the tumble of colors, sounds, and smells of the *mercado* and immediately felt better. We tentatively tried out our five words of Spanish and had a ball choosing among the varieties of mangos and *aguacates* (avocados). We stared down fish heads, cow brains, and pig cadavers. We bought a large *bolsa* (woven bag) and stocked it with the freshest fruits and vegetables we'd ever seen. The kids gaped in slack-mouthed amazement at the sights around them. We bought fresh tortillas on the corner, amazingly cheap baked goods in the *panadería* next door, and on the way home, we stopped at a *tienda* and bought coffee, sugar, milk, fresh orange juice, bottled water, and food disinfectant. It was clear that tomorrow morning we would be much better prepared to greet the new day. Welcome to paradise indeed.

> *"One son is a vegetarian and so it took us a little while to figure out how to find and order meat- and egg-free dishes. Once we got the hang of it, we did pretty well. Pasta is ubiquitous and the basic fast food here is a French bread sandwich with cheese, so these were always available."* — Frances

Tip: If you're moving to a city where the water quality is questionable, bring enough bottled water with you to last until you find a safe supply of drinking water. Figure on at least six to eight glasses per person for the first 24 hours, and make it a priority to find purified water immediately after you arrive. If you're traveling with a baby and aren't breastfeeding, be sure to bring along a month's worth of supplies to give you time to locate all the necessities abroad. Needless to say, breastfeeding makes living abroad with a baby much easier. No need for sterilizing water or buying and storing expensive bottles and formula.

Venturing out the first time — Daypack supply list

Don't feel the need to walk around overburdened and ready to do battle with every eventuality that might befall your family. You really only need a daypack filled with the following basic essentials to allow your family to wander around for most of your first full day abroad without forcing you to return home before you're ready:
- Disinfectant wipes and/or antibacterial liquid for dirty hands.
- Water (bottled).
- Extra diaper/pull-up if necessary.

- Small, portable changing pad if necessary.
- Map of city.
- Small bilingual dictionary.
- Small ball, Frisbee, or hackeysack for impromptu play.
- Snacks.
- Tissues or toilet paper.
- Sunscreen/small first-aid kit (with lip balm, bandages, and anti-bacterial ointment).
- Empty bag for carrying food or other items home.
- Money in secure carrying pouch or money belt.

Staying Safe

Depending on where you spend your sabbatical, you may or may not want to advertise the fact that you're Americans. I'm not saying you should lie and tell everybody you're from Toronto (although I have done that once or twice), but it's wise to be sensitive to the political and cultural attitudes of your chosen destination. Educate yourselves about the place you're living in, take commonsense precautions, and don't invite unwarranted attention. The American government and its international presence and policies are extremely unpopular in many parts of the world. By extension, all Americans are suspect in some places. Try not to take hostile or suspicious attitudes personally. Be friendly and pleasant whenever possible, and avoid overtly political discussions with strangers. Perhaps your low-key presence will go some way to softening the attitudes of those around you. Having kids along immediately makes you more approachable since being parents gives you something in common with the locals even if you are from an alien culture. Don't walk around with your passports unless they're necessary to transact some sort of official business. Keep your money hidden on your body whenever possible and avoid carrying large bills. (See *Chapter 6: The Money Thing* for more information about dealing with money safely.) Try not to look like tourists. Act as if you know where you're going, dress as much like the locals as possible, and resist the impulse to carry a camera slung around your neck. When you're traveling in a foreign culture, it's much safer to blend in rather than drawing attention to yourselves. Squeaky wheels abroad are more likely to get fleeced than greased.

There is a great deal of information on traveling safely with children available on the Web and in numerous books (see *Resources* for suggestions). Look it over just to be sure you understand the basic safety rules, but try not to get overly protective. There are commonsense ways to protect your family without living in gated communities or being afraid to move about. Just as at home, don't mark your children's names and address on their belongings in a visible spot. Find an inconspicuous area to put this information. Dress younger children in brightly colored clothing for easy visibility and put their names and address in a pocket in case they get lost.

The "don't talk to strangers" rule won't work during your sabbatical because everyone you meet will be a "stranger." Instead, teach your children to be alert to potentially dangerous or uncomfortable situations and play the "what if" game often as a family. If you get lost, what should you do? If someone offers you food or candy, what should you do? If someone you don't know takes your hand and starts walking away with you, what should you do? If you need to go to the bathroom and there isn't one close by, what should you do? If someone tries to talk to you and you don't want to, what should you do? Spin as many scenarios as possible and go over them frequently. If something should happen to your child and you're not around, at least you will have talked about it and given your child some idea of how to deal with it.

It's a good bet, especially if you have younger children, that somebody is going to get lost at some point during your adventure. Kids are kids and they wander away despite your dogged attempts at constant surveillance. Asher, at three years old, was constantly wandering off. We could usually spot him easily — the only platinum blonde head bobbing among a sea of black and brown ones. But there were a couple of times we really couldn't find him and we were beside ourselves with panic. There's almost nothing worse than realizing how ultimately powerless you are to prevent bad things from happening sometimes. And it's difficult not to imagine the worst. In the event that you do lose one of your kids, try to remain calm and enlist the help of others around you. Everyone really does want to help. Here again, dressing your kids in bright clothing is helpful because it will help you describe them easily and quickly to someone else. But of course it's nearly impossible to remain calm when your child is missing. When you do eventually find your lost son or daughter playing happily with a new puppy two doors down, or inside a nearby restaurant laughing with the owner, smile and be gracious and try not to have a nervous breakdown right there. Go home, open a bottle of wine, and do that deep breathing thing again. And then hug your kids and tell them how much you love them.

Regarding safety and older kids, it's very important to trust your own instincts about a particular situation. It's also important to teach your kids to trust theirs. Sometimes you don't know why, but you just "know" that a specific situation or person doesn't feel right. It's important to trust this feeling and leave immediately, even if it creates an uncomfortable or awkward situation. Our bodies often sense danger before our conscious minds can register what that danger is. If you wait until you actually "know" there's a problem, it might be too late. (I tell you this from experience.) There may be someone in your family who is more sensitive in general to these kinds of feelings. Or it may depend on a specific situation. Your family may want to have a special code word (ours was "banana") that gets used if someone ever gets a "feeling" that something isn't right. If this word is used, it means everyone gets up to leave wherever you are immediately — no questions, no discussion. Save the discussion for later, when you're all feeling safe. The "feeling" may have been nothing or there may indeed have been some trouble brewing that not everyone could see. Better to trust those feelings than experience something unfortunate unnecessarily.

Cleome was seven when we arrived in Mexico. Over the next year and a half her language ability and sense of independence blossomed. She had much more freedom in San Miguel than she'd ever had back home. She took buses home alone after tutoring. She ran around the neighborhood to buy tortillas. And she often went alone to the *pape-laria* several blocks away to buy school supplies. We wanted to help her have realistic expectations about the world and to develop the tools to explore prudently without dampening her enthusiasm for explora-tion. So we talked a lot about the clues her body might give her in a situation that somehow doesn't feel "right." A "funny feeling" in her stomach, a strange prickly sensation at her temples or behind her ears. We tried to sensitize her to things her body may "know" before her mind actually registers whatever isn't right about a situation. And we made it clear that it was important that she trust her body even if she wasn't completely sure there was a problem. She knew to shout loudly if someone was bothering her and also how to say in Spanish, "Help me, this isn't my parent. He's bothering me," if she was in a situation where she couldn't just walk away.

It's critical to empower your kids with this information rather than scaring them or going the "victim" route. Your kids are going to be encountering a lot of unfamiliar places, people, and situations. They may not "know" what something or someone is supposed to be like and that's when those "feelings" are usually pretty accurate. We can't always protect our kids and they're eventually going to have to learn how to negotiate their own paths through the world. We felt this was our op-portunity to start helping Cleome along her path. If she did encounter a sticky situation, we wanted her to know enough to get out rather than feel paralyzed by fear, helplessness, or a lack of concrete information.

Other good sources for safety information in your new home are locals and other expats. Ask their opinions regarding how safe a per-son, situation, or area might be for your child and take their advice to heart, even if you don't immediately understand their concerns. Dur-ing our first month in San Miguel we said hi to everyone we met and felt perfectly comfortable doing so. One morning a neighbor pointedly suggested we be pleasant but not linger near a certain house down the block. Turns out the man who lived there was a very rich and powerful pederast. No one in the neighborhood dared speak against him pub-licly. I think they were afraid of his power and money. I felt blessed that the neighbors cared enough to warn me and horrified that I had not picked up any strange vibes from this guy on my own. I was trying to be open and friendly and perhaps I let my guard down too much during those first several weeks. It's a hard line to walk, that of being open to new people and adventures and also protective of yourself and your family. Really, all you can do is be pleasant, use common sense, get to know your neighbors, and be aware of your surroundings. Don't walk around fearing the worst. Even if one or two unfortunate people cross your path, don't let those isolated moments of ugliness destroy the beauty of your adventure.

Tip: One more time: dress kids in bright clothes so they can be easily found in a crowd and so you can describe them quickly to others if they get lost.

Sanitation: Food, Water, Air

Sanitation is a major concern in many countries. Obviously you want to be careful with food and water. Drink and brush your teeth using only bottled water unless you're absolutely sure the tap water is safe to drink. Initially this may seem onerous, but you'll be surprised at how quickly it becomes second nature. In most areas of the world where the water is unsafe for human consumption, the locals don't drink tap water either and there are systems in place to make the use of bottled water easy and convenient. For example, in Mexico seemingly every home is outfitted with water dispensers that hold five-gallon (19-liter) plastic water containers. These containers are delivered by truck to your home regularly and are extremely inexpensive, about $1.50 per five-gallon bottle. An average family goes through one or two of these a week. Unless the tap water is contaminated with serious chemicals that will cause injuries to your eyes or skin, it's usually fine to wash your hands and take showers and wash dishes in water that you can't drink. Just make sure you dry your hands and body well and allow your dishes to air-dry completely before using them.

Foods bought in markets, on the street, and in grocery stores may need to be disinfected before you consume them. Foods grown in many parts of the world can have heavy concentrations of fertilizers, pesticides, and/or "night soil" (human and animal feces) on their surfaces. To be safe, soak fresh fruits and vegetables in a solution of water and iodine for 30 minutes. (Use 5 drops of 2% tincture of iodine to one quart or liter of clear water and 10 drops to a quart or liter of cloudy water.) In Mexico, tincture of iodine is marketed under the name "Microdyne" and is widely available in pharmacies and grocery stores. Alternatively, you can get tetraglycine hydroperiodide tablets (iodine pills), such as Globaline, Potable-Aqua, and Coghlan's, at some pharmacies and sporting goods stores and substitute them for the tincture of iodine. Just follow the package directions. The Centers for Disease Control and Prevention (CDC) website (see *Resources*) provides detailed information about how to avoid contaminated food and water while traveling as well as recommendations for how to disinfect food when needed.

Note: You don't have to soak produce that will be thoroughly cooked or peeled, such as bananas and avocados.

Use good judgment regarding restaurant food. Generally speaking, restaurants that either cater to tourists or at least have some tourist clientele will have an awareness of the "sensitive tummies" of their clients and will soak their produce in iodine and use bottled water in their preparations. This may also be the case in restaurants frequented by locals since restaurant owners don't want to risk losing business by having anyone get sick after eating there.

Street food is a different kettle of fish altogether. I urge you to be very cautious about eating food from street vendors. You just can't be sure of their sanitation practices. We did eat off the street eventually, but only after receiving recommendations from other gringos and after watching the vendors to see exactly what their sanitation and cooking procedures were like. We wanted to make sure the food was kept cold until it was cooked, that the turnover was heavy so nothing sat around too long, and that once the food was cooked it was served immediately and piping hot.

You will also want to be aware of any health concerns in your new home due to increased air pollution from vehicles, chemical toxins from factories and artisan manufacturers, and microscopic particles in the dirt and dust that may carry animal feces and other biohazards.

Note: Whatever the levels of pollution or air and water quality in your sabbatical city, it's going take some time for your systems to adjust to the changed microbial environment in your new home. It's not so much a matter of good or bad germs; it's more a matter of *different* germs. You're as likely to get sick from the germs back home after living abroad as you are to get sick from the germs abroad as you begin your sabbatical. That's why it's important in the early weeks to be especially cautious with food and drink, to allow your bodies to adjust leisurely to all the environmental differences.

We were quite careful with food the kids ate and it seemed that their natural inclination was to stay away from highly seasoned food until their bodies could handle it. Eventually, Asher began sucking limes like candy (they're a natural disinfectant) and Cleome began to sprinkle chile on everything. We ate a lot of ice cream cones and frozen treats, but only at ice cream stores with a consistent source of electricity. We almost never bought anything frozen from a street vendor because we were concerned that inconsistent freezing and thawing of foods might have created a perfect growth medium for weird bacteria. You're fairly safe with fresh juices off the street, however, especially if they squeeze them right in front of you. And there's almost nothing more delicious or refreshing. Soda pop is available everywhere in Mexico, and I mean everywhere. You can be miles from anywhere and someone will drive by selling Cokes out of the back of a rusty pick-up truck.

Despite our careful precautions, each of us did manage to come down with some kind of minor gastrointestinal bug early on in our sabbatical. We each spent a few days with the runs and Asher got hit with a bug that had him running from both ends (I think some of this came from drinking his bath water). But after those initial adjustments, we were healthier overall during our 18 months in San Miguel than we'd ever been back home in Minnesota, where wintertime is a six-month siege of invading viruses.

Basic Health and Sanitation
Guidelines for Living Abroad

• Drink bottled water and use it for brushing your teeth as well. Don't sing or gargle in the shower and don't allow children to drink the bath water.

• Cook with bottled water if the water will be consumed or absorbed in large quantities, such as when you are making soups or rice. For pasta, boil the water for several minutes before adding the pasta. Ditto for cooking vegetables.

• Initially, as your bodies are adjusting to the different germs in the air and dirt, you may want to wash your hands in a foaming iodine hand soap that we found in pharmacies and drugstores throughout Mexico. This soap is also available on the Web and is often used by medical and veterinary professionals. It is called iodine hand soap and is marketed under various names including "Han-San" and "Santi-Wash." For the first six weeks we washed our hands with this soap whenever we came in from outside. It was especially important for the kids, who were playing hard and touching everything in sight, including the ground, their clothes, and their lips. After the first six weeks we made sure we washed our hands with normal soap several times a day, particularly before eating.

• Soak all veggies and fruits in an iodine solution especially formulated for this use (see above) for 30 minutes. While you don't need to soak produce that will be thoroughly cooked or peeled, we erred on the side of soaking almost everything else.

• Avoid street food and choose restaurants carefully, especially until your systems have had time to adjust to the new germ environment. Err on the side of caution and give yourselves a couple of weeks at least.

• Always carry bottled water, wipes, and toilet paper with you when you go out.

"Because Quito is two miles high, we all suffered from lack of oxygen for a couple of months and we also learned that you really can't drink the water." — Tani

Unwanted Visitors: Scorpions, Cockroaches, Assorted Vermin

Speaking of bugs, you may discover a vast new world of insects, reptiles, and other exotic fauna waiting for you abroad. Depending on your relationship to creepy crawly things, it may well challenge you. Let me admit right up front that I'm not a bug person. It's not that I run shrieking away from bugs (much). And truly, I made my peace with spiders many years ago. But in general, I prefer bugs to hang out somewhere other than in my house (or on the back of my leg, as a scorpion briefly did). Living in Mexico truly broadened my insect horizons. After our experiences with scorpions and cockroaches, those centipedes in our basement back home in Minnesota seem downright cuddly.

Overall we had fewer bugs in our second house than we have here in Minnesota. But our first house in San Miguel was a completely different story. We discovered the cockroaches first. They weren't numerous but they were LARGE. Someone told us they were actually "palmetto bugs." That was reassuring until we looked up the term "palmetto bugs" on the Internet and found that it was just a dressed-up term for cockroaches. Because we'd lived with cockroaches at other times in our lives they didn't cause us much of a problem. Their significance waxed and waned depending on their numbers and of course we quickly lost all interest in the cockroaches after we discovered the scorpions.

Scorpions in Mexico come in two flavors. The darker, larger kind can give you a nasty sting more or less equal to a bad wasp sting; the smaller, translucent kind can kill you if you're old, sick, or very young. Luckily, we had the dark kind. (It seems odd to use the words "lucky" and "scorpion" in the same sentence, but there you have it.) It was actually our maid who found the first one. She came running into the kitchen looking for the "Rah — eed." In English, you pronounce it Raid. I'm thinking, "Oh, she's found some kind of bug." I followed her upstairs and she pointed underneath a couch in my writing studio.

"*Hay un alacrán,*" she informed me calmly. I crouched down and peered underneath, wondering what kind of bug an *alacrán* might be. A big, black scorpion is what an *alacrán* might be! I tried to follow her example and remain calm but my involuntary shriek reflex kicked in. Michael came running and against all logic decided he needed to capture the scorpion in a jar (it must be a boy thing). He put the jar on a little shelf near our bed where the scorpion died a painful death over many weeks. We did learn, during this sadistic science experiment, that scorpions can live for a long time without food, water, or even air. At times, I confess, I wished the jar had been big enough for both Michael and the scorpion.

Anyway, that was the tip of the scorpion iceberg. Turns out the 300-year-old stone wall bordering the garden was home to a scorpion colony. Every couple of days we found a few scorpions at the base of the wall and we'd chop their heads off with the gardener's spade. Only a few ever made it inside the house. They don't move quickly and they're not typically aggressive. They don't charge at you or set out to sting you. They're actually quite reclusive, but you don't want to accidentally step on one in your bare feet or meet up with one inside a pair of slippers. We didn't tell the kids too much about our scorpion hunting. We showed them what one looked like and told them to stay away and let us know if they ever saw one so no one would get stung. That was about it. We didn't want to freak them out. I figured I was freaking out enough for everybody.

11. Surviving the First Month Settling In: Tension, Grumpiness and Other Early Adjustments

"We're settling into a routine of sorts — which is good and bad. So much of the value of traveling is simply in disrupting routine; the opportunity presented is less one of experiencing new things than of experiencing things anew. Not that we can't do this wherever we are, regardless of how long we've been there. It's just that we don't — or at least tend not to. And it's not that easy to steer out of the well-worn furrows we trace each day. But the good part of routine is returning as well: we know where we will be sleeping tonight; we wake up (finally!) to a predictably good cup of coffee; the confinement of our meager possessions to a box or bag or satchel has been relaxed and they have been furloughed to spread throughout our new space, to colonize shelves and tabletops, drawers, closets, ledges, and nooks. I still can't find my sunglasses: we're almost back to normal!"

El Grito #2

After you've worked out the initial arrival kinks and have a dependable source of food and money, you'll probably spend a week or two just marveling at your wonderful new home. You'll kick around town each day discovering the odd and unusual, and gather for dinner each night to debrief each other on the day's events. "Wasn't that parade cool?" "Can you believe there are burros living down the street?" "What was the name of that roll we got from the bakery this morning?" "I talked to the neighbors in Spanish and I think they understood me!"

For a couple of weeks everyone is filled with such incredible energy and excitement that each day seems to last forever. And you're all moving at warp speed. Not only do you want to explore all the nooks and crannies of your new home, you have a long list of tasks to accomplish. You have to find schools for the kids, get yourself hooked up to the Internet, figure out how to handle your mail, look into language classes for yourselves, help the kids find new friends. This burst of fantastic energy is one of the most wonderful parts of greeting your new home. By all means enjoy it.

But don't be surprised if you wake up one morning a couple weeks into your sabbatical feeling unusually grumpy. Nothing's exactly wrong but you're tired of dealing with the kids and their problems 24 hours a day. You don't want to search out another hardware store and explain to the guy behind the counter which small, impossible-to-describe item you need today. You don't want to take another family jaunt to the ice cream store or down to the center of town "to see what's going on." You don't want to stop at the market to pick up a few things for dinner. All you want is to be left alone to work on your novel without anybody bugging you! You're sick to death of everyone needing you all the time! Why can't everybody just leave you alone! (Rest assured that after a couple of days of yelling, everybody will definitely leave you alone.)

But when you're stretched out in the sun with a nice cool drink in one hand and a book in the other, how come you still feel restless and bored? You find yourself impatient with that novel you were dying to write. The sun is out but you've lost your enthusiasm for it. You can feel the tension in your back and shoulders. Instead of enjoying yourself and your family in paradise, you wish the kids and your spouse would just disappear and leave you alone to face the miserable person that is you.

Sound unlikely? Maybe, maybe not. We definitely hit some rough times early on where everyone was really grumpy. Nothing obvious was wrong, but there'd be some part of each day when all hell would break loose and we'd just bark at each other. Worse than we'd ever done back home, even on our bad days.

Withdrawal From What's Known

My theory is that we were going through some sort of withdrawal and we were doing it cold turkey. No more work to organize our lives around and buffer us from the kids each day. No set schedule or routine to fall back on when we were tired or wanted to get away from each other. No friends to call when we wanted to complain about something the other one did. Michael, in particular, became something of an ogre. He had set himself up with these grandiose plans and goals for his time away and, upon landing, he realized nothing was going to happen overnight. No book would be written the first day; no rock song composed in the first week, the first month, or even the first few months. It's like he thought that because he wasn't working, he'd immediately have 24/7 to work on his own projects. No way. Settling in takes time.

Same goes for the kids. All the adjustments they were making to their new lives required a great deal of our attention and energy. Back home you may actually deal with yourselves as a family very seldom relative to what you will suddenly experience during your sabbatical. Without the usual rounds of "enrichment" activities, community events, and other family commitments, you may not know what to do with yourselves much of the time.

The most critical problem we encountered was our inability to relax. It seems like relaxing should be the easiest thing in the world, but it wasn't for us. And depending on how busy and stressful your lives are now, it may not be for you either. After an hour of sitting in the sun with a book or roaming through the Indian market with the kids, we'd start fretting about if and when the artistic life was going to swoop down and carry us away to the bestseller list. We were pathetically unprepared to live in a world where our main goal in life wasn't achieving "results."

Tip: Try to remind each other that relaxing into a new, less regimented life takes time. This may help soften some of the brittle moments you'll encounter early on.

"We felt like we needed to do everything right away. We needed to find out where the stores were; where to pay for telephone, electricity, water; when trash was picked up. We also needed to look for a tutor right away to get the kids started with learning the language. Our house needed basic things like dishes; the toilet needed fixing and so did the shower and washing machine. Mostly small stuff, but doing everything all at once and throwing in the language and cultural barriers just added to the confusion."

— Rob

Establish a New Routine Right Away

It may seem antithetical to the nature of your family sabbatical, but consider establishing some sort of family routine, however minimal, right away. Get up at the same time each day, eat breakfast, and then get going on an activity that lends some type of structure to your day.

At first, we balked at establishing any type of routine not only because we were trying to "relax," but also because we were attempting to live a more "Mexican" lifestyle. It was a big adventure to go to the open-air market and see what new fruit or vegetable we could bring home for dinner that night. Michael cooked elaborate meals that took hours to prepare and we'd lounge around the table after dinner, bellies and heads full of food and wine. We might head out for a walk at dusk and then meander home to get kids to bed and fall into bed ourselves, exhausted by doing little or nothing all day long. Mornings were spent getting kids to school and then a stroll here or there or reading on the roof or whatever. Afternoons sort of came and went in our new, decidedly grumpy family fashion.

Our rather aimless existence would have felt fine for a two-week vacation, but it was obvious it wouldn't work over the long term. After a while we realized that as much as we loved jettisoning the old routine, everyone felt a lot more relaxed when there was a sense of structure to the day. We also needed to feel more purposeful even as we were learning to slow down and feel the different pace of life in Mexico. So we created a routine that was much less structured than the one back home, but that had a loose structure we could all plan our days around.

We divided the days into chunks. The morning chunk was school for the kids and writing or reading for us. The afternoon chunk (the kids were home by 2:00 p.m.) was homework or Spanish tutoring for Cleome, a nap for Asher, and eating *comida* (early supper) at around 4:00 p.m. The early evening chunk was a sports activity or a walk downtown to see who or what we could see and then back home for a snack and kids into bed by 8:00 p.m. We eventually sprinkled a few more scheduled activities into the weekly mix: a regular night out for Michael and me together, Spanish tutoring one evening a week separately, a movie night midweek for the kids, and on rare occasions, other activities that popped up connected to school or friends.

Of course everything fell apart on the weekends. Weekends back home in the States were a jumble of classes, play-dates, errands, and shopping trips. These things just weren't part of our Mexican lives and each weekend felt like it stretched on for years. We filled our first couple of months of weekends with sightseeing and bus trips to nearby communities. But you can't do that every weekend, especially with young children and a limited budget. So we decided to impose some sort of routine on the weekends as well. We started doing a major grocery shopping expedition on Saturday mornings out at the big shopping center on the outskirts of town. Without a car, this was a major, all-morning adventure involving buses and taxis. Making the decision to go back to the more American way of a large shopping trip once a week felt a bit like selling out, but we had to be clear about our goals for the trip. Yes, it was to experience another culture, another language, and another way of life. But it was also about finding time to write, and we suddenly realized how little time we had to ourselves each day for our personal projects. Developing a daily schedule that moved in chunks became imperative to accomplishing anything creative and really enjoying our time with the kids. Compared to our lives back home, our Mexican daily schedule was anything but busy. And once we fell into this general routine, everything and everyone started to feel more comfortable. Our general grumpiness dissipated and it felt like we were finally starting to settle into our new home.

Living in Limbo

It may sound bizarre, but one of the hardest things we encountered was figuring out what to do with all the time we suddenly had and nothing concrete to fill it. And the urge was very much to fill it. Back home we filled our time with working, or vacuuming, or calling around for the best price on car insurance, or ferrying the kids to and from some activity. Suddenly we had no house maintenance to speak of (three cheers for our maid who came with the price of the rent), no car and thus no car maintenance, and minimal have-to-do-this or must-get-this-done-by-Friday. That whole mundane, chore-ridden level of existence had been removed in one fell swoop. And about two and a half months in — when most of the novelty of moving to the new place was wearing off — there was this yawning chasm of, OK, what do we do now? Learn an instrument? Take a pottery class?

It drove us nuts. Were we already bored with this new place? How were we going to last for another year or longer here? Did we need to consider moving to someplace different already?

It wasn't so much boredom with the new place we were feeling, but rather our preoccupation (good Americans that we are) with filling every moment of every day with some sort of "meaningful" activity. This is ironic considering that back home our days are filled with the distractions of basically meaningless activities that are at once so overwhelming and transparent that you don't even notice how much of your existence is devoted to them until they aren't there any longer.

How to Fill the Distraction Void

Obviously, if you have work set up abroad this won't be nearly the issue for you that it was for us. However, if you're not working or working only occasionally, this sense of idle desolation may very well creep up a couple of months in. So here are some suggestions for how to settle into your new home and fill the distraction void more quickly — and satisfactorily:

• *Get a library card immediately* if there's a library nearby, and go there several times a week. Read all the time.

• *Sign up for language tutoring or classes* at a nearby school to learn the language and get to know teachers and other students.

• *Sign each of your kids up for one extracurricular activity* that is sports or arts oriented. This is a great way to meet other people, both kids and their parents. (Be careful not to inundate your kids with too many activities, however. The idea is not to replicate their lives back home but to give them the gift of learning how to daydream and spend time "without anything to do" so that they can discover how to fill that time on their own.)

• *Find a way to connect with the community* through volunteering at your kids' schools or the local library, teaching English at a community center, working on some environmental issue, or plying your volunteer skills with some other organization.

• *Take a class or do one activity together with your spouse* at least once a week. This will get you away from the kids and help create an active and energetic bond between you and your partner.

• *Start experimenting as a family.* Find a few activities out in the community you like to do together, parents and children.

• *Consciously slow yourself and your kids down.* Take a yoga class. Meditate. Read for two-hour stretches. Play an instrument. Ban yourself from the computer for a week or perhaps two (or longer!). Don't read or listen to or watch the news. Let your kids be "bored."

Remember, the goal is to extricate your minds and bodies from your old routines. It takes time but eventually you will be able to establish a relationship with yourselves and the world that is new and different and something you're truly comfortable with.

"While we were in living in Mexico, we went to a Club Med in Ixtapa over spring break. It was mostly filled with Americans and many of the mothers asked me what kind of activities our kids were involved in. After a lot of thought, I realized our kids were not signed up for the usual soccer, music lessons, religion classes, and the like. Our kids loved the less structured time with fewer commitments. We marveled that they liked *the one park in San Miguel more than all the parks in Hinsdale. They liked it better because it was a large centralized park with basketball, soccer, running, playground, food vendors, fountains, flowers, and a creek and was great for hide-and-go-seek. You could usually find pick-up basketball games and someone you knew there. Back in Hinsdale we have 13 different parks with little critical mass to draw enough kids for pick-up games."*   — Kim

Looking back, it seems ludicrous that it took us so long to fully enjoy our lives in paradise without having to get up and go to work or do anything we didn't want to do. Call it "Psychosis Americano" or "Retirementitis." But we did eventually get there. After three or four months of nervous hand-wringing we were finally able to get up every day and look forward to the lazy hours ahead of us with relish instead of dread. We'd stand up on the roof deck with a cup of coffee in one hand musing about some bit of writing, a chord progression, or nothing at all. And eventually one of us would catch the other's eye and say with a hint of amazement, "Hey, can you believe it? We're living in Mexico!"

12. I Love My Kids But They're Driving Me Crazy! Staying Sane While Living Abroad With Your Children

"After three or four o'clock things relax a bit. We head out — Cleome slapping the flagstones out front in her sandals, Asher on Michael's shoulders like a midget camel driver — perhaps to the mercado for some veggies or flowers or some goofy thing Cleome insists she needs for school; perhaps to stroll through the jardín (garden) in the town square to kick a ball around the cobbles or chase lazy pigeons in front of the parroquia (church), finally succumbing to compulsory helados (ice cream) for the kids. Weekends could be just about anything — dinner with neighbors, a video for the kids, swimming at a hot spring or a nearby hotel pool, a video for the kids, a day trip to some nearby town (to look for more helados). And of course no weekend would be complete without a trip to Gigante, San Miguel's only large modern grocery store. We bus there and catch a cab back with a trunk load of groceries and a couple of treats to be fought over in the back seat. And then maybe a video for the kids . . ." El Grito #4

Living abroad with your children will be marvelous. You will spend your days patiently and wisely counseling them about topics of interest and they will be attentive and energetic listeners. They will forget all of their unpleasant habits and will become fascinated by life in another culture and eagerly follow you wherever you lead them. When it's time to eat, they will eat everything on their plates, no matter how odd or unfamiliar. They will never ask for things they know you disapprove of. They will turn into charming, lovely, and respectful world citizens thanks to you and this wonderful adventure you've taken them on.

Enough fantasy? Good. Because day-to-day life abroad with children is going to be much the same as day-to-day-life back home. Kids are kids no matter where they are. Especially U.S. kids. They're going to want what they want, when they want it. And that's usually now! In fact, life with kids abroad can at times be worse than life with kids back home. Back home, you've already fought your battles over food, treats, television, clothes, money, and such, and (for the moment anyway) everyone generally knows what the rules are. Get ready to rewrite those rules, and the earlier the better.

Flexibility Is Key

Time for a disclaimer: Back home in the U.S. we were (and still are) quite rigid about the amount of television and sweets the kids get. They would say they get almost none of either. We would say they get a little of both. But while we lived in Mexico the rules about both of these contentious items changed a lot, and they did so with us kicking and screaming every step of the way.

Mexicans adore sweets and salty treats and they consume these snacks constantly. There's a *panadería* (bakery), an *helado* (ice cream) stand, and a *tienda* (store) with an exotic collection of Mexican candies and snacks on every corner. Everything is dirt cheap and at kid-eye-and-hand level. The kids' school buddies all ate treats. The adults walking down the street ate treats. They served treats at school. Our maid brought the kids treats every time she came. Of course we know all that fat, sugar, and salt is terrible for you. So do our kids. But it was a normal part of daily life in San Miguel and our kids really felt left out.

Eventually we allowed them a small treat nearly every day after school except on "movie nights," when they got to run across the street to the little *tienda* owned by our maid to pick out a salty *and* a sweet treat. We made it clear that this relaxing of rules around snack foods was a "while we're in Mexico" thing and I don't think it's done any long-lasting damage to our children. It did reduce our family conflicts considerably, and those might have been more damaging in the long run.

We also reached détente on the movie-watching issue. This was and continues to be a battleground issue for us in the States because we're pretty hardcore about how much television the kids consume. But in Mexico, they had movie nights twice a week and were allowed to watch movies, sometimes nonstop, on the weekends as well. In our defense, kid movies in Mexico are in Spanish. Watching an animated Disney flick in Spanish is still a passive activity, but it's a bit more educational. We also didn't have television reception, so watching movies and the occasional computer game was all the screen time there was. And because there was so much less available in terms of playgrounds, toys, and neighborhood friends, we had to look for other things to fill those endless hours after dinner and before bed. There was an additional benefit to the kids' movie nights for Michael and me. We spent so much time with the kids in Mexico that finding time *away* from them became the challenge. Movie dates for the kids gave us some much-needed together time up on the roof with a glass of wine.

In retrospect, I wish we'd been better prepared to make changes early on and had been able to relax some of our rules more gracefully. It would have cut down on a lot of tension and made things more pleasant for everyone — which is really important when you're spending so much time together.

We finally decided to stop fighting endless battles over treats and movies because we knew that our time abroad had definite starting and ending points. Our kids understood very well that there were different rules for different places and living in Mexico was a different place that ultimately called for different rules. It also got back to that old cliché "when in Rome (or Mexico, or France or wherever) . . ." For good and for bad, it's important to be sensitive to the culture around you as well as the pressures on your kids and attempt to be flexible within reason. I guess it comes down to picking your battles and realizing that the battles abroad may be different from those back home. If you remain rigid and unyielding about every aspect of family life during your sabbatical and expect rules to remain unchanged, expect daily (and losing) battles.

Of course, you have to do what's comfortable for your family. Friends of ours who spent seven months in San Miguel brought a SEGA system down with them for their teenaged boys. That wouldn't have been our choice but it worked for their family just fine and made it possible for everyone to have a good time while living away from home. We also lightened up on the "authentic" food issue. At first, we ate only Mexican food but after a few months, we started ordering Domino's pizza every other week for the kids.

Remember that you're thrusting this sabbatical experience upon your kids. Unless they're begging to go, they're not the ones asking to be separated from everything familiar. Ironically, they may be much more open to experiencing life in another culture if they don't have to give up every last piece of their own — or even better, if they feel like they're getting away with something abroad that you'd never let them do back home. Decide where you can bend and where you can't. Flexibility is the key to making the experience more pleasant for everyone.

> *"We had to compromise a lot. We got better and better at how to travel – how to keep the kids happy and also satisfy our own interests. We also did things as a family that Orin and I would never have done alone – like going to McDonalds and KFC every once in a while, going swimming at the fancy western hotels for fun occasionally, and things like that. Orin and I also took turns going out on adventures and being with the kids. Sometimes while the kids were at school we would try a new restaurant or go someplace we knew the kids would not enjoy."* — Rachel

Getting to Know (and really like) Your Kids

Soon after arriving in Mexico we took a bus trip to the small town of Dolores Hidalgo. It quickly turned into a daylong tour of ice cream stores, parks, and *tiendas*. Asher got a ball, Cleome got a book, and

Michael and I got an enormous headache and 15 minutes or so in a museum. Typical. I just sort of shrugged off the trip and chalked it up to life with kids. But Michael came home so angry and sad after that bus trip I thought we might really be facing some sort of family crisis. He sank into a depression and was convinced that our Mexico sabbatical was going to be one big bummer that revolved around satisfying the kids' desires and none of our own. He withdrew into himself and wanted nothing to do with the children or me. This went on for a week and I finally suggested he move to Mexico City and find some garret to write in for a month before we made page one of the Mexico Daily News ("Gringa stabs husband with stale tortilla").

It was obvious that he and I had completely different expectations about what our sabbatical with kids would entail. He'd been working fulltime since the kids had been born and was completely unprepared for the switch to fulltime parenting. He was under the impression that because he wasn't working, he'd have his days completely free to pursue his dreams. It wasn't until our sabbatical that Michael truly understood that we were not 28 and childless anymore and that the rules of lives with kids are seriously different.

During our sabbatical, Michael got a crash course in the reality of life with kids and at first it was tough going. Until then, he'd been largely on the periphery of their lives and didn't truly know them or accept them for the unreasonable beasts they can often be. He'd been more of a weekend parent and was used to picking and choosing the nature of his interactions with them. After a period of really disliking our children (and feeling terrible about it), he grew more relaxed and comfortable with letting the kids be kids and also developed a greater appreciation of how tough and valuable it is to be a fulltime parent. Ultimately, I think the sabbatical helped us become more patient and flexible as parents and really made the difference between Michael and me not just loving our kids but truly liking them (and vice versa).

Take Regular Breaks From Your Children

Learning to like your kids is important, and getting away from them regularly is a critical part of the process wherever you're living. It is perhaps even more important during your sabbatical when there are different pressures and fewer built-in breaks. Language tutoring, art classes, dinners out, drinks with friends, walks after dark — whatever activity you choose, make a plan to get out and enjoy yourselves without the children on a regular basis. If you already build breaks away from the kids into your weekly schedule back home, make sure you continue this practice abroad. If you don't get away from your kids back home, learn to do so abroad. You'll find that you have much more energy and patience during your time *with* the kids if you recharge your batteries by getting *away* from them regularly. Also, if you don't get out on your own and experience different aspects of the exciting swirl of new life around you, you'll diminish the potential of your time abroad.

A family sabbatical abroad is partly about stepping away from your home culture to explore yourself, your kids, and your partner away from everything familiar. There is much to discover about ourselves when we look through a different lens for a period of time and it's critical to do it with and without your kids. Don't forgo having adult experiences just because you're a parent. Use this opportunity to reconnect with yourself and your spouse in an exciting way. Get a babysitter, go for a walk together, and practice speaking in another language. Have a romantic evening somewhere. Watch the sunset from a rooftop restaurant or have a glass of wine under the stars. I guarantee that ordering your first meal together in a foreign language will be good for a few laughs.

Finding trustworthy babysitters, daycare, preschools and other caregivers

Finding quality care for your children while you're living abroad is not difficult. But when you're operating in a different culture and language, there are some specific challenges to keep in mind. Typically you'll find the same child-care options available abroad that you have back home. These include home daycare, daycare centers, a person (babysitter) who comes into your home and watches your child for a specific period of time, and a live-in nanny. Each has its advantages and disadvantages and the old adage that you get what you pay for is usually true.

The best way to locate quality child care is through word of mouth. Ask everyone you meet with children if their kids go to nursery school or if they have any suggestions for how you can find someone to watch your kids. Talk about the going rate for quality child care and what sorts of experiences they've had finding care for their kids. The biggest dilemma for the people you ask will be whether they want to spill the beans about someone wonderful they've found, because then you become competition for their caregiver's time. But keep asking. Check bulletin boards and classified ads. Ask your maid, gardener, the neighbors, or an older child's teacher for recommendations. Eventually someone will give you a lead that pans out and you'll contact that caregiver and go from there.

We initially put our two-year-old in a Mexican daycare center that was connected to our daughter's elementary school. There were approximately ten kids in his class and there were two teachers watching and guiding them. The facilities were adequate although we mostly looked at it as glorified babysitting that included fun toys, mats, games, dances, and songs. There wasn't anything in the way of a teaching philosophy or a specific curriculum, but it was clean and the teachers were kind and conscientious. We paid approximately $45 per month (yes, per month) and a one-time $50 registration fee for Asher to attend this school from 8:45 a.m. to 12:45 p.m. five days a week. We provided diapers and snacks each day, and Asher really liked it a lot.

"We put our daughter into private Italian preschool immediately. While there were some other English-speaking students in the school, Claire's teacher did not speak English. The teacher felt it took Claire about nine months to really get a grasp of the

language but Claire always loved school and seemed to enjoy discovering a world she quickly divided into English and Italian." — Channing

During the summer break we employed Fabiola, the 19-year-old sister of our maid. We paid her about $2 an hour to take Asher to the park, the library, and just out to play each morning for a few hours so we could get some work done. It was mostly fine, although our communication with her was spotty due to our language differences. This is one of the primary areas of concern for hiring caregivers abroad.

When working through language and cultural barriers of any sort, it's critical to make sure that basic information is understood by everyone, even if it feels awkward or that you're repeating yourself constantly. Keep in mind that your child's welfare is at stake. In the States, everyone operates in more or less the same way. The basics such as pick-up and drop-off times, payment schedules, and health, safety, and discipline expectations are usually spelled out clearly and effectively through daycare manuals, conversations, and accepted practices. This may not be the case when you're living abroad. It's easy to let things go unsaid because you assume things are going to be done in a certain way or perhaps because it's uncomfortable or difficult to communicate. But it takes only one frightening moment to make you realize that assumptions aren't enough — such as when you expect your child to be returned by 1:00 p.m. and there's no sign of him at 3:00 and you realize you have absolutely no way of knowing where your babysitter has taken him. Did he get injured? Did she forget? Has he been kidnapped? The most horrible thoughts race through your mind when you realize someone you barely know has your child.

In our case, Fabiola eventually showed up with a smile and a napping boy on her shoulder. She said he'd fallen asleep at her house and she didn't want to wake him. Up to that point we'd been making babysitting arrangements through her sister Sonia and it was only then that I learned Fabiola didn't have a phone at her house so there was no way for her to let us know. After I expressed how very worried I'd been, we agreed that she would find some way to call us if it ever happened again and soon thereafter, she got a cell phone. The point is that even though it may be awkward, it's absolutely critical to go over all the basics with your caregiver and make sure your wishes are understood and observed. Also, make sure your children are respectful of your caregiver and that they don't take advantage of the situation. In some cultures, the employer's children are treated like little "masters" who get to rule the roost like little tyrants. Caregivers can pass along wonderful local traditions to your children in the form of foods and songs and games. But they can also engage in negative stereotyping and questionable discipline and safety practices. Just make sure you communicate your expectations clearly with both your children and caregiver and monitor their interactions regularly.

> *"We arrived in early July, and had been warned that we would need to find an apartment soon because the whole country closes down in August, so we needed to get started quickly. We contacted a nanny service we found in a tour guidebook and arranged to have someone come and be with our kids the second and third days we were there. This was a bit of a leap of faith, but the young woman who turned up was awesome."*
> — Frances

Nannies, grandmas and other fulltime caregivers

Some families living abroad have a full or part-time nanny (which, like a maid, is a potentially affordable luxury abroad). In many cases the nanny eventually becomes part of the family and the situation works out well, *más o menos*. But not always. We know of many instances where awkward moments have arisen between caregiver and employer and it usually comes down to a lack of communication. If a caregiver from another culture is going to be a regular part of your family's life, it's important to anticipate the potential for misunderstandings and deal with them proactively. I'm specifically talking about your rules regarding safety, cleanliness, food, bedtimes, and discipline. Your caregiver may have very different ideas about these things. Don't assume you share the same attitudes. Tell your caregiver plainly what your expectations are and make sure he or she understands and agrees to adhere to them. You may have to show your caregiver how you want things done in terms of cleaning or cooking for your children. Even if it feels a bit silly, demonstrate diapering, bathing, and bedtime procedures. Better to risk over-explaining than letting something go unsaid and return home later to find a problem waiting.

> *"Finding support for Marcel has been wonderful for us in Norway because Gretha is a Norwegian citizen. Child care in Norway is close to free when you consider the governmental help and subsidies, and health care is nearly free for everybody. It's a good feeling not to have to worry about these issues, but the choices are limited."*
> — Ali and Gretha, with Marcel (age 3), who are living in Husnes, Norway

Another caregiver option is to employ a family member as a nanny for a period of time. Maybe Grandma is up for an adventure with the grandkids for a few months or a niece or nephew is old enough to spend summer vacation living abroad and helping with the kids during your sabbatical. Perhaps a friend or babysitter from back home would like to come for a visit over school vacations and during summer break. Pay their airfare and throw in nominal spending money, and they've got an exciting adventure and you've got time and space to breathe and have adventures of your own.

Entertaining Your Kids Abroad

One of the biggest challenges we faced during our sabbatical was figuring out how to entertain ourselves and our children without blowing our budget. Back home we're blessed with (and take for granted) a bazillion playgrounds and parks with marvelous facilities. In less wealthy countries (and therefore cheaper to live in), there are often no parks to speak of. If there is some sort of park, the playground facilities are likely to be nonexistent, decrepit, or possibly even dangerous for children to play on.

Finding inexpensive or free activities to keep the kids active and en-

tertained was an ongoing struggle in San Miguel. Part of it had to do
with not knowing the city well enough in the beginning and being unable (due to language barriers) to ask all the questions we needed to ask.
Part of it had to do with our emphasis on not wanting to immediately
become a part of the Gringo community and wanting instead to live a
bit more of a "Mexican" life. And part of it had to do with our limited
budget and not being able to afford the rather expensive activities and
programs aimed at foreign visitors.

> *"We loved going to new places that our children loved. The first time we went to Thai-
> land we went to a place called Sukothai – it was a kingdom from the 1200s where the
> Khmer had lived and it was not a heavily touristy place. To get there we took a second-
> class train ride, since the first-class trains did not stop there. Since it was second-class,
> the windows opened and at every stop women got on the train and sold Phad Thai and
> fish cakes wrapped in banana leaves and the train wound through hilly jungles. It was
> magical. At the ruins of the kingdom it was very uncrowded and the kids played so hap-
> pily among the ruins. They were taken off guard by how intriguing a place it was."*
> — Rachel

When choosing a place to live, it's critical (and I do mean critical)
to check into some of the basic kid facilities nearby or at least budget
for activities to keep your kids (and you) happy. Depending on where
you're living, finding free or affordable kid-oriented adventures on the
weekends and in the late afternoons may not be easy, especially if you
don't have a car. There may not be playgrounds and rec centers right
down the block. Swimming pools, tennis courts, and soccer fields usually charge a fee or are associated with hotels or kids' programs that
aren't always open to the public. It's important to investigate all avenues
of entertainment for your kids to find different adventures that work.
Do any of the schools have a playground or offer after-school programs?
Is there a library? Scouts? Do you have the money to pay for additional
help? Can a nearby teenager take your kids on a walk? Are there other
kids living nearby? What do they do for fun? Do they play in the street
(which is often the case) and is that OK with you? Eventually, we found

a hotel in town that let us use its pool for about $3 a person. We started spending long Saturday afternoons there with a picnic and it became a wonderful and affordable part of our adventure.

> *"The festivals in Mexico were terrific and unique for us. Días de los Muertos in Patzcuaro was spectacular. The older two children were free to go to town or to Internet cafés, markets, and friends' houses on their own. They had more freedom and access to "city" activities than they do at home. Just walking everywhere was great for us. The hot springs, the food. The kids took metalworking the entire time and loved it. They also studied piano and guitar and really had some great teachers."* — Karen

> *"Figure out early on how to get info on local festivals and just go to them. They are almost always worth it."* — Frances

Camps, sports, classes

Although I'm certainly not advocating that you fill every moment of your child's day with enrichment activities as we have a tendency to do in the States, an occasional sports activity or music, dance, or art class can be wonderful. Not only does it help fill up the day, it helps your kids make friends and learn about their new language and culture, and it lets them have some fun away from you. Cleome had Spanish tutoring twice a week and chose one other weekly activity to be involved in. She tried out a dance class at the local rec center and eventually gave that up to start Tae Kwan Do. Both activities were quite inexpensive and were taught completely in Spanish (or Korean). During summer vacation, she did a month-long art/language day camp and that was about it. There were all sorts of other possibilities but enrolling in them would have quickly busted our budget and would have gotten us back to the pace we had consciously left behind. We know of many families who essentially traded a busy American lifestyle in America for a busy (and expensive) American lifestyle in their home away from home. Horseback riding, Flamenco dancing, soccer leagues, jewelry-making classes — your new home may offer many of the same activities (sometimes with a twist, like the Flamenco dancing) that your kids were involved in back home. I urge you to resist the temptation to over-program your children, even if they are starting to drive you crazy. One of the great benefits of keeping your kids' time relatively unstructured is that after an interim period of "I'm bored" and "There's nothing to do," kids quickly discover the joys of reading and imaginative play.

Note: It's OK to be bored. Boredom is often the key to the door that opens your imagination. We're afraid to let our kids be bored and because of that, we program the imagination right out of them.

Tip: Have a regular supply of books available. If there's no library nearby, then order books online through Amazon or another service and build that expense into your budget. Books for general reading, language learning, and research are critical for everyone's mental health and intellectual development.

"I loved the slower pace of life and the emphasis more on people and relationships rather than on always doing something."   — Kim

Surviving Day Trips, Vacations and Other Travels with Kids

Taking trips away from your home base can be a great way to spend time with your kids and explore your home away from home. These adventures can be as simple as hopping a local bus and taking it to the end of the line to kick around in a new part of town and get an inexpensive tour of the city. Or, you can take a longer journey by bus or car and plan to spend a few nights in a distant city.

During your sabbatical, you may find that you have a lot of flexibility in terms of when and where you can travel. One way to take advantage of this and see different parts of your new country inexpensively is to set up house exchanges during your sabbatical. House exchanges are becoming more and more popular and are an excellent way to see a country on a budget. Use the Internet to locate a house exchange service (in Mexico we used Mexconnect). Think about where you want to travel, plug in your dates and lodging requirements, and you might end up with some fabulous opportunities to travel for very little money.

Caution: Make sure your rental agreement abroad doesn't specifically prohibit this type of exchange and consider any responses to your posting carefully. As a renter, you generally have fewer worries and far more flexibility but you're still responsible for any damage to your rental house.

Day trips and vacations with children can be wonderful but they can also be unsatisfying marathons of snacks, treats, and bathrooms. You may find that your level of frustration during any trip increases in direct proportion to the number of museums, churches, restaurants, and stores you have to either leave prematurely or abandon completely to accommodate the decibel level of your children's whining. During a day trip to the Mexican city of Querétaro, the only way we saw any of its beautiful plazas and Spanish colonial architecture was by convincing our children that the best ice cream shop in the city was on the other side of a historic church, across two plazas, and around the corner from Francisco Eduardo Tresguerras' amazing Neptune fountain (like I said, in Mexico there's an ice cream shop on every block).

> *"The kids were not so comfortable going to places that were far out of their comfort zone, especially since most of where we were was already out of their comfort zone. I remember traveling in Southwest China in a very ethnic town that was celebrating a Buddha's birthday. There were women coming down from villages in the hills and making fires on the sides of the road and making amazing dishes for offerings at the Temple. The Temple itself was very crowded. Music was being played with these ancient instruments. Fires were burning and candles were lit and old women were chanting. It was the most amazing scene and Orin and I couldn't believe our good fortune in being in the right place at the right time. There were no tourists around and we freely wandered around and nobody cared at all that we were there. It was an incredibly rich adventure. But the kids were so uncomfortable that after a certain point they flat out refused to go into the Temple and down the dirt paths where all these women were cooking. There was so much whining and moaning that finally Orin and I took them back to the guest house and we took turns all afternoon going to watch the festival."*
> — Rachel

Sometimes simply getting to a place is the hardest part of traveling with kids. Traveling with young children by bus, car, or airplane for more than a few hours can challenge any parent's patience. By all means bring the usual supply of books, toys, art supplies, and snacks. (And consider toting along Benadryl or some other sleep-inducing medicine.) Do all the singing and road games you can summon the energy for but also consider letting the kids zone out by watching movies or using a Game Boy. If you reserve this brainless activity for traveling, your kids will really think the trip is special. Besides, expecting kids to stay in their seats for long periods without exploding is a losing proposition unless they don't notice they're doing it.

One other potential area of compromise, and this is much touchier, is safety. Seatbelts are simply not a fact of life in many parts of the world. Nor are guardrails, crosswalks, traffic lights, or a multitude of other safety systems considered "standard" in the U.S. By necessity we tossed out many of the safety rules we take for granted in the States during our 18 months in Mexico. We didn't wear seatbelts because in most vehicles there weren't any available. We didn't use car seats because we didn't have a vehicle with us and none of the vehicles we rode in had one. If you're traveling in your own vehicle, obviously you get to make the safety rules for your family. But if you're relying on alternate transportation, it's likely you'll have to compromise on safety along the way.

Tips for Surviving Outings With Your Kids

Over time, we adjusted our expectations regarding travel with the kids and the kids gradually became better travelers as well. But it was hellish at the start and some of our lowest moments as a family occurred either during or immediately after a day trip or vacation. With that in mind, the following suggestions may help quicken your family's learning curve and improve chances that everyone will have at least a modicum of fun during your various adventures right from the start.

1. Be flexible when it comes to treats and food. The rules are different on the road and even young kids can understand that. Sometimes an ice cream cone "right now" instead of after lunch can save the day. Flexibility is the key. Try to bend rather than break.

2. Plan for things not to go smoothly. If you're prepared for the worst, you'll be able to face tough moments with more grace and good will. Because "the worst" rarely happens, everyone will feel extra cheerful when you're prepared for things to go badly and they actually go well.

3. Whenever possible, build a visit to a beach, swimming pool, or lake into your trips. Water plus beach plus sun adds up to big, big fun. No matter what. And it doesn't have to be a beach. Hotel pools, hot springs, even a sprinkler can quickly turn a bummer into a blast.

4. Don't let your kids' reluctance to explore the unknown sway you. Plan to be adventurous. Although it initially took ice cream bribes to get our kids interested in new adventures, they eventually looked forward to all the fun surprises that inevitably happened along the way. After a little whining, your kids may discover how much fun embarking on new adventures can be.

"Being with the kids made us do a greater variety of things because all of our activities revolved around so many different kinds of interests." — Kim

5. Plan trips with your kids' energy levels and interests in mind. Be realistic. Surrender to the reality of young children or be prepared to be frustrated. Plan outings carefully. Don't try to do more than one activity per outing. For example, hit a museum in the morning *or* go for a swim (or to the park) with a picnic lunch in the afternoon. This can be disappointing to the adults, but it makes for a more relaxed and ultimately more enjoyable trip for everyone.

"We had to plan our time with the children's schedules and tolerance for museums and such in mind. In general, our children did really well in museums, archeological sites,

art galleries, and the like, but we were always careful to do these types of activities in small doses." — Julie

6. ***When all else fails, go swimming.*** This is a critical piece of advice.

"We did bring board games and sports toys for our kids and invested much more time in playing these with the kids than we do in the U.S. (which was good for us). We only brought two computer games and that seemed to be fine. We did rent videos two times a week at least. And it was very useful to find a regular place to go swimming. That's important." — Marline

Tip: Maintaining a sense of humor can save the day when maintaining a sense of perspective is impossible.

---

35 THINGS TO DO WITH KIDS (WHEN YOU'VE ALREADY DONE EVERYTHING YOU CAN THINK OF)

1. Star gaze.
2. Sing songs.
3. Have a water balloon fight.
4. Paint pictures.
5. Do a family art project. For example, make "mail art" collages with the bus tickets, brochures, and other items you've collected along the way. Cut them up and glue them to generic postcards or postcards from your travels and send them to friends back home. Or use the same materials to make a family scrapbook of your adventures.
6. Take a walk.
7. Find a garden to enjoy.
8. Cook something together.
9. Call a babysitter.
10. Fix something broken.

11. Download a new computer game.

12. Research something new on the Internet.

13. Go to the library or bookstore.

14. Go to the park.

15. Go to the most kid-friendly restaurant you can find and have lunch.

16. Rent a movie.

17. Ride on every sidewalk and dime-store kid ride you can find.

18. Shop for shoes.

19. Shop for a new fruit.

20. Buy a small, low maintenance pet like a mouse or rabbit.

21. Do some American homework.

22. Make a funny postcard to send to a friend.

23. Play cards.

24. Fly a kite.

25. Call a friend.

26. Buy someone back home a gift.

27. Turn up the music really loud and dance.

28. Make homemade musical instruments.

29. Teach the kids to do the waltz or to salsa dance.

30. Let the kids make dinner.

31. Get in the bathtub with them and blow bubbles.

32. Have a laughing (coughing, farting, snoring, yelling, burping, whistling) contest.

33. Tell knock-knock jokes.

34. Go up on the roof and scream and then come back down and do a group hug.

35. Go to the dentist. (Going to the dentist for a routine cleaning is one of those activities that families often put off both at home and abroad. It's a good idea to fit some of these mundane but important chores into your adventure abroad.)

13. Getting Sick

"Our only medical emergency occurred when we were returning to Guatemala from a visit to Mexico. Zeb had been running a mild fever for several days. While overnighting in a hotel, his fever went so high that he was hallucinating even after I gave him ibuprofen. We knew it was time to give him a cold shower but there wasn't any water! We poured our drinking water over him to try and cool him down but it didn't help, so at midnight we set off for a nearby public hospital. It was a very hot, rather sad place with worn equipment, hand-drawn posters showing 'ways to prevent cholera,' and 'how to recognize diphtheria,' and a case of labeled indentations where vials of emergency medications should have been. Even so, the doctor and nurse saw him right away and gave him what he needed – a shot of antibiotics, more fever-reducing medication and a 15-minute cold shower. We were reassured to be there but extremely grateful that it was nothing more serious than tonsillitis!" — Sarah

Unfortunately it will happen sooner or later. Despite all your careful precautions — the iodine soaked veggies, the constant hand washing, the bottled water — someone, maybe everyone, will get sick. And then what will you do?

An Ounce of Prevention . . .

This is an area where it pays to do your research and gather information before you actually need it. As in finding babysitters, good schools, and the like, your network of local and expat friends are going to be critical allies when you need advice about finding good medical care. You may find a wide variety of specialists, homeopaths, clinics, and hospitals available nearby. Or you may be limited to one or two general practitioners, the local hospital, and a network of pharmacies scattered around town. In many countries, pharmacists often train with doctors and may be quite knowledgeable about treating common illnesses. Diarrhea, nausea, headaches, sunburn, food poisoning, fevers, coughs, colds — these and other minor illnesses can be taken care of, in many cases, without a visit to the doctor. Common medicines that require a prescription in the States can often be obtained in pharmacies abroad at a reasonable cost and without a prescription. The trick is to ask around and find a reputable and knowledgeable pharmacist.

> *"The first things to do are locate a school, a park, and a pediatrician."* — Channing

> *"Although we brought a large variety of medical supplies, we found most of what we needed was available locally anyway, and we had confidence in the doctors we visited. Apart from one infection of stomach parasites (sounds worse than it felt and was easily treated), we have so far only experienced the kind of mild ailments and sicknesses that we would expect to go through in a normal year at home. In fact, ironically, we noticed during our first week here that Zeb's stool was teeming with worms that he had obviously brought with him from Vermont, probably from eating unwashed apples in our neighbor's orchard the previous fall!"* — Sarah

You will have better success using a pharmacy to treat a minor illness if you can describe the problem and request a specific treatment or medicine using the local language. If you're looking for a specific medicine, try the common name but throw a Spanish, French, or Italian accent into the mix. Be aware that a misplaced accent can make something as simple as a request for Benadryl get you a shrug and nothing more. In Mexico, for example, Benadryl is pronounced "Bay-NAH-dreel."

> *"We had access to a Western clinic, which was great — Chinese hospitals are pretty scary places. But none of us was ever very ill, thank goodness. One experience we had was*

interesting. Stanley had to have a physical at a particular children's clinic in order to go to his daycare. All the children stood in lines and were examined in front of each other. Stanley found this humiliating and it was hard. He also had to have a blood test for TB and I was worried about whether they would use clean needles. I did bring an interpreter along with me and we determined that the needles were clean and it turned out okay." — Rachel

Trust your instincts

If someone in your family comes down with diarrhea that persists beyond a few days, it might be a simple bug or it could be something more serious, perhaps an intestinal infection or parasite requiring an antibiotic. You can start by explaining the symptoms to a trusted pharmacist. If a pharmacist can't solve the problem he or she will recommend that you see a doctor. If you are dispensed medicine at a pharmacy, double-check the expiration date and don't take anything you're not familiar with. Occasionally a pharmacist will suggest a medicine that is no longer recommended or that has been banned in the States, but this is relatively rare in Western countries. Most sicknesses will blow over on their own. A couple of days of laying low and pushing the liquids along with a few doses of Pepto-Bismol, and you'll be up and around again just slightly the worse for wear. But if your two-year-old is running a high fever and is also battling diarrhea and nausea, a quick trip to the doctor or hospital emergency room is certainly in order. Don't mess around with something that could be dangerous.

Finding Quality Medical Care

Locating a good doctor and pharmacy is important and something you should do soon after arrival rather than waiting until an emergency. Along with the advice of other expats and friendly locals, your child's school might be able to suggest a good pediatrician and the parents of your children's schoolmates might also have some ideas. Make sure you bring along important medical records for each member of your family. These include vaccination histories, physicals, prescriptions, blood types, X-rays, and anything else you consider important to your family's health history. If anybody in your family has an ongoing serious illness or chronic condition, it's important to personally visit a potential physician to introduce yourself and make him or her aware of your situation. It's not a bad idea to ask your home physician to recommend a doctor in the country you're headed to even if that doctor is located in some other city. In an emergency, it can be very reassuring to have the name of someone who knows your doctor back home and be able to give this name to the local doctor treating you or your child.

> *"I was seven months pregnant when we left the U.S. It was a bit of a puzzle trying to figure out if our U.S. insurance would cover the birth and finding a doctor who spoke English. Before we left I found an English-speaking OB about an hour away thanks to online contacts and the presence of an American military base 45 minutes from Lucca. We did import things like children's Tylenol from the U.S. but also relied on the counsel of the Italian pediatrician and the pharmacist."* — Channing

> *"The U.S. Embassy had a list of local docs who spoke English. We had a physical with them before school started and thus felt connected to someone when the first medical problems arose. This is certainly one of the scary parts, even though the medical system was quite fine, it's a touch stressful to think of dealing with something complicated in another language. Talk to other expats up front, find out who's had good dealings with medical problems so you know who to call if it comes up."* — Frances

One thing I suggest you do soon after you arrive is jump in your car or grab a cab and go to the nearest hospital. Just for a visit. How long does it take to get there? How quickly did you find a cab? Where is the emergency room entrance? What sorts of documents do you have to have with you to be treated? Does anyone speak English? Are interpreters available? Does your health insurance cover you at this particular hospital? These are things you may never need to know, but if you do end up with a medical emergency, knowing the answers to these questions could make a difference. And visiting a hospital in another country is really an interesting experience. That initial visit is probably the only time you'll get to see the inside of a hospital during your sabbatical. Let's hope so anyway.

"Our daughter had one hospital visit, an emergency in the middle of the night. It sounds like a recipe for disaster, but the visit to the hospital went exceedingly well. We got great care and paid very little for it." — Julie

"Our kids were only sick once, with a very bad throat infection. We went to the local doctor and he suggested penicillin injections. (I had already tried penicillin over-the-counter tablets with no luck.) We did this for four days until an American friend who was a physician told me to stop. She said it was a very outdated, poor practice. The penicillin was having no effect and it wasn't strep and it just went away on its own. The local orthodontist suggested gargling with lime juice and vinegar. It packs a lot more of a punch than gargling with salt water." — Kim

Thankfully, we had relatively few experiences with doctors abroad. I did visit the emergency room of a local hospital after ripping my calf muscle on the beach during one of our vacations. Nobody spoke English and I was very happy to be able to speak Spanish well enough to describe my situation, ask questions, and understand the diagnosis and treatment. It would have been extremely frustrating, particularly in a true emergency, to rush to the hospital and not be able to communicate with the healthcare professionals. Think about this in advance and call around to find out if different facilities offer interpretive services. These might be very helpful to you should you encounter some kind of medical emergency during your stay.

Tip: Ask locals you trust or other expats for recommendations about doctors and other medical services. If all else fails and you're worried about receiving appropriate medical care, go to the largest hotel in town and ask if they can recommend an English-speaking doctor.

"It was very hard being sick with the flu, all five of us, with only one bathroom work-ing! We kept trying different doctors for different things. Most of them looked at us briefly and said, antibiotic." — Rob

Sources of medical information

The Internet can be an excellent resource for researching nearly any-thing that ails you or your family. Keep in mind, however, that anyone can post information on the Internet. An informative and well written website doesn't necessarily establish medical credentials. So it's impor-tant to use common sense when you're conducting medical research on the Net. Check a variety of sources and compare and contrast informa-tion across different websites. Also, bring along an easy to understand medical reference book and a book that illustrates basic emergency medicine procedures and keep them close at hand (see *Resources* for sug-gested titles). If someone in your family experiences a medical emer-gency, turn to those books to check for what to do while you're waiting for the ambulance, cab, or doctor to arrive. Clearly written books can also help your children do the right thing in the event that a sibling or parent gets hurt and they must act quickly. Sit down with your kids and page through the books together so everyone knows how to use them. Walk through an emergency scenario and discuss how to contact a hos-pital or other emergency service if something goes wrong. Make sure your older children know where your medical supplies are kept and that your first-aid kit is stored out of reach of younger kids.

The Internet is also a good way to double-check the treatments for common illnesses and remind yourselves of what to look for if a sim-ple problem seems to be turning into something more serious. When you're far away from home, it's comforting to have a place to go for information in English to assuage your fears, answer questions, and do some basic research before you head to a doctor to have a problem checked out. Being prepared with questions and concerns, particularly if you're operating in a different language, will make you a much better advocate for someone in your family needing medical attention.

Health Insurance Abroad

To protect yourselves in the event of some serious illness or injury during your time abroad, you will want international health insurance coverage for everyone in your family. Check your current health insurance policy carefully to see if it includes adequate coverage when you are outside of the U.S. or your home country. The majority of HMO or employer-sponsored U.S. health plans either will not cover you internationally for longer than a two-week vacation or will offer only minimal coverage abroad that may not be adequate for your family's needs. If your current policy is not satisfactory for your sabbatical, you will need to purchase international health insurance.

This is one area where it really pays to surf the Net. There are many different companies offering a mind-boggling array of international health insurance products, all with different pricing options, deductibles, and coverage types and amounts. The two basic types are *travel* health insurance and *expatriate* health insurance. The length of your sabbatical will often determine which type your family needs. Travel health insurance policies are quite expensive and typically cover travel outside of the U.S. for two weeks to 70 days. This is short-term vacation health insurance. If your sabbatical is longer than 70 days, you will most likely be looking for expatriate health insurance.

Finding the right expat policy

Type "international health insurance" into your search engine and sit back and watch hundreds of options appear. Don't despair. Although there are many different companies and policies out there, checking for a few specific items will narrow your search significantly. First, decide what type of basic expat coverage you're looking for. Do you want a *comprehensive policy* (significantly more expensive) to cover every little possibility? Or are you fairly comfortable playing the odds and going with more of a *catastrophic policy*, which will cover serious emergencies but leave you to pay for smaller medical expenses out of pocket? If you go with catastrophic coverage, decide which deductible amount is right for your family. A larger deductible means a smaller monthly premium. It also means you'll have to pay that deductible should you ever actually need to use the policy.

Start with a broker

A good place to start researching your family's insurance needs is with an international health insurance broker. Insurance brokers represent a variety of different companies and insurance products and are a good basic source of information on this confusing topic. Make sure he or she understands that you're looking for expatriate coverage. Insurance brokers make a commission when you purchase one of the health insurance policies they represent. However, using a broker doesn't increase the cost of your policy because his or her commission is paid by the insurance company, not you. You can find insurance brokers listed online and can contact them by phone or email.

Brokers are worth contacting even if you ultimately decide not to use one. They have access to policies offered by insurance companies around the world, and the best international policy for your family may be one offered by a British or German insurance company. At the very least, an initial conversation with an insurance broker will give you a good general idea of the types of policies and options available to your family. I spoke with several and each conversation helped bring some aspect of this confusing issue into better focus.

Geographic coverage options

One important decision you will need to make early on is whether you want expatriate insurance that covers you strictly *outside* the U.S. (much cheaper) or expatriate health insurance that covers you both outside *and inside* the U.S. as well. This is a critical difference. Many expatriate health insurance policies can offer excellent coverage at a third of the cost of U.S. policies because health care in the U.S. is the most expensive in the world. If the policy does not cover you in the U.S., it will be much cheaper but you will not be covered if you return for short vacations or if something happens abroad and you decide to return to the U.S. for treatment. There are some inexpensive policies that will cover you for short periods (visits of two weeks or even up to 30 days) if you live predominately outside of the U.S. There are also policies that will allow you to be covered in the U.S. if you live continuously outside the U.S. for a specified period of time, typically a minimum of six months. You will narrow your choices significantly based on your decision regarding this issue.

If you're looking for coverage specifically outside the U.S., you can usually find inexpensive high quality expatriate medical coverage to suit your needs. Depending on where you're going, you may well have access to medical care of equal or even better quality than what you have available at home. In our experience, competent health care abroad for minor illnesses, broken bones, and minor surgery is available in most larger cities and is far less expensive than similar care in the States. The costs of medicines, doctor's visits, dental care, and even hospital stays are, in most cases, a fraction of what they are back home. That emergency room visit I mentioned earlier for my ripped calf muscle cost a grand total of $15.

To investigate medical care in your sabbatical destination, hop on the Internet and ask other expats living there about the local facilities as well as the costs, quality, availability, education, and training of health-care professionals in your city. Check to see whether any local hospitals or clinics offer information online. Perhaps your medical practitioners back home will have some helpful information about facilities and doctors in your intended destination. Physicians back home are often tied into a professional network of international medical facilities and practitioners. Your own doctor or dentist may be able to recommend a colleague or provide a website or telephone number to a specific medical facility or international healthcare service that can provide more specific information. All of your research will help you narrow down the type of international health coverage your family will need during your travels.

"Our 11-year-old son had an appendectomy while in Quito. We had been referred by friends of friends to an American-style hospital, funded by American missionaries, before we even went to Ecuador. We were quite pleased with the care he got and were amazed at how inexpensive it was. Our son also had a problem later on in the year that was quite scary. He began getting terrible headaches, eventually leading to dizziness and the inability to walk unassisted. Of course, I thought, 'brain tumor.' Among other things, we consulted with the top neurologist in the country, had a CAT scan done on him, ruled out most fevers and other diseases. Nothing turned up. We finally decided to treat him with antibiotics on the off chance he had an inner-ear infection. Antibiotics are something you buy over-the-counter in Ecuador. We did and he did get better. We're still not sure that he had an inner-ear infection, but he hasn't had any recurrence of the problems, so perhaps that's what it was. My daughter fell at a playground and had emergency plastic surgery at the same hospital that my son had had his appendectomy. The results were as good as anything that could've been done in the U.S. The total charge for the plastic surgery was only about $150. David's appendectomy only cost about $450 for a five-day stay in the hospital including surgery, sonograms, and everything else." — Tani

Read the fine print

Whichever insurance you go with, check the policy carefully to make sure it covers everything you need completely, at an anticipated price tag. Most policies include exclusions for "dangerous activities" which refer to things like scuba diving, motorcycling, parasailing, and the like. If your sabbatical will include these types of activities and you want them covered, you'll either need a different type of policy or have to pay for a separate rider to cover them if one is available. Also be aware of pre-existing condition exclusions. Some policies will provide coverage for pre-existing conditions after continuous coverage for a specified period of time. Other policies don't offer riders for pre-existing conditions and simply will not cover specific items.

Make sure you understand the terms of your international family medical insurance policy regarding the following important items:

• Emergency medical evacuation, reunion, and repatriation.

- Coverage amount for accidents and sickness.
- Choice of hospital or doctor. (Are you covered for out-of-system services? Can you reduce out-of-pocket costs by using "in-system" care?)
- Home-country coverage for visits or treatment of an accident or sickness originating in a location abroad.
- Maternity coverage (if this is an issue).
- Types of exclusions and limitations.
- Pre-certification requirements.
- Method of payment to providers — direct pay or reimbursement?
- Whether you must reside outside of the U.S. for a period of time and if so for how long.

Once you find the right policy for your family, be certain you understand how to access your health insurance should you need it. Can you flash the card at any hospital? Do you need to call someplace first and get authorization? Is there a toll-free number you can access from abroad? Do you need to pay on the spot and then send documentation to your insurance company for reimbursement? Which documents do you specifically need to send?

Health insurance is something that is not necessarily interesting or fun to deal with and for that reason, it's easy to put off. Don't. Dig out your current health insurance policy right now to see if your family will be covered during your sabbatical. If not, bite the bullet and start looking for international healthcare coverage now. The irony about health insurance is that you're paying for something you hope you never to have to use. But if you do have to use it, you realize very quickly that the price of health insurance is worth every penny.

Vaccinations

Before you leave for your sabbatical, make sure everyone in your family has a complete physical and that all your immunizations and boosters are up-to-date. Discuss your travel plans with your doctor, or even better, take advantage of the medical travel specialist or travel clinic associated with your current health insurance. These travel specialists can help you check to see if any specific immunizations are required or recommended for your destination. Hepatitis vaccinations in particular are often required and several others may be suggested depending on the location of your sabbatical. Give yourselves plenty of advance notice to get any required shots since some immunizations require specific waiting periods between doses or need to be given in certain combinations. The Centers for Disease Control (CDC) has a very thorough and up-to-date website listing disease risk areas and recommended and required vaccinations by location. Make sure any vaccinations you receive are recorded on World Health Organization-approved forms and keep these records with your passport in case immigration officials ask to see them.

Because many families around the world don't receive preventive health care, it's not uncommon for communities abroad to administer childhood vaccinations at school to ensure that kids are protected from common diseases. Usually, but not always, a notice is sent home a day or two in advance of these vaccinations. If you do not want your child vaccinated, you must state this in writing and submit it to the director of the school. It's helpful, in this instance, to have your child's vaccination records along so you can provide the names and dates of your child's previous vaccinations. Sometimes the school requires proof that your child has really had the necessary shots. It's also common for schools to administer additional medical/health treatments such as vitamins and anti-parasite medication. Again, if you do not want your children to receive these medications, you must state it in writing.

Dental Care

It's a wise idea to visit the dentist before you leave home. Get everyone a check-up and have any necessary dental work done. Depending on the length and location of your sabbatical, you may never need or want to visit a dentist overseas. In fact, in some parts of the world the last thing you want to do is have an unfamiliar dentist messing around in your mouth using potentially outdated tools and techniques.

However, dental care abroad can be both excellent and a bargain. A number of our friends had dental work performed in San Miguel on either their children (orthodontia) or themselves with only positive things to say. One of our friends had done the math and concluded that it was actually cheaper to get her ten-year-old daughter braces in Mexico and come back down a few times a year for check-ups (and mini vacations) than to pay for braces in the States. Another family started their three boys on braces and retainers abroad, reasoning that their dentist back home could continue the work but at a reduced cost since so much had already been accomplished.

> *"It was great working with our dentist/orthodontist. The care is much cheaper and very competent but not as sophisticated as in the U.S. Well worth checking out."* — Kim

In our case, my 25-year-old dental bridge broke the day before we left for Mexico. The Mexican woman who eventually became our family dentist was not only well educated and pleasant, with a very modern office and the latest technology, but she spoke English to boot. I spent half what I would have in the States for a new dental bridge. We all got our teeth cleaned before returning to the States and our dentist charged us $30 for each cleaning, which included a fluoride treatment and X-rays for the kids. We brought back copies of the X-rays to show to our dentist back home. Of course, it's extremely important to ask around before committing your mouth and your pocketbook to a stranger's care.

Eye Doctors

If you or your children wear glasses or contact lenses, be sure to bring along an extra pair for each child as well as recent prescriptions. If you need to see an eye doctor for some reason while you're living abroad, you shouldn't have any problem finding quality eye care, even in the most unlikely places. Ask your doctor back home, a local doctor or pharmacist, or friends for a recommendation.

Caring for your family's health abroad is no different from caring for it back home. To a greater or lesser degree, any time you deal with healthcare professionals abroad or in the States you place yourselves and your children in a relative stranger's hands and begin a doctor/patient relationship based largely on trust. You make an educated leap of faith using the information available to you at the time. This includes recommendations from others, your own research, and your gut instinct about what's best in a given situation. Granted, you may have more healthcare choices back home than abroad, but having more choices doesn't necessarily guarantee success or even satisfaction. Trust your own instincts and teach your kids to trust theirs. Set off on your trip with the goal of keeping everyone healthy during your sabbatical. But if someone does get sick and needs medical attention, feel confident that you'll be able to quickly find the right treatment to make them well again.

14. Making Friends Abroad

"Hands down, the advantages of going abroad with kids far outweigh the disadvantages. Kids facilitate an incredible entry into the culture. They open all kinds of doors to meeting families and others. Through their activities and school events you meet all sorts of people. We had Americans who lived in Guanajuato say repeatedly to us that we had made more Mexican friends and been invited into more Mexican homes and events than they had in six years. And your kids' friendships may well lead to future exchanges between families — them sending their children to live with you and vice versa. You also get a look into Mexican family life and youth culture that you might not otherwise get as adults living alone abroad."   — Marline

One of the most wonderful surprises awaiting you abroad are the friends you will meet. You'll undoubtedly develop a tight circle of friends with whom you'll share holidays, travels, dinners, and adventures. And you'll be surprised at how permanent some of these "temporary" friendships will become.

Expat Friendships Are Special

Forming friendships abroad with other expats happens surprisingly easily and, in some respects, these friendships can become deeper and more rewarding than many friendships back home. You're likely to feel an immediate kinship with some of the people you meet during your sabbatical. You're linked by a shared sense of adventure and a desire for something greater than can be found in your own backyards. There's an unconscious recognition that you've made similar choices and share specific core values that are the driving force behind your decision to leave home even for a relatively short period of time.

In many cases, your children will be the sparks that ignite these new friendships. A play date with a new friend from school or a chance conversation with another parent at the park can quickly lead to a rewarding friendship, for traveling has a way of opening you up to new experiences. And parents anywhere naturally gravitate toward each other to provide playmates for their kids and support systems for themselves. Making friends with other parents abroad means sharing many of the same adventures and challenges as you feel your way together through an unfamiliar culture, language, and location.

> *"A big challenge for us was connecting with other Jews. In Nanjing there were a few Jewish students so we invited them for the Jewish New Year and Passover. That was fun and I think it showed the kids how you can make community and celebrate your holidays wherever you are."* — Rachel

Although we did eventually make a number of excellent Mexican friends, our expat friendships happened far more quickly and easily. We had fewer obstacles to overcome because we were "foreigners" together. We shared a common language and culture that made us allies in sifting through the more confusing aspects of life abroad. Our expat community became our extended family, which was especially nice in Mexico where extended families are the norm.

One particularly interesting aspect of developing expat friendships abroad is that you do so despite differences that would normally prevent your paths from crossing back home, such as location, profession, educational background, and even religious, racial, ethnic, economic, and political differences. The sense of "us" as expats cuts across your differences and connects you on some very basic level, which can be an incredibly enriching experience. The shared context of living as outsiders in a different culture provides everyone with exciting fodder for discussion and your new friends, with different perspectives, backgrounds,

and life experiences, may offer up viewpoints that cause you to reconsider your own opinions and even your future goals.

> *"Living abroad was very enriching and got Andy and me talking more about what
> kind of lifestyle we wanted to live once our kids were in college. We met so many
> other people with varied backgrounds — artists, musicians, writers, restaurateurs,
> midwives, jewelry designers, etc. It made for so much more interesting conversation
> and more meaningful friendships."* — Kim

It's through this network of friends that you'll exchange invaluable
information about doctors, dentists, religious communities, schools,
and much more. You may practice speaking a foreign language together
(and laugh hysterically while you do it). And these friends may ultimately become future business partners, collaborators, and colleagues.

Your children will also develop friendships in your new expat community and these relationships will transcend boundaries as well. Kids
who may not gravitate toward each other back home will become instant
friends thanks to the shared (and rather desperate) search for playmates
who speak their language and share a common country and culture.
After your sabbatical is over these friendships can turn into wonderful
pen-pal relationships and future opportunities for visiting "old" friends
who live in other parts of the U.S. or the world.

Tip: Developing friendships abroad can help kids reach out to new
friends when they return home as well. Your kids will have a very different sense of what it means to be an outsider and may be more sympathetic to newcomers in their classrooms.

Getting to Know the Locals

Making friends with local native speakers is typically much more
difficult. Yet it can be an enormously rewarding entrée into another
culture and community that most foreigners don't experience. So while
many gringos we met weren't motivated to traverse the cultural and
language barriers in order to meet local Mexicans, we resolved to try.

After our first six months in San Miguel, we moved out of the center of town in order to live in a more traditionally Mexican neighborhood. Our children went to Mexican schools and we worked very hard to learn Spanish so that we could converse with our neighbors as much as possible. Despite our best efforts, however, it was still hard to meet local Mexicans who would exchange more than a simple hello, even after we'd lived there for 18 months.

It's important to have realistic expectations about how quickly locals will invite you into their homes and what sorts of relationships are really possible with local families while you're living abroad.

> *"The atmosphere was much more open to meeting people, although it was harder to make connections with Mexicans. We had been told by a friend who grew up in Mexico City that most Mexicans had lives so full of family obligations that it was tough to find social time with them. They suggested seeking out Mexicans who are from other areas or who have one spouse from somewhere else, because they have less time committed to extended family. And indeed the people we came to know fit this description."*
>
> — Kim

In a town geared to tourists, the natives are less likely to go out of their way to meet you. Why should they continually open their hearts and homes to relatively transient relationships? And in many cultures, including Mexico, family is everything. Developing new friendships takes a backseat to cultivating and attending to the daily obligations of extended families. Language difficulties can make communication awkward and cultural differences can make it feel that you'll never crack the wall of polite distance that separates you from native speakers.

Note: We Americans also have a tendency towards openness that isn't shared universally. So even if you do develop friendships with local people, you may not feel the ready intimacy you're used to back home.

Eventually a few exceptional locals did reach out in unusual ways to befriend us, and we ended up making some wonderful Mexican friends. These were typically transplants to San Miguel from other parts of Mexico or Mexicans interested in striking up friendships with Americans in order to practice speaking English and learn more about American culture. They were willing to overlook our rotten Spanish to help us improve and could themselves speak at least some English to get us over the inevitable rough spots in any conversation.

It may be a bit disappointing initially to learn that other English speakers will probably be your primary source of solace, companionship, and information. But don't let that prevent you from working hard to establish relationships with the locals. Be patient and keep in mind that finding native speakers willing to bridge the language and culture gap to become true friends takes both patience and perseverance.

> *"Making new friends, both natives and gringos, was definitely one of the greatest joys about living in another country."* — Leah

Kids Pave the Way for New Friendships

We knew that helping our children make friends was one of the most important things we could do to ensure their sabbatical experience was a good one. What we didn't realize was how important *their* friendships would become to making *our* sabbatical experience a successful one as well. On numerous occasions at school, in the park, at the library, or in the market, our kids introduced us to other local and expat families who became very important parts of our community. Your kids can be particularly good ambassadors in meeting native families, which as I mentioned above, can be rather tricky. Kids are good at meeting other kids and it forces you to meet their parents as well.

> *"Rather than a liability, we found that children are a great calling card, an icebreaker and a cultural universal, even if you do things differently."* — Sarah

> *"Having our kids with us greatly enhanced the experience because we were enjoying the place not only through our own experiences but also through theirs. It made it much easier to meet people at the playground or the park or even the 'jardin.' We met many parents through the school our two youngest went to. It was much tougher meeting*

people through the traditional private school our oldest attended because the school had a much more settled environment with fewer new students coming in." — Kim

Where to Meet New Friends

School is an obvious place to make new acquaintances. Classmates and their families will undoubtedly become friends over time. Each birthday party, school outing, or after-school activity offers an opportunity to rub shoulders with other parents. Volunteering at school in a variety of capacities (whether it's teaching English, serving up tacos at lunch, or sitting on a classroom committee) can help break the ice and convince people that getting to know you might be worth their effort. Organized athletics and recreational activities are excellent ways to connect with families with similar interests. Tennis, swimming, soccer, gymnastics, dance, music, writing workshops, and many other activities are offered in cities across the globe. Some may be organized through neighborhood recreation centers, schools, or the city itself. There may be a network of private sports teams or just a fledgling group of basketball hopefuls down the block. If there's nothing available in your city, perhaps you can ask around and help organize something for the kids or adults in your area.

"Try to get your children involved in activities that involve other families (like soccer), as it is a good way to meet and make friends with natives." — Leah

"We mostly met people through our activities with our kids, especially sports activities like soccer and basketball. We also met people through our kids' schools, the park, and our kids' tutors." — Jody

Extracurricular classes can be a good way to meet natives, depending on the community. Sometimes the locals are simply too poor to afford activities beyond basic schooling, so you might find yourself in a dance or karate class filled with other gringos. Check your community center or local library for activities that attract native residents as well.

"Connect with local park/community centers and take a class of some sort. It almost doesn't matter what — anything to connect you with people. Do something like yoga or cooking, where it doesn't matter if you know the language perfectly because you see it demonstrated. Same thing for the kids; we found a great ping-pong association where they took classes — other kids we knew were taking fencing. Act on things like this quickly, as the year goes by very fast. Connect with anyone even vaguely known to you in the city or country. (If you tell everyone you meet the last few months before you go you will get some connections). Then be daring and contact people! The local exposure this way is irreplaceable."   — Frances

Staying in Touch When You Move Away

The wonderful friendships you've established abroad will undoubtedly change when you or your friends move on, but it doesn't have to mean an end to your relationships. All those shared adventures will remain an important part of your sabbatical story and it's worth keeping those ties alive when you move back home or on to wherever your adventure takes you next. Re-entering the life you left behind can be a challenging experience and nobody back home will understand your experiences abroad like your expat and native friends do. Exchanging emails, letters, and telephone calls with people going through the same thing can make the process easier.

We know families who have become business partners after spending time together abroad and others who visit each other regularly in the States and spend vacations together at home and abroad. A few of our friends have become permanent residents of San Miguel and they continue to draw us back to Mexico year after year. Our kids email quick hellos to their friends around the U.S. and Mexico. Every email, letter, and visit is a reminder that our families shared an amazing experience together. These ongoing relationships are constant reminders of what our family accomplished in the past and the potential adventures we can look forward to in the future.

15. Bridging the Great Divide: Cultural and Language Differences

"There is a very real sense in which our wealth leaves us bereft, and the apparent poverty of those around us here is a treasure. Of course, this is not to say that I would blithely give up my 'wealth' or that they aren't working ceaselessly to escape from their poverty. Simply that it would be foolish to think that our apparent gain has not also cost us something — something perhaps essential to our ability to fully enjoy our bounty, as though we had traded our eyes for something worth looking at." El Grito #3

Depending on where you go, you're likely to discover that some of the cultural assumptions and values you hold dear are not universally shared. Some of these cultural differences will be obvious and others a bit more subtle, but they can at times leave you feeling confused and frustrated. An awkward situation might simply be the result of your inability to speak the language — or something more culturally profound. But no matter how you perceive these differences in attitudes and behavior, it hammers home the fact that people around the world have many different beliefs that are as valid and strongly held as our own.

"Make sure you realize that you are going to be a guest in someone else's country and avoid thinking too often why things are so different in a negative sense. Usually

you can come to a realization that there is a positive or at least an interesting angle, or perhaps some humor to be found in why things are done so differently. This mental process is also key to how your children will perceive the differences." — Kim

Different Doesn't Mean Wrong

Sensitizing your kids to the differences between cultures is a gentle way to help them understand that there is more than one "right way" to think about things. Some of the differences will be obvious, like the language, foods, houses, ways of dressing, types of greetings, schools, traffic laws, shopping, and different mealtimes. There may also be more subtle differences such as personal space, when and how to make eye contact, gestures, taboos, and gender roles. The following is a very incomplete list of some of the cultural differences your family may discover during your family sabbatical abroad:

• *Time and punctuality.* Every culture has a different sense of time. Other cultures may be much more laissez faire about when things begin and end, or open and close. Few cultures have as rigorous and exacting a sense of scheduling as our own and being late in another culture is not necessarily a sign of disrespect or laziness. Differences in the overall pace of life may initially be a source of frustration. To enjoy your time abroad and really engage in a foreign culture, try your best to adopt the indigenous sense of time.

• *Consumerism, entitlement, wealth.* We Americans have a tendency to assess a situation based on what we can take, buy, or own from it. We often enjoy the world by consuming it. We feel that it's our right. But other cultures don't always share this same sense of entitlement. Most people don't have the kinds of opportunities or disposable income Americans do and may have a completely different relationship to money, jobs, work, and what constitutes success. Additionally, the consumer culture exported by American media to the rest of the world creates the impression that all Americans are "rich." While you may not consider yourselves especially well off relative to your American neighbors, compared to your neighbors abroad, you may be very rich indeed.

This can lead to some awkward moments that require sensitivity and tact. Neighbors or employees may ask you for money to help solve their families' problems or, conversely, may offer you things they can't afford to part with themselves. The very meaning of giving and receiving may be different from what you're used to. Beggars and vendors may ask for money or try to sell you trinkets you don't want or food you'd rather not eat. It takes time and discussion with other expats and natives to understand the context — whether or not you're being taken advantage of, or even if you can help someone without offending them.

"Children wouldn't come to our house to play because parents were afraid that then they would have to invite us to their house and they were ashamed that their houses were not nice enough to have us over." — Rachel

• *Ownership of public space and sense of civic responsibility.* Some cultures don't share the Western belief that every square inch of the world can or should be owned, tamed, or controlled. Streets, sidewalks, and alleys may be considered a "no man's land" and the rules around their use much looser. Or conversely, you may find that public spaces such as parks and playgrounds may be less user-friendly than those back home. On the other hand, other cultures may have a more highly developed sense of civic responsibility that sublimates individual rights to the greater good. Public buildings and spaces may receive extensive care while little funding is directed at providing for the general population.

"It's not a big deal, but it has been hard to deal with how some people cannot think outside of their prescribed boxes. As a result I am having a hard time finding out how to obtain a Norwegian driver's license without losing my American one." — Ali

• *Concern for the environment and animals.* Animal and environmental rights are considered an unaffordable luxury in many places. You and your family may be disturbed by serious environmental hazards and diseased and unkempt animals in the streets while the locals may simply consider them a fact of life. Differences in education, traditions, available funding, trust in civic leaders, and existing public infrastructure all influence the amount of energy directed at these issues. If such things upset you, consider finding ways to improve them. Pick up the trash in your neighborhood, work at an animal shelter or start one if nothing like it exists. These efforts will make you feel like you're actively engaged in doing something positive for the community.

• *Attitudes toward children.* In many cultures around the world, kids are loved and valued in a way they just aren't in the United States. Kids aren't simply tolerated (or worse) but are truly enjoyed. Children are often present in places they aren't allowed in the U.S., including bars and pool halls. You may quickly find that your children become ambassadors of good will, coaxing smiles and opening doors to new relationships and opportunities.

> *"Italians are unbelievably sweet and welcoming to children whether in the street where they all compliment you and squeeze your child or in restaurants — even though high chairs are a rarity!"*
> — Channing

• *The role of religion* can be profoundly different. The separation of church and state in the U.S. is the exception. In many other cultures religion plays a central role in every facet of daily life and directly influences political, educational, and social systems.

• *Acceptable noise levels.* This was one of the most difficult things for our family to get used to in Mexico. Loud music, roof dogs, roosters, eternal construction, fireworks, and late night parties were ever present, and our impulse was to lean out the window or knock on the neighbors' door and ask them to please quiet down. That simply is not done. Even if you do ask, nothing will change except that you will be disliked and rebuffed by your neighbors. If the same is true where you sabbatical, plan to get used to all the noise or get earplugs.

• *Public safety standards.* Traffic enforcement, playground safety, seat belt use, building construction regulations, and pedestrian safety may be more or less stringent than what you're used to back home. Act accordingly.

"Derek was often commenting on things that were different in San Miguel from Hinsdale, so one day I encouraged him to write down a list of what all those things were. He commented on the lack of large commercial signs, and the lack of the big picture windows in stores. He talked about how there was hardly any grass but lots of flowers. He talked about all the funny noises from the guy with the crooning voice announcing peanuts for sale, to the firecrackers in the middle of the night, to the roosters crowing, and the dogs all barking. He loved how kids played in the streets and how kids could hop on the bumpers of pickup trucks for a ride up the hill. They rarely went more than 10 to 15 miles per hour and it was tolerated by the drivers well." — Kim

"Zeb (age 4) really appreciated breaking some of the laws of home and how much less safe and more exciting life was in Guatemala. This included occasional rides in the back of the SUV, skipping the seatbelt for slow rides through the cobblestone streets of Antigua, or riding in the back of a pickup truck. He enjoyed raiding the fruit from jocote trees or nispero bushes with the other kids and finding and chewing on cano de conejo. He liked throwing stones at chickens and dogs and playing with firecrackers with the other kids when we weren't looking. Zeb also enjoyed seeing guns all over the place, civil police, army, Pepsi-truck guards, and even armed doormen at the local pizza parlor. Obviously we didn't share his enthusiasm on this one." — Sarah

When "Your Way" Isn't the Way It's Done

Many of our American acquaintances felt a sense of frustration while living abroad at what they perceived as ineptitude, corruption, laziness, or inefficiency on the part of the local population. A Mexican storeowner will enthusiastically assure you he can get a specific item, but two weeks and many visits later the item still hasn't materialized. Each time, the storeowner will shrug and reassure you that it will definitely be here *mañana*. For Americans who are used to prompt and predictable service, this can drive you nuts. But it's not that the storeowner is lying to you. It's that he doesn't want to disappoint you. He doesn't really know when the truck with your part on it will arrive but it might very well be tomorrow. *¿Quién sabe?* (Who knows?) He has no control over your item's whereabouts, but he genuinely wants to make you happy.

"A big problem was being promised by our landlord a phone line — with which to plug in our computer — and never getting it. The first month we had great difficulty doing email or communicating by phone. We were told that Mexicans hate to say no and disappoint you, but the upshot was very frustrating." — Marline

"The most pleasant surprise for me was the enjoyment I got from adopting another way of life. I find tremendous pleasure in doing things differently, like grocery shopping for example. I like going daily to the market and finding something fresh to prepare for dinner. The most unpleasant is learning to deal with the inadequacies of the system. In the U.S., if the phone service or electricity or Internet service or whatever goes out, things get fixed. Here, people just learn to say 'ni modo' (oh well). It's hard, when you have certain standards of expectation, to learn to live with substandard quality and not be frustrated all the time." — Jody

This difference in the way things get done (or not done) is exemplified by Telmex, the national Mexican telephone company, which is notorious for its lack of reliability and customer service. A lack of telephone service obviously infuriates both Mexicans and gringos alike, but a major cultural difference is illustrated by how Mexicans and gringos react to the situation. The Mexicans typically accept the inconvenience as one of those uncontrollable parts of life. *Ni modo* — what can you do except wait for phone service to be repaired? The gringos react by storming the gates, demanding repair service, and threatening lawsuits. The interesting part is that the amount of energy expended seems to have little bearing on how quickly the repair actually occurs.

"Getting connected to the Internet (my husband needed an ADSL line because of his work) was a challenge. The phone company was less than efficient, and dealing with technical matters on the phone with even pretty good Spanish skills was another challenge. After six weeks and multiple phone calls it did happen." — Frances

"We really didn't believe what we heard and read about the bureaucratic process in Italy. We thought since we both had a background in government, we could work out anything. Wrong." — Channing

A true story

American friends of ours living in San Miguel lost their phone and Internet service one day. They woke up and it just didn't work. They called the telephone company from a pay phone, went to visit the company in person, spoke with numerous officials, and so on — all to no avail. A week later, with their telephone and computer service still out, they strolled into the Telmex General Manager's office and demanded to sit down at his desk and use his phone and Internet service since theirs hadn't been repaired. The General Manager smiled, welcomed them in, listened to their story sympathetically, and then invited them to use whatever they needed as he got up and walked out of the office to do his work in another room. Their service remained out of order.

Our friends finally thought they were on their way to restored service after they found their way to a woman in top management (already an unusual occurrence) who declared her steadfast commitment to fixing their problem. "If you don't get your telephone service back by tomorrow, come to my office first thing tomorrow morning and I'll personally see that it's fixed." They woke up to find their phone service still out and returned to the woman's office the following morning to discover that she'd left for a two-week vacation. Vindictive? Hostile? Not at all. Everyone was being as nice as possible without actively involving themselves in someone else's problem. Why invite trouble?

Corruption?

There are numerous stories and complaints of corruption in other cultures but what we may perceive as "corruption" may also simply be the way things get done. Giving a cop 100 pesos to avoid a parking ticket seems to a Mexican no more unusual than tipping a waiter 15% on your bill.

"Graft and corruption have trickled down in Ecuador to the most basic aspects of everyone's life, and everyone has personally and directly experienced both. Whereas

in the U.S. they manage to keep most evidence of it out of mainstream, middle-class white culture. Because of our "improved" standard of living, we in the U.S. are able to hide our heads in the sand about the corruption in our own country in a way they can't in third world countries. So, even though it was a pain to deal with in our own lives (though it occasionally worked out very well for us because we caught on how to bribe people pretty quickly) it was a real eye-opener to the degree corruption really surrounds us all the time."

— Tani

Belief in the future

I also noticed that Mexicans truly don't have the same confidence (arrogance?) that they'll be here next year or next month or really, even tomorrow. A common expression here is *"ojalá,"* sort of a Spanish/Arabic "God willing." And they mean it. They don't pay in advance here. They don't buy in bulk. Tampons don't come 40 to a box. That would imply a belief in the future as well as the ability to pay for more than you need *"ahorita,"* right now. *Now* is what the Mexicans concern themselves with. Today. I'm alive today and I need *x*. Tomorrow, if I'm alive, I'll worry about what I need then. This is a place where you can buy bandages, pieces of tape, nails, cigarettes, and much more individually. No one thinks twice about opening a package of four light bulbs to sell you one. Why would you buy four when tomorrow the lamp might break or the electricity might be shut off?

Until we moved to Mexico, I didn't realize how much time and energy we Americans expend planning for and making assumptions about the future. We're confident that if we work hard enough or believe in something enough, it will come true. And for us, it often does. That's the American dream. That's what the insurance industry is built on. That's what mortgages are all about. And the stock market. (And our ability to take this trip.) But the same can't be said about life in Mexico because too often some invaders have swept through or a flood raged by last week or some disease ravaged the village yesterday. They don't have insurance here. Or mortgages. (Although this is rapidly changing thanks to all the Americans interested in owning property in Mexico.)

They don't assume longevity or a consistent source of income. Not that it doesn't happen. They just don't assume that it will. *Ojalá*.

Traverse Cultural Barriers: Learn the Language!

The most important thing you can do to bridge cultural barriers is to learn the local language. Bridging the language barrier makes all the difference between visiting a culture and truly experiencing it. It paves the way to really *living* in the place you've landed and counters the sense of isolation you and your family will feel at times. Learning a new language, however, takes time even for young children. Many people give up in frustration or don't even try. I urge you to give it a go and stick with it even if it feels hopeless. The rewards of learning a second language — of simply making the effort regardless of your ability — are enormous and lifelong.

We were surprised at how relatively slowly our kids picked up Spanish. We'd imagined that their brains were like sponges that would just absorb the new language from the world around them. But our seven-year-old didn't even start to get interested in learning Spanish until we'd already been in Mexico for a month. It took another month for her to really commit to learning the language without us pushing her. By that time, she was excited about going to her tutoring sessions twice a week and was the one instituting the "we're only going to speak Spanish" rule while we were out of our house or at dinner. Our two-year-old had even less interest in learning Spanish and he struggled with it for nine months or longer before he could speak it comfortably.

Again, learning a language is a slow process. It helps that we were forced to speak it every day, but you do have to get out there and be willing to make a fool of yourself. Some days it goes well, and other days it just goes. Even though I had asked for the same quantity of tortillas at the same little *puesta* for months, there were days I still messed it up. I'd end up asking for who knows what ("I'd like a half-kilo of mud, please.") and my request would be met with a quizzical expression.

Practice makes better

If you expect yourselves or your kids to just "pick up" another language, you're going to end up frustrated and disappointed at how little you all come away with. It doesn't happen that way. The best way to learn another language is to find some sort of structured language program at whatever level and learning method suits you and your kids best. These include private tutors, conversation classes, academic courses at universities or language schools, and private study aids like books, cassettes, and interactive computer software. Spanish camps, soccer, art or theater classes, dance lessons, and other activities conducted in another language can be wonderful language learning opportunities. Depending on your interest, budget, and desire for fluency, you may want to opt for some intensive classes early on or take a basic class to get you started and then jump into something more intensive after you've gotten your feet wet.

Think about each of your individual learning styles and what might be the most effective setting for your language learning. Do you do best in small groups? One-on-one? Are you a more visual or aural learner? Do you like studying books or do you want it up on the blackboard? Do you like using flash cards? Do you need someone else to set concrete goals or are you motivated enough to do that for yourself?

Language schools can offer excellent classes and have a stake in your success. You can also meet other expats there and expand your social network. The classes can be pricey, however, so comparison shop both online and on foot. Ask to sit in on a class before signing up to make sure the teacher, materials, and language level feel like a good fit.

Private tutors can be wonderful. Again, shop around and get recommendations from others who have taken classes with specific tutors to narrow your options. Make sure your tutor is really a teacher and that your sessions incorporate some rigor and structure and aren't simply conversation periods that may not advance your language skills very quickly. A native speaker may not always be a good teacher. Be prepared to try different teachers and tutors to find one that complements you or your child's learning style. (For more specific information about finding language tutors and language schools, see *Chapter 8: School Daze Part Two*.)

There are also informal ways to learn and practice another language. Listen to the radio. Get the local newspaper and commit to reading a couple of articles from start to finish each day. Read books out loud in your new language to work on your accent and pronunciation. Tape the words for household objects on furniture, clothing, utensils, and food items. Spend dinners and breakfasts trying to converse in the new language you're trying to learn. (Plan on *very* short conversations in the beginning.) Watch movies in either the native language or sub-titled in your new language. Look through children's books for good basic vocabulary written rhythmically or in rhyme, which can help you memorize phrases and words. Make dates with your expat friends to speak only the native language at parties or for a period of time during a dinner date. Invite native friends to expat gatherings. Everyone is more likely to speak the native language to make your local friends more comfortable. Learning a new language comes down to practice. Always carry a pocket dictionary and cross-check often. Don't be afraid to look dumb or make mistakes. The most important thing to do is laugh and have fun.

Learning the language or at least embarking on the process won't erase cultural differences. But it can help you more fully understand the differences and perhaps even allow you to appreciate them on a deeper level. Whether these cultural differences remain a source of amusement, enjoyment, or frustration, they'll undoubtedly be excellent fodder for discussion between you and your kids.

> "My biggest suggestion is to find out more about the specific culture of where you are going. The Chinese culture profoundly affected our experience, and we were somewhat unprepared because we had compared and planned based on suggestions from people who had lived in Central and South America and France, which have cultures that are very different from China's."
>
> — Rachel

Surrender to the Differences

Once you accept the fact that things are done differently, you'll really be able to start enjoying yourself in your new home. Talk about the differences with your kids. This is an excellent way to help your children develop an interest in world affairs and to cultivate a global perspective on solving problems at home and abroad. It will open their minds to other cultures and with any luck promote a lifelong interest in travel and maintaining friendships abroad. It can also help cultivate a more tolerant attitude toward others and a greater sense of patience and flexibility in every aspect of your life. There's something wonderful about the Mexican perspective on life where nobody's absolutely sure that *mañana* will really appear or that you'll be in one piece to greet it. If tomorrow does happen by and you're still here, then whatever needs to be done, fix that lamp or buy an extension cord, can be done. *¿Cómo no?* Today is here and you must take advantage of it. All you can be certain of is this moment. Everything else? *Ojalá.*

16. Marooned in Paradise: Singing the Homesick Blues

"After the last of an initial flurry of visitors left and our email slowed to a trickle, we found ourselves a bit like a small research expedition watching our supply ship recede slowly over the horizon, marooned with a few beat-up crates of hardtack and toilet paper, our backs to the jungle of our fantasies and before us all the work of transforming a big lazy dream into some sort of reality. Granted, somewhere in those crates were some little paper umbrellas for our drinks . . . " El Grito #4

It creeps up without warning at around the three-month mark. Everyone appears to be adjusting fine and getting acclimated to the food, altitude, language, new friends, and new schedule. Then suddenly, Wham! You find yourself constantly thinking about home and feeling an overwhelming desire to go back.

Homesickness can be an intense and haunting sadness or just random thoughts that flit in and out of your consciousness throughout the day. Our now three-year-old suddenly started talking about his room back home and some of the snacks he was missing (goldfish crackers and rice cakes) that we couldn't get in Mexico. We'd be riding the bus to school, staring out the window at passing burros, 500-year-old churches, and busy tamale stands, when he'd turn and say thoughtfully, "I love the JCC [his daycare], Mama. Remember the JCC in Minnesota?"

I found myself checking email constantly and writing lengthy missives to friends begging for information about my garden and their lives. It wasn't that I wanted to leave Mexico; it's just that I suddenly realized that we weren't in Minnesota and I felt the distance profoundly. The novelty of arriving in a new place had worn off and I was able to truly feel, for the first time, how long we were planning to be away.

> *"For me, when I got homesick I would go to the one coffee shop and have an expensive coffee and a pastry. For the kids, sometimes it was just talking about what we missed, sometimes we would make a phone call, sometimes send an email, and sometimes go to McDonalds."* — Rachel

I Miss — Everything!

Homesickness is about missing friends and family and the ease of the familiar. It's not necessarily about wanting to move back home, but more about wanting to think about the things you've left behind. It often comes on when you've finally shaken off all the old baggage and you feel a void that will eventually, but not yet, fill with new friends and new connections to the place you've plopped down in. That's about the time you've begun to feel forgotten by your friends and associates back home. The easy connection you had with everyone has started to evaporate as they attend to busy lives that you're simply not a part of.

> *"My oldest spoke of going home daily and complained often. I let her complain in the afternoon for 15 minutes. She emailed friends back home and that helped."* — Karen

When we returned to Minnesota, people kept saying, "You're back already? It didn't seem like you were gone that long." For them, the days of our adventure slipped by unnoticed as they pounded the same old paths oblivious to the passage of time. But living abroad and freed from the mundane tasks that gobble up time, the days often felt 72 hours long. At the beginning, we spent so much time exploring and figuring out all the new rules of our new home that we fell into bed wondering when we'd ever stop feeling tired and excited by all this newness. Right around the three-month mark. At that point, your life starts to feel somewhat familiar again. You've carved out some new routines but there's plenty of time and space to start longing for some of the things you've left behind.

"Once you go you'll miss your home but it'll pass and then when you leave you'll miss your new home." — John, age 9

"Our kids missed their friends the most. They didn't miss the U.S. or our house or the school, but just their friends. We addressed this by having them use AOL chat, email, and occasionally letting them make long distance phone calls. The calls seemed to lift their spirits the most. They were most homesick after about three months but then we talked about how our stay was almost half over." — Kim

Coping with Homesickness

So, what can you do about homesickness? What if your kids are really bummed out about being away from their friends and their school? What if you become obsessed with back home and being away from everything that's familiar? Truthfully, nothing but time will make homesickness go away completely. Eventually, your life will fill up with friends and activities in your new home and you'll make peace with the minutes and hours that click by. But in the meantime, there are a number of concrete things you and your family can do to keep homesickness manageable:

• *Keep in touch with the folks back home* through email and digital pictures. This really helps a lot. It's so instantaneous you feel like you're not that far away.

• *Play a familiar game* — cards or a board game.

• *Watch American movies every once in a while* and search out a pizza or make spaghetti. Familiar things from back home will cheer everyone up. At least for a while.

• *Download some favorite songs from the Internet* and dance around the living room together.

• *Talk about being homesick* with your kids and your spouse rather than bottling it up and hoping it will go away. This helps enormously and goes a long way to creating that "we're in this together" feeling.

• ***Pick up the phone and call someone*** (or even better, use the computer or a callback service to chat with a friend or family member from back home). Careful with this one, though. It can be expensive and can also backfire and just create more of a longing to be back home.

> *"I still miss the U.S. I also think Gretha misses her friends, but she does not talk about it much. Marcel still talks about his friends from his Montessori preschool and how he is going to marry Madeline, his sweetheart from the Montessori. We do get to travel once in a while and we keep in touch via the Internet. We also have visitors."* — Ali

> *"We had long discussions about the gains of being there and playing the comparison game. We did that a lot. 'What I like about Mexico is . . . Mexico is better than home because . . .' or 'Home is better because . . .' and let them reminisce and get out their frustration."* — Leah

Try playing the "What do you miss the most?" game. "Which foods are you missing the most?" "Which toys are you missing? Friends? Teachers?" Write a letter. Send an email. These are opportunities for your kids to feel how lucky they are to have so many wonderful things waiting for them at the end of their trip. You can also flip it around and play the same game but ask, "What's the best thing about being in a new place?" "What's your new favorite food?" "What can you do here that you can't do back home?" Homesickness can actually highlight some of the big positives about being away on your adventure.

> *"My kids definitely miss their friends and I work hard to maintain contact with them. One teacher was willing to do ongoing emails from her class throughout the year. We do a postcard swap with a friend, sending postcards every couple of weeks back and forth. On our trips back to the States we make sure everyone gets to visit their friends. This year, our second year here, a lot of that has tapered off. We now have good friends here and don't miss everyone so much."* — Jody

"One son would get teary in the evenings when tired, missing his friends. He felt out of place frequently in the culture at first and missed things American. We just talked through it and tried to keep focused on the positive things. Incidentally, now he's the most vocal about missing his Spanish friends and wants badly to go back."

— Frances

Holidays in the Key of Blue

Homesickness can feel especially profound during holidays and birthdays. Celebrating without friends and family can make things seem a bit sad and empty. To combat homesickness during these times, bring along familiar objects and adapt your family's familiar rituals to the new traditions of your temporary home. Use a cactus for a Christmas tree (but be careful stringing those ornaments!). Learn how to make turkey tamales for Thanksgiving. Asher's third birthday was a raucous four-hour piñata/water balloon fiesta with a homemade American chocolate cake and a traditional Mexican *tres leches* birthday cake as well. Cleome's eighth birthday included her favorite lasagne dinner and a second piñata/pizza birthday party a month later when her cousins came for a visit from the States. Use extended school holidays as an excuse to go on a special family adventure. Arrange parties with your expat friends and encourage visitors from back home to spend their holidays abroad with your family. Indulge the kids with a few more presents than normal during these times and bug the grandparents, aunts, and uncles to send gifts from the States so the kids will know they haven't been forgotten by people back home.

"Zeb suffered from homesickness much more than we would have imagined. For the first six months, even though he was having plenty of fun and was very interested in the experience, he would repeatedly ask to go back to Montpelier. He would talk about the friends, places, and (mostly) the toys (his own and his friends') that he missed. When he talked about missing a particular friend, or his former daycare, we got postcards and he dictated a message to send. When it was a particular toy, we took the next opportunity to buy something in its place, subject to the usual terms and conditions.

We would also gently point out that he had far more toys at his disposal than most of his playmates. We tried to maintain as many of the home rituals as possible — warm milk with maple [syrup] every morning (brought with us and by any visitors), regular trips to the library that we were lucky enough to have on site, the National Geographic (forwarded to us) every month, and so on." — Sarah

"The only one who really felt true homesickness was our older son (age 11). He really missed home and his friends. There wasn't a whole lot to do about it but lend an understanding ear. He was also able to email his friends a lot. It's hard to tell if that helped or only made it worse." — Rob

Ultimately there's no cure for homesickness and everybody's bound to suffer from it at one time or another. All you can do is accept it as part of the adventure and help your kids understand that it's OK to feel sad and to miss things from back home. Encourage the people you love to keep in touch and remind them well in advance of special moments in your family's life abroad so they can acknowledge them with a call, card, or gift. Homesickness isn't fun, but it can be an opportunity to count your blessings and remind each other how lucky you are to be able to go on such a wonderful adventure and still have so many equally wonderful things waiting for you back home.

17. Welcoming Visitors: How Long Is Your Mother Staying?

"We've had a consistent influx of visitors, and it's been great to have friends and family here to experience Mexico and this gorgeous city with us. It looks like our next sojourner will be Michael's mother in June for a couple weeks. After that, we're not sure. We're hoping to see Elisa's brother Dan and family in August, as they weren't able to make it over spring break, and then Grammy Arlene joins us at the end of the month once school starts again. In the past few months we've had great visits from Michael's friend Sean and his daughter, from Elisa's dad who visited at the end of October, and from Michael's dad and stepmother who left earlier this week. We'll still have room for visitors in the new place — in fact, more. So you might want to think about getting on our calendar."
                                                                    El Grito #3

As you prepare for your journey, the most natural thing in the world is to invite people to come visit you in whatever exotic location you've chosen. Most people will excitedly agree to the idea and a few will actually take you up on it. Be careful. I know it seems like a good idea to invite everyone you know to join you in paradise and it can be a wonderful thing to see friends and family from home. But having visitors during your sabbatical is also a potential minefield.

Our friend Nancy's mother-in-law arrived for a two-week visit while they were spending a year in Madrid. Somehow the visit stretched into two months and although the mother-in-law was a nice enough woman, Nancy got increasingly frustrated by someone taking over the living room of their already tiny apartment for so long. The situation came to a head during a party at a neighbor's when the mother-in-law asked if they could leave because she was tired and wanted to go home. Nancy, who had sampled a bit too much fine Spanish wine that evening, told her husband Chuck to go ahead and take his mother and the kids home. "Your mother can sleep on my side of the bed," Nancy said, glaring at her husband. "Because I'm staying on the damn couch until she goes back to Cleveland!" Chuck got the message and called a travel agent the next day. This may be an extreme example, but thinking through your "welcome" strategy in advance can definitely help make everyone's time together less explosive.

Decide on the Rules of Engagement

Before that first friend arrives on your doorstep, take the time to seriously consider how you want to handle visitors from back home. The following is a partial list of things to consider:

• Will friends and family stay with you or in a nearby hotel?

• If they will stay in your home, are there adequate beds, bathrooms, towels, bedding, and such? Or do you need to set up some temporary accommodations?

• If they will stay in a hotel, who will make all the arrangements for their stay?

• Will they need a car? Who will make those arrangements?

• Will you spend the entire visit together or only meet for specific meals and adventures?

• Will you buy all the food and liquor or will they chip in?

• Will you play tour guide or provide them with maps and suggestions and wish them well?

• What type of visitors are they? What are their expectations of you?

• Will you interrupt your routine completely or ask them to respect certain schedules you've developed?

• What impact will visitors have on your children and their schedules? Will you need to hire babysitters? Will you need to put additional safety measures in place or make such measures explicit to your visitors? (Think medicine kits and poisoning if you have young children.)

"I would think carefully about who you invite to come, which may depend in part on the reasons for your trip. In our case, we were careful not to ask too many people because we only had five months and wanted quiet family time. Still, we probably had guests at least a week out of every month, which was too much in retrospect, though I would have a hard time saying that we didn't enjoy every single visitor." — Julie

Timing is everything

Typically, visitors will want to schedule their visits around specific vacation periods at home, especially if they have children. Christmas, Easter, and summer break are the most popular and you'll have clusters of visitors, some even overlapping, during these times. During one Easter break, we had four different groups of visitors with three of them overlapping by a few days coming and going. It was fun, exhausting, exciting, and pure hell all rolled into one. The kids never got enough sleep and were dragged from event to event and meal to meal. They adored having other (English-speaking) children and adults to play with and played with such intensity that by the end of the visit they were reduced to teary, screaming lumps of flesh equally likely to melt over a dropped piece of candy or a playmate "breathing on me."

We made the mistake of saying yes to everyone who wanted to come when sometimes we should have gently said no or at least suggested an alternate time for the visit. We probably should have put more people in a hotel rather than sticking them on mattresses on the floor as was often the case (or sleeping on those mattresses ourselves and giving our beds over to our guests). One book I read suggested you urge your guests to come visit during the first part of your stay abroad, before you've gotten all your routines down. This makes a great deal of sense, if your guests will cooperate. If they won't and make plans to show up throughout your stay (as ours did), making some of these decisions beforehand and sticking to your guns can make everyone's experience more pleasant.

We eventually smartened up and realized that we had to stick to our routines somewhat, regardless of visitors, or else the kids got ornery and so did we. We also started to help people "pitch in" on costs by asking each visitor to bring us a care package of specific items that we emailed ahead. That way, we could buy all the basic supplies for visitors and provide most of the meals (except restaurant meals where visitors inevitably pick up the tab) without breaking the bank or feeling taken advantage of.

> *"We encouraged visitors to make their plans early, because inevitably they wanted to all come at spring break so we had to space them out. We rented a house for family that stayed for two weeks and friends offered their house to our friends who stayed one week at spring break. Other times, people stayed at hotels or B&Bs."* — Kim

Eventually, after a few sets of visitors had come and gone, we had the routine down pat. We'd hand them a map of the city and a key to the house. We'd make a few suggestions about what to see and which adventures to take and then we'd wave goodbye as we pushed our friends and family out the door (sometimes with our children in tow). This way, not only did we manage to find a bit of privacy amidst all the extra bodies, voices, trash, laundry, and so on that visitors bring, but also our visitors got the chance to experience the place more as we did when we first arrived. They'd arrive home breathless and excited by the morning's discoveries. If we'd gone with and just led them to all the waiting wonders, the sense of adventure would have been much diminished.

¿Mi casa es su casa?

It's actually not a bad idea to choose a house with visitors in mind if you know they'll be coming and intend to stay with you. If your house isn't set up to lodge visitors comfortably, be sure to make potential guests aware of that ahead of time and help them find suitable lodging nearby. We had four bathrooms in our first house and although we had only two bedrooms, each had its own bath. So, we gave one bedroom to our guests and had the kids join us in ours (king-sized bed) and the visitors who shared our house were usually so grateful for the free digs and hospitality that they went out of their way to be helpful and unobtrusive. But still, it's tiring to have extra people in your space all day and night long. The routines you've fought so hard for are inevitably messed up and once the guests are gone, you have to work out bedtimes, naptimes, and study times all over again.

> *"Try not to have visitors come in the beginning of your time abroad. My mother came about two months after we had been in China and while it was great to see her, I still didn't have good language legs yet and I felt frustrated that I could not show her around as much as I would have liked."* — Rachel

Look Who's Not Coming to Dinner

It can be surprising who actually does make the trek to see you and who, ultimately, doesn't. In our case we were surprised at who didn't. Almost none of our friends made it down despite having made noises about doing so early on. Why? Their lives were too busy, it was too expensive, it seemed too far away. We felt a combination of sadness and relief when, by the end of our trip, the guests had dwindled to nothing. For the last six months of our trip we didn't have a single visitor other than people we'd met on their own sabbaticals earlier in our trip who were returning for a brief vacation. People who are travelers, travel. And people who aren't often don't — ever. No matter how wonderful they think you are or how exotic and exciting the place that you're offering promises to be, they'll find a reason (often a good one) not to come.

It's not altogether surprising, given that we'd kidnapped their grandchildren, niece, nephew, or cousins, that our visitors were mostly family. And it's also not surprising that those who do make the trip will have a better sense of your adventure and that upon your return you will value their relationships that much more. You'll have to explain it (or not) to everyone else. The folks who lived it with you will be a part of your sabbatical story for a lifetime.

18. Epiphanies, Such as They Are: Expectations vs. Reality

"The easy thrills of nonstop novelty and picture-postcard adventure are pretty much a thing of the past. The visceral compass, calendar, and clock that never really believed we wouldn't be returning to Minnesota any time soon have all quietly made the necessary adjustments. When we wake up in the morning we are now here, and here now: for the time being this place is home. Some things have changed, but not much really. We're pretty much the same people, living out the same quotient of pleasure and pain, encountering the same set of obstacles and opportunities by which we've come to recognize ourselves for some time now. We're just doing some different things, and some things differently, and eating a lot more beans and rice."   El Grito #3

When we left home in January 2002, Michael and I envisioned a sabbatical filled with big decisions, important conversations, and epiphanies that would shake us to the core and alter our family's course for the next decade or so. But interestingly, while we had a wonderful and intermittently exciting adventure — spending 18 months in Mexico writing, making music, learning a second language, hanging with our kids, and meeting people from all over the world — we never actually experienced anything you could describe as life-altering.

"I believe we and our children will be so much more open to other cultures and other people for having had this experience. I know that what we have done will have an empowering effect as well. I believe my children will feel that because they have moved

*to another country, mastered the language, and learned from its culture, there won't
be anything in this world they can't do."* — Jody

Same Old Same Old?

It's not that we didn't go through changes. Moving to a new country
and into a new home, learning another language, and experiencing different schools, foods, and friends caused dramatic changes in our daily
lives. But the more significant long-term transformations were much
subtler than we'd expected.

Our sabbatical was really about sowing seeds that will come to frui-
tion sometime in the future. How can we possibly know or even anticipate the long-term impact of Michael being such a significant force in
our children's early lives? It will probably strengthen his bond with the
kids, but who knows? It may contribute to some kind of family murder/
suicide thing when Asher turns 16. The kids seem to have an affinity
for learning languages and we hope this has enhanced their sense of
how wide and interesting the world is. But how can we know? While in
my heart I believe this sabbatical experience has significantly increased
the chances that our children will be more interesting and active global
citizens, there's no guarantee. You just have to hold your breath, leap
in, and hope for the best.

> *"For the kids, it's made them more comfortable and confident with going into new situ-
> ations. They have a concrete sense of how big and diverse the world is. They appreciate
> what we have in the U.S. — a yard, parks that are clean and have grass, more foods
> they like, family close by. They have a lot of perspective on lifestyle options — that
> there are many choices available to us, that it is possible to create opportunities for
> yourself, that travel is great."* — Rachel

Minor Epiphanies

Perhaps something very dramatic will occur during your sabbatical,
as it did for some of our friends who chucked careers and remained in

Mexico or moved on to other adventures rather than returning home. For us, however, the permanent epiphanies were of the minor sort. We didn't experience any life-changing events rating a 10 on the Richter scale, but we have continued to feel the aftershocks of our sabbatical in a number of surprising ways. The following aspects of our lives abroad have left an indelible mark on our family:

• *Living a pedestrian lifestyle.* The biggest single change in our lives abroad on a daily basis was that we spent no time sitting in a car waiting to leave or arrive or for the light to change or for the traffic to clear. We didn't wait. We walked — to school, for ice cream, as entertainment. Walking was our way of life and we noticed serious differences in our stamina and leg strength. You see the world differently when you walk. You meet people's eyes. You touch the ground with your feet and feel the sun on your shoulders. It makes you sensitive to your surroundings and ultimately to yourself in a way that's easily lost when you schlepp around in the car all day long. Back home we remain a one-car family and continually search for ways to live a more pedestrian lifestyle.

"We loved the custom of taking leisurely walks in the early evening and seeing the world wandering by." — Frances

• *Dietary changes.* Having access to good, cheap, fresh food makes a world of difference in what you buy, cook, and eat. We are now more willing to spend money on fresh organic food and we have invested in a high-quality water filter. Our heightened awareness of pesticide and fertilizer use in Central and Latin America has also convinced us to continue soaking all our produce back home in a specially formulated cleanser or iodine solution.

• *Slowing down — finally!* One hard-won change was becoming more comfortable with a slower pace and not seeking out constant distractions to fill the empty time and space. I think this paring down of our activities and the concentration of our energies on the creative rather than the mundane continues to inform much of what we do back home.

"It's not often that both Rich and I have that much time where we aren't constrained by the issues of a job. We had the time to pursue several interests we each have, as well as having lots of time for travelling around the country. And also, so many people helped us both here at home and abroad. It was good to feel so well-supported." — Tani

• *Reading books.* We read more books in 18 months than we had in probably the same number of years. We read books for hours instead of minutes. Sometimes we read books for days at a time. One of the most important reasons we decided to stay in San Miguel is because it has the largest bilingual library in Mexico, which allowed every member of our family to develop an amazing relationship to books and reading. This was a huge, unexpected, and incredibly wonderful development for all of us. Even our three-year-old started spending long periods of time paging through books, or being read to or pretending to read to himself. Our eight-year-old embarked on a lifelong love affair with books. By the end of 18 months abroad she had read perhaps 200 books including every children's classic, every series we could find or order. She had also upped her reading level by at least two grades. For Michael and me, it was heaven. We read books that were often 500 pages long. I can't remember another time in my adult life feeling confident that I'd be able to sustain the patience, time, and interest in reading books of that heft.

"I learned how to be more comfortable with spending time both alone and with people I didn't know well and relating to people in a different cultural environment. I also got re-focused on what I wanted to be spending my time doing when we returned." — Rachel

• *Simplifying our lives.* Thanks to being renters without a car and having cheap household labor available, we spent almost no time doing chores or maintaining our stuff while we were away. It became obvious to us how much of our time back home had gone into maintaining our material possessions. In Mexico we shopped for food, liquor, and other supplies once a week. We wore the same few clothes we arrived with and, as you can imagine, we were an amazingly threadbare, ragtag bunch at times. We studied. We read. We sipped wine and watched the sunset from our rooftop. And we watched our little pot of savings dwindle each month. We did, at times, wish we had more money to travel and take advantage of the concerts and restaurants San Miguel offers in abundance. But even more often we thought about how lovely it was to boil life down to a tiny box of money, thoughts, activities, and belongings. I suppose that's actually the most Mexican of anything we did. We slowly reduced our sense of entitlement and acquisition. Back in Minnesota we continue to reduce the amount of "stuff" we own. We buy and use recycled materials and we limit the amount of time and money we devote to buying and maintaining things.

> *"We moved for the experience of living in a foreign culture. It ran completely against our grains to almost exclusively raise our children in Minneapolis, Minnesota. Ecuador was incredibly beautiful and it was exciting to learn a new language. It was also amazing to do things we would not have had the opportunity to do in Minnesota, like climbing an active volcano, hiking deep in the tropical rainforest, and drinking 'chiche' with the natives, or, for my oldest daughter, getting to participate quite actively in a demonstration/riot which involved getting tear gas thrown at her."* — Tani

- **Establishing long-lasting new friendships.** These relationships are some of the best and most enduring souvenirs of a sabbatical adventure. We never anticipated meeting so many interesting and like-minded people. And we have been amazed at how close we remain, even as the months and years have flown by since our time abroad together. Truly, this is one of the most precious and unexpected treasures of our time in Mexico. See *Chapter 14: Making Friends Abroad* for more on the subject.
- **Gaining clarity of vision.** Living somewhere else helps you see more clearly the place you are not. We became aware of many of the things we'd taken for granted back home. Things like clean playgrounds with good equipment, bathrooms and drinking fountains, quality plumbing, clean water, and clean sidewalks. These things seem inconsequential until you don't have them anymore. Our sabbatical helped us develop a ten-year plan for our family that emphasizes community

service, giving more of our income to charitable organizations, keeping our kids less "programmed," and enhancing the creative aspects of our daily work. We also have a greater commitment to keeping Spanish a part of our lives through classes, speaking Spanish at home, immersion camps, bilingual schools for the kids, and getting involved with the Latino community.

> *"One of the things that has been both challenging and surprisingly wonderful for me is the language. Norwegian is not my first language and I do not think it will be my strongest anytime soon, but I have come to like it."* — Ali

• **Discovering how cool our kids are.** This was enormous. We developed a genuine love and respect for our children as individuals and discovered new strengths and different aspects of their personalities at the same time they did. We figure part of our job now is to remind them (and ourselves) of these strengths during the tough years of adolescence ahead.

> *"I suspect that my children will see the world differently. That they will be more open-minded and not get so caught up in trying to be like everybody else. I hope that they will be better people for having seen that individual differences and group differences do not have to mean dislike and that they will be able to see the world more as it really is — how small it is and how big it is — and take on their own adventures with courage and curiosity."* — Leah

• **Developing a strong sibling relationship.** There were far fewer distractions in our lives abroad and the kids became adept at finding things to do alone and with each other. When they became bored, they found ways to amuse themselves together through books, drawing, baths, and long hours of fantasy play. At times the kids felt deprived of specific things, but they also seemed to have a greater overall sense of contentment with what they had, which was mostly each other. Living away and living lean cut the extras to almost nothing except the very experience of our daily comings and goings. Their relationship blossomed through the challenges they faced together and they continue to share an unusually close and active bond for siblings with a five-year age difference between them.

• *Discovering ourselves as creative beings.* Being able to write and do other creative projects for several uninterrupted hours a day was definitely an epiphany in terms of getting something done! Our kids are better able to see us as creative people now and, thanks to enforced boredom at times, they continue to have the opportunity to discover the creativity inside of themselves as well (despite much whining and gnashing of teeth). Ultimately, our sabbatical experience reinforced the importance of making creativity the center of our lives.

> *"As for our family, I think that we will travel again in the future. It has been a great bonding experience and we have discovered how much we like hanging around together (although, of course, there were plenty of "those moments" with the kids). I think that Marc and I will more actively pursue our dreams. More seems possible now. We are not so stuck in the jobs, savings, security, insurance, retirement cobweb (or do I mean safety net?) as we were."* — Julie

• *Discovering ourselves as a family.* During our sabbatical our family began to feel like an actual thing, a solid object like a table or a house. It wasn't something we could touch or necessarily name, but it existed like a cozy bubble we floated inside of on sunny mornings and an anchor that moored us during bad weather and stiff winds. This sense of our family as an entity, something existing outside of ourselves as individuals, something we constructed together and feel an allegiance to, is perhaps the most subtle and permanent part of our sabbatical experience. We've laughed long and hard with each other. And yelled. And cried.

Each of us carries something different from our sabbatical and we can only guess at what it will mean for our family in the future. But small changes have been effected and it has changed our family signature. Cleome, who was an undemonstrative and physically shy child, now demands a different and wonderfully physical loving sign-off from us each night. She requires kisses and affectionate words to be exchanged in a specific order and with heartfelt energy before she's willing to relinquish her hold on the day. Asher, always demonstrative, continues to be the family memory jar — our own little oral historian who constantly pipes up with some obscure but wonderfully touching family moment from long ago. And Michael and I are just proud as hell that we did it. We planned it, lived it, and know that we'll do it again. Our family. It's so cool. (We are, without a doubt, the coolest family on the block.)

19. THE GOOD, THE BAD AND THE UGLY: DIFFICULTIES

"This sabbatical was no longer the vast blue-sky dream of pure possibility we'd lived with for several years of preparation. It had coalesced now into a definite, circumscribed, thoroughly time-bound mortal reality along with all the limitations that implies. We had to begin watching our money. We'd picked up just enough of the language for it to begin to get difficult and frustrating and to feel acutely what novices we were. We'd been without our friends and family for long enough to start missing them. We were spending a lot more time with our children than we'd anticipated and consequently a lot less time out having adult adventures than we'd naively expected. But we got beyond all that. 'Más o menos.' When push came to shove it never took much of a shove to remind each other (with a Carol Merrill wave of a hand) where we'd landed (door #1 — ooh!), how we'd gotten here (door #2 — ahh!) and just how fortunate we really were (door #3 — squeal and cover your mouth and jump up and down and kiss the host). Correction: we are." El Grito #4

I won't pretend that moving to a foreign country with your children will always be a wonderful and energizing experience. It will be both demanding and rewarding, and some days it will feel only demanding and not at all rewarding. But that's no different from at home, right? There are always those "moments" because life everywhere has its up and downs. Here then is a summary of some of the downs you may encounter while living abroad along with a few words of advice about how to deal with them:

1. You will feel bored at times.

Having more time on your hands is probably one of the main reasons you're going on a sabbatical in the first place, but it's not necessarily easy to suddenly have time at your disposal and nothing to fill it with. When you move abroad and plop down in a place where not that much is actually required of you, you may feel a bit out of sorts. And nervous. And bored. It may take several months for you to become truly comfortable with the slower pace of your lives abroad. Gradually you will become more comfortable with daydreaming and, yes, even getting bored. You just have to give this one time.

2. Attending to your children's needs will take a lot of your time.

I guarantee that your kids will require more attention abroad than you initially anticipate. Especially for the first few months as they settle into school and slowly start to make friends in their new home. If you can plan to give them a significant amount of your time early on, you will feel less resentful and they will feel less needy.

"We had no idea how much of a full-time job it would be to help two kids integrate into a foreign culture. We had this idea that we'd (parents) have lots of time to write and relax. Well, we had much less time than we thought. Homework became a two-hour family affair with us all working on translating, etc. (But that was kind of nice too.) And then there were social outings and get-togethers with the kids that we had to help arrange. It was useful to have at least one of us in the background to help when the kids got stuck with language with their friends." — Marline

"Having children makes the transition much more difficult because you don't just have your own feelings, anxieties, and fears to overcome, you have theirs as well." — Leah

"I felt a greater sense of responsibility to set the right tone as our kids experienced difficulties at school or just adjusting in general." — Kim

"You have to make a lot of time for your kids, pay a lot of attention to them to allow them the safe space they need to deal with all the changes." — Tani

Tip: Although it may be hard at first to find time to hang out in cafés and wander aimlessly around the city, make sure you build kid-free time into your schedules so you don't end up resenting the amount of your time and attention your children require.

"We came second in terms of what we wanted to do. Our classes needed to fit within our children's school schedule or we had to take turns. One month we both took classes at the same time and that was very difficult. Two days into our month-long classes, our kids were asking us to stop going to class." — Rob

"Our children found it very hard not to have English-speaking friends because they knew so little Spanish. Of course, this improved as their language got better, but the first month in particular was rough. My children would probably also say that they missed TV, but for me this was a good change." — Julie

3. You're likely to experience marital stress.

In my opinion, if your marriage isn't strong, taking a family sabbatical abroad is a recipe for disaster. While you're likely to encounter less stress in terms of deadlines, commuting, and other daily concerns, there may be more stress on your relationship as a result of spending so much more time together as a couple and as a family. There were moments when Michael and I felt closer than ever and others when we wondered how in the hell we ended up in a foreign country with such a jerk. Be prepared to give each other a lot of latitude during the inevitable bumpy moments and have the hugs and kisses ready when everyone's claws have retracted. You'll find you have many more opportunities for intense intimacy as well as opportunities for intense hostility.

"At times when Orin and I felt stressed about our relationship I had little support and felt very alone and isolated. We could have worked harder to go out more often on

our own without the kids, maybe to even have done a short weekend trip without the kids. We had spent time in therapy preparing before we went, but we still hit snags and sometimes it was just hard." — Rachel

Tip: Budget for a trustworthy babysitter and find one early on to make sure you get out without the kids. This is a priority. (See *Chapter 12: I Love My Kids But They're Driving Me Crazy!* for more on finding a babysitter.)

4. Learning the language will take longer than you think.

Don't fool yourself into thinking that learning a new language will be a breeze for you or your children. It takes time and practice and isn't something that's likely to happen through osmosis. Decide whether you will make the effort to learn another language and what concrete steps you will take to achieve it. The rewards are incredible but it's definitely going to take some work to get there. Classes and tutors can help you along.

"The only disadvantage of going abroad with kids is that the parents can expect their language acquisition to go much more slowly. Your kids will be in school all day immersed in Spanish. When they get home they want to speak English and so you do. So just accept it — you won't be learning as fast as you might have when you were younger, footloose, and on your own traveling or living abroad." — Marline

"Our son is a nonstop talker in English, but he took longer to learn Spanish than we had hoped. We had tried to teach him some before leaving but, out of context, he was very resistant to learning. This led to frustration when we arrived and he found himself unable to communicate his desires and resolve conflicts with other children. Unfortunately, that frustration led to aggressive behavior on his part. In retrospect, given the problems we encountered before Zeb could communicate effectively with others, we should have made a greater financial and time commitment to having him learn Spanish before leaving." — Sarah

5. It takes a while to feel at home.

Try to remain patient and expect a bit of discomfort when you first move abroad. Be confident that you will eventually get to know your neighbors and your new community and that wonderful friends and activities will eventually fill the hours of your days. But be aware that it's not something that's going to happen overnight.

> *"I wish I would have brought my husband, and stayed for a year. In six months you are finally just getting adjusted. Your children have finally accepted the place and are making gains and then you leave."* — Leah

> *"I would have stayed the entire school year and would have arrived several weeks prior to school beginning to check them all out and make a better decision. The 'school bus' was challenging and not safe, the elementary school had safety issues. The high school was tough and tedious for my daughter. I would also have checked out houses after arriving so I could see them first."* — Karen

> *"Because of the language barrier, we didn't know how to use the phone or ask how to use it. We didn't know how to find information or where we even lived. No one seemed to give us a straight answer. Our biggest challenge right off the bat was discovering that our oldest daughter's school was across town, not next door to our apartment as we were originally told. It only got worse when we were told she was not welcome — they'd established a new policy of not allowing foreigners who weren't staying the full academic year. We had to beg our way in and luckily it worked."* — Marline

6. You and your children will feel isolated and lonely at times.

Homesickness, loneliness, sadness, and tears will all be a part of your adventure just as laughter and fun will be. Being able to anticipate and weather difficult moments together will do more than simply help you cope. They'll become opportunities to grow stronger and more resilient as individuals as well as a family.

"Being away from their friends was hard on the kids and they were sad if they felt they missed something fun back home. Drew had given little thought to missing his eighth grade graduation but when he found out how much fun it was, he did feel left out. It was also frustrating to the kids that they couldn't speak Spanish better at times. Drew could carry on a one-on-one conversation but got somewhat lost when it became a group conversation. He also had difficulty understanding humor or jokes. Kyle was just very appreciative that most of the kids in his class spoke English because he said it would have been very lonely if they didn't, since he couldn't speak Spanish well."

— Kim

"I wish I would have spent more time learning the language before going. For me it was a very isolating experience because I was so hung up about not being able to express myself to non-English speakers."

— Tani

7. Living on a budget will get tiresome.

Pinching pennies all day long is no fun, which is why Michael and I decided early on to spend every single penny in our sabbatical savings account. Obviously we had to watch our money carefully and we cut our spending significantly compared with what we'd spent back home. But we didn't deny ourselves things we truly wanted. One of the primary reasons we chose Mexico for our sabbatical destination was because of budget concerns. There were days we wished we had an endless supply of money to blow on something outrageous like a $500 ride in the colorful hot air balloons that floated above the San Miguel hills each weekend. But we didn't do it. There were other things we wanted more, like our two-week beach vacation and a family horseback riding adventure.

"I think the most important thing is to remember (and remind yourself constantly!) that you are not living in America and to anticipate lots of surprises (culturally and financially). For example, the dollar lost 30% of its value vs. the Euro when we were

there . . . not much we could have done about that. On the other hand, we realized that we could have a live-in nanny (for less than it would have cost in the U.S.) so we were able to bike, hike, and explore the Italian countryside in ways we never would have imagined."

— Channing

In order to live cheaply but well, pick your splurges carefully. Going out to eat abroad can be as expensive as in the States, especially if you're on a relatively tight budget and there are a lot of wonderful restaurants nearby. This can get frustrating because sometimes you really want to eat out. Build these splurges into your budget by finding inexpensive ways to do it. We found the street food in Mexico to be cheap, delicious, and if we chose carefully, very safe. The kids loved it and so did we. We did occasionally eat out in pricier places, especially if guests were visiting and then, as often as not, they picked up the tab. It's really a matter of being disciplined in all of your expenditures so that when you feel like splurging and heading out for a nice meal or a hot air balloon ride, you can do it without breaking the bank.

20. Going Back

"I had hoped that we would make a lasting change to a less frenzied pace of life. Now, six months after returning home, I can say that this has definitely not occurred. I always feel like I have more things to do than I could possibly ever get done, and that is stressful. (Maybe the contrast is even sharper since our life was on Mexican time so recently.) On a positive note, we are exploring our lives and how we want to live more deeply than we would have ever done a year and a half ago. I know that we will upset the apple cart again as a family — maybe in a year or two, maybe not for a while. Either way, we have rekindled that adventuring spirit that was such an integral part of our younger, non-parent selves."
— Julie

It may be hard to believe, but the moment will come when it's time to return home. It's certainly possible that your lives have changed so completely that your family has decided to remain abroad beyond your original end date. Your kids are thriving, you've found a way to make some money, and your affairs back home remain manageable from a distance. If so, congratulations and good luck on the unknown adventures ahead: your family sabbatical has changed to a new life abroad.

For most, however, a family sabbatical will end at an agreed time. The money runs out, affairs at home require your attention, and the children miss home and their friends; so you have to go back, and perhaps, you're ready. You and your family will return home full of stories and altered perceptions and if you're lucky, some opportunities to tweak the life you left a year or more ago.

"It is hard to imagine going back to the life we led before and the material burdens that await us at home. Ward is determined to spend less time commuting and more time with his family and himself. We hope that Spanish and perhaps a third language will come easily to Zeb at school and that his interest in other cultures will continue."

— Sarah

Preparations for Heading Home

Compared with the extensive preparations required to embark on your sabbatical, preparing to return home is a breeze. Because you have so many fewer entanglements and complications in your lives abroad, the preparations for returning home will be largely psychological as opposed to physical. Still, there are a variety of tasks you'll want to get started on as you look homeward.

Gifts

A couple of months before you head home, start thinking about what kinds of gifts you want to buy for family members and friends who have helped facilitate your sabbatical. Buying gifts for the special people in your lives will get the kids excited about the last phase of their adventure and it will make the idea of going home suddenly very real. Strategic gift-buying is also a way to honor the people you've met during your time abroad. You can spread your dollars around by buying from those merchants with whom you have developed special relationships.

Now is also the time to start packing up any gifts that you've bought along the way. Consider sending a box or two of gifts back with your last few visitors to help save on exorbitant mailing costs and also to give you a chance to go on some fun shopping expeditions with friends from back home. Buy in bulk for the best deals. Think in terms of weight if you will be shipping things back. Obviously soft, lightweight things like scarves, tapestries and cloth bags will be easier to transport than pottery or metalwork.

Gift giving is also a great way for your kids to reconnect with their friends back home. Offering small tokens of affection bought during their adventure abroad can help generate discussion about their time away and break the ice with friends our children haven't seen in a while.

END OF SABBATICAL CHORE LIST

Tying up loose ends abroad

• Begin sorting through your belongings and make decisions about what you will give away, sell, or take back with you.

• If you're going to be sending things home, start researching methods and costs so you're not surprised by mailing costs, packaging requirements, and possible size or weight restrictions.

• Make final travel arrangements with airlines, trains, etc.

• Inform teachers, tutors, and others of your departure date and plan for a goodbye party at your children's school and/or at your home to formalize your departure.

• If necessary, get any required documentation from schools, doctors, or employers abroad to take back home with you.

• Close out foreign bank accounts and wrap up your other sabbatical financial affairs.

• Exchange foreign currency for dollars. Better yet, spend what you have and be careful about withdrawing more than you need in the local currency.

• Update your master address/email list to include the addresses of your new foreign and expat friends. Make sure you get both the home-country and foreign addresses of your expat buddies. Have your children do the same with their friends, tutors, and teachers.

• Give your and your children's local friends, teachers, tutors, and employees small thank-you gifts prior to leaving to formalize the end of your relationships — or at any rate, this phase of your relationships. You will likely maintain friendships with some of these individuals.

Chores to take care of before arriving home

One thing you can do to stem the tide of craziness that will meet you upon your return is to take care of some of the mundane administrative responsibilities of life back home before your sabbatical ends. Thanks to the Internet, you can check off a number of these tasks before you head back. Doing so will help cut down on the number of chores you'll need to accomplish immediately after arriving home.

• Reinstate car insurance to take effect on your arrival date if it isn't current.

• Renew your driver's license if it expired while you were gone.

• Check into camps, daycare, and other children's education and activity programs if you are returning during the summer break.

• Communicate with your children's schools back home to ensure their spots and get any necessary administrative paperwork and documents from their schools abroad. Check once again to see whether the kids need to do any catch-up homework to prepare for their return to school.

• Communicate with your renters to confirm their date of departure, conditions of departure, return of damage deposit, etc.

• Make appointments with accountants, tax advisors, and insurance agents for soon after you return to deal with any financial matters you've put off during your sabbatical.

• Put out feelers for employment or confirm with your existing employer your return date, conditions of your return, etc.

• Let everyone on your master address/email list know when you plan to return home.

• Have your kids send postcards, letters, and emails to let their friends and relatives know they're coming home.

• Research medical insurance if yours will be expiring after you return home. If you will be insured through your employer back home, make sure you know the date when coverage will start (or restart).

• Make dentist and doctor appointments for camp physicals, eye checks, and other health concerns for soon after your return.

Welcome (to a busy and slightly overwhelming) Home!

The reality is that no matter how much you manage to accomplish from abroad, you will still return home to a long list of chores and business matters that will need your immediate attention. You will need to get your things out of storage and put your house back in order if you've leased it. You may need to search for a new living situation if you sold your home or were leasing a place prior to leaving. You'll have to arrange for the start-up of all your utilities and go to the post office to make sure your mail is routed correctly. You'll need to notify your banks and search through all your belongings to locate important papers. If you didn't have your car with you, getting it back on the road again will take time and money. Family and friends will inundate you with phone calls and invitations. If you weren't working overseas, you probably won't have a lot of cash on hand and someone will need to start bringing in some money soon after you return. The kids will need attention and they will want to see their friends and toys and visit all the places they were pining for while they were gone. They may also feel a sense of "foreignness" that may catch them unawares and leave them feeling strangely different from their peers. At the end of your first week back, you may feel like you haven't yet taken a deep breath to enjoy being home. By the end of your second week back, you may wonder why you returned at all.

Transition shock in reverse

The first few days back you may be riding the high of being home again. Seeing neighbors, unpacking treasures, and finding the coffeemaker and drinking your old brand will feel energizing and soothing all at the same time. But don't be surprised if within a week or so your energy levels begin to flag and you start to feel deflated. Part of it is a lack of routine again. Your days may have a distinctly haphazard feel as you pick up the flotsam and jetsam of your old lives and examine each chunk waiting to feel, well, something. You may be homesick for the life and good friends you left behind in your sabbatical city. It can also be hard to acknowledge that your overseas adventure is at an end and that you're now faced with the decision of what's next. And you may pine for that hard won sense of peace and relaxation that just isn't a normal part of life in the United States.

"We were really frustrated by having to get in a car so often and sit in traffic. After a year of walking and a well-functioning metro system, this was hard." — Frances

"When I returned, I realized I spent more time in one day in the car than I did in a week or more in San Miguel. I really enjoyed walking more in Mexico and experiencing everyday life on a more personal level. I felt more connected to people because of the warm and charming greeting of 'buenos días,' 'buenas tardes,' 'buenas noches.' There was more of a human connection because it was coupled with a smile or with direct eye contact that felt open and respectful. I have really missed it a lot since I've returned." — Kim

The contrast between our lives in Mexico and our lives back home hit us like a ton of bricks. U.S. culture is fueled by a pervasive, transparent tension and it was obvious to us that while we'd been away, we'd been fueled by something altogether different. We loved seeing our close friends again but they had a wound-up edge to their energies that made us uncomfortable. People remarked on the changes in our body language and postures. They said we were different. Somehow more open and relaxed. At times we felt like astronauts returning from 18 months of weightlessness and having to learn how to negotiate gravity all over again.

"I notice I feel more comfortable with fewer friends. We have many friends but they are all flung out across our town and in different contexts and thus, I often actually feel a lack of community. I was very happy in Mexico having just four families as friends – just four families to coordinate with. I liked that." — Marline

"Returning was a really wonderful time for purging the house of unneeded stuff. Somehow things we had never been able to throw out seemed easy to get rid of after a year without them."   — Frances

Calming the Homecoming Whirlwind

Although it can be hard to resist the "jumping back in" syndrome (and you can't eliminate the frenzied moments completely), there are things you can do to make your homecoming less hectic. The following steps may help transform the tornado of returning into something closer to a spirited gale:

• As a family, discuss the possibilities of feeling grumpy, sad, depressed, and alienated for a period of time once you return home.

• Reassure your children that whatever they are feeling, including feeling homesick for the places and friends they left behind to come home, is perfectly normal.

• Remind each other to be patient. Things will gradually begin to feel more comfortable after a few weeks back home.

• You and your children may be surprised that friends and family aren't really very interested in your sabbatical trip. Encourage your kids to talk about hobbies, sports, and other topics of mutual interest rather than spinning tales of life abroad. Wait for people to ask before offering long-winded descriptions of your adventures.

• Get together with other families who have lived abroad. Compare reentry notes and share tales of life abroad and how strange it feels to come home.

• Reestablish some sort of basic routine quickly.

• Communicate with your friends abroad soon after your return through emails and letters.

• Limit your social engagements. See people one-on-one or family-by-family rather than having a big, splashy "we're back" party. More than a small group can feel uncomfortable and overwhelming at first.

• Seek out foods and cultural events from your sabbatical country.

• Exercise regularly and slowly work your way back into one or two

social networking activities such as a book club or school organization.
• Make conscious decisions about allowing media back into your lives.
You may want to severely limit exposure to radio, TV, and periodicals.

> *"We experienced virtually no transition difficulties although Rich is still pining for fresh, cheap, wonderful fish. We were amazed that we could go anywhere and drink tap water and not notice immediate side effects."*
> — Tani

Because we returned during the summer, we had several months to
find our sea legs (or remain adrift, depending on your point of view) before school and work started up. But if your family returns on a Sunday
and heads back to jobs and school the following day, your transition will
obviously be different. I'm not sure which is the more difficult, picking
up your old lives without missing a beat or gradually picking up a "new"
life bit by bit. Whichever way you go, you're bound to hit a few bumps
and grumpy moments along the way.

Make Your Child's First Weeks Back at School Easier

It's likely that your children will feel nervous about returning to
school. They may be sad at having to leave friends overseas and worried that their old friends back home will have forgotten them. If your
child hasn't been communicating with her friends during your sabbatical, make sure she emails or sends postcards to her best friends back
home just prior to returning so that everyone can get excited to see
each other. Again, have your child bring back a few small gifts for her
friends and perhaps a small gift for her teacher as well. And do follow
up on your promise to return with materials for the school no matter
how small or insignificant they feel.

Before classes start or at least during the first few days of class, speak
with your child's teacher and explain that your child has been away for a
period of time on sabbatical. Discuss any remedial work your child may
need to complete during the first few weeks of school. Don't hesitate
to get your child temporary tutoring if there are one or two academic

areas where she needs additional help to make her feel comfortable and on equal footing with her schoolmates. And have your child's teacher help facilitate the potentially rocky terrain of peer relationships.

Although Cleome never experienced any noticeable gaps in her academics, she had a few rough moments transitioning back into school after being gone for 18 months because her old friends had formed new cliques in her absence. Having to navigate peer group acceptance back home was perhaps harder after Mexico, where she had been something novel and everyone wanted to be her buddy. Back in Minnesota she was simply one of the pack and diving in again was a whole different adventure. Luckily, the friendship issue resolved itself quickly and within a week or two she was fine.

> *"When you're older you'll really appreciate all you learn and the languages you learn. Plus it makes you 'different' when you get back. Kids will know you have done something cool."* — Henry, age 11

> *"Lilly had no issues on reintegration. Before leaving, we had her attend a sixth grade class on Take Your Daughter to Work Day so she would have a feel for middle school. We had also walked her around the school. Emory reintegrated well although she had a lot of work in the first two months. She's in advanced algebra and we got her a tutor to help her catch up. She also got hit with writing essays to apply to TAG [accelerated] classes in high school. It all had to happen very fast upon returning."* — Marline

> *"After a year of real Spanish life, it was hard for our kids to ease back into the Spanish classes their grades were in. See what you can do to jump your kids up a level or two."* — Frances

Carry Your Lives Abroad Back Home

Given the pervasive and overwhelming pressure of U.S. culture, is it really possible to live the lessons you learned abroad once you return home? Can you maintain those hard won changes such as giving yourself more creative, contemplative space and spending more time with the kids and less time working and over-scheduling? Can you continue to engage with a language and culture different from your own? Frankly, I have my doubts whether it's possible to achieve a lifestyle similar to the one you had abroad while living in the U.S. It means working less, wanting less, and actively resisting the most seductive and potent aspects of American culture. It means not buying into the "American dream," which is obviously easier to do when you're living outside the country.

Trying to pursue a slower, simpler, more family-directed lifestyle in the U.S. can leave you feeling unimportant and spectacularly "out of the loop." But based on your family's experience abroad and your desire to continue a more creative and intense family interaction back home, you may decide it's worth a try. We did and so have some of the friends we made abroad.

> *"At least at the beginning, we moved through our lives in a slower, easier fashion. Our children were very content to hang around the house, puttering with their toys or talking to us. They would often say no to play dates in favor of going slow, a change for them. We were all also very aware of the positives and negatives about living in the U.S. On the positive side, life is very easy. There are so many choices for food at the grocery! There is hot water; there are bathtubs! We can understand everyone! On the other hand, I immediately noticed that I stopped walking as much, often to save time, which I really thought I wouldn't do. I also noticed that I was sitting in the car an awful lot because I wanted to go places that were too far to walk. Time had stopped its lovely meander."* — Julie

Live the lessons you learned

If your family is interested in trying to carve out something less frenzied and more akin to the lifestyle you lived abroad, here are a few suggestions for things to try once you return home:

• Provide for a buffer period. Have a little money in the bank for when you return so that you can get yourselves acclimated and settled without feeling tremendous financial pressure. You don't want to have to start (or start looking for) full-time employment immediately.

• Avoid returning to the same job, same hours, same responsibilities. Reorder your priorities and find employment that suits your desired lifestyle and puts your family first.

> *"Living abroad gave my husband the space to make some huge changes in his work life. He would never have been able to do this without getting away."* — Marline

• Find a job closer to home or consider working out of your home to increase your flexibility and independence.

• Read books about simplifying your lives immediately after you return to inspire you to actively resist the forces around you encouraging consumption.

> *"I clearly didn't want to return to the hectic life I used to lead. We went about reintegration pretty slowly. We haven't unpacked our house yet. We have just the basics out. And, we don't really miss all that stuff."* — Marline

• Trim back your needs significantly. Buy a smaller refrigerator or don't fill to bursting the one you have. Buy fewer clothes, fewer furnishings, fewer toys. Own one car and use mass transit.

> *"We really noticed how much our culture is based on accumulation of stuff and shopping for stuff and getting better stuff. What was hardest was seeing our friends, people we love, being very concerned, even overly concerned with getting nicer stuff and getting a nicer house and getting a nicer car while we just felt happy to have water coming out of our tap that was clean enough to drink. For me the hardest thing continues to be this obsession with stuff and that I see myself being seduced back into caring about it. Then I catch myself and I really dislike the way stuff can be seductive and how marketing can make you feel like you need so many things that you don't."* — Rachel

• Talk frequently with your kids about lifestyle choices, environmental consequences, and remaining vigilant about the media you consume and your role as consumers in general. Actively discuss your family goals and the lessons you've learned abroad that you all want to continue. Then live them.

> *"Mostly, for the kids, I think they now 'get it' that there is life and culture and points of view different from the U.S. experience. I don't think you ever lose that. They already are talking about how they can get back there, via school or eventual work. In the case of our sons, because soccer is such a big deal there and is played constantly, they got really into soccer – the chance to see a lot of coverage of the World Cup also has biased them against American baseball and football now."*
> — Frances

• Program your kids less. Sign them up for fewer dance, piano, ice skating, soccer, you-name-it lessons. One extracurricular activity a week will do.

• Cut back on entertainment expenses. Hunt for free family activities in your community. Take more walks. Have everyone in your family take up an instrument.

• Consciously resist the "warp speed" lifestyle so many others are breathlessly pursuing. Make take-out food a treat and continue to cook meals at home. Resist passing like ships in the night in order to head out the door to evening meetings or classes. Sit in the backyard and drink a glass of wine after dinner while the kids play with others in the neighborhood. Build book-reading time into your evening and weekend schedules. Just say no when too many activities and invitations threaten to overwhelm your lives.

> *"I feel really good about Andy's and my ability to take a dream and make it a reality and that we were able to share it with our kids. As our kids get older I think they will be more amazed that we packed up and moved to Mexico for seven months. Perhaps reflecting on this will make it easier for them to make change happen in their lives when they are older."*
> — Kim

• Lighten your financial load so you can do more with less.

• Continue learning your new language and become involved some-how in the culture of the community you were immersed in abroad. Practice your new language in your house at meals and while you're walking around the neighborhood. Teach your neighbors and children's friends simple phrases in your new language.

• Stay in touch with the friends you met during your sabbatical and visit each other over time.

• Build travel into your long-term family plan. Every five, seven, or ten years, take another family sabbatical so that you can renew your life plans along the way. You did it once. You can do it again!

> *"I'm guessing that my children will all be more interested in further travels abroad as they each grow up. Both of the older ones have expressed an interest in learning several other languages. My husband continued traveling abroad and we ended up adopting a child from Haiti, something neither of us was looking for and which wouldn't have happened if we hadn't lived in a third world country ourselves."* — Tani

> *"It's one thing to take an inexpensive holiday in a developing country and observe life from a comfortable distance, but to share in others' experiences on a day-to-day basis is obviously more profound. We realize in a more meaningful way how lucky we are. We rarely bemoan the lack of variety in our diet but feel grateful that we are always well nourished. The petty annoyances of living in our peaceful suburb at home will (hopefully) seem insignificant after learning to tolerate much greater disturbance."* — Sarah

Remember: No One Cares Like You Do

Let me offer one last word of warning. Don't be surprised if the folks back home seem less excited than expected about the time your family spent abroad. While you were experiencing the richness of another culture, life continued back home without you. Despite the fact that you're bursting with stories, many of the people you love just won't be that interested in the details of your trip. They may be remarkably content to hear that things went well and, after a polite question or two, they may not ask another thing about your journey. It's not rudeness. They just may not have a clue about what to ask. Of course an eager few will press you for details and page willingly through your photo albums, but most will not.

Take the initiative to continue your family sabbatical at home. Take it upon yourselves to generate the energy, the interest, and the excitement by discussing your family's adventure. Continue to learn more about other languages and cultures. Do it! The challenges are enormous, but so are the rewards.

RESOURCES

Books

A Family Year Abroad: How to Live Outside the Borders by Chris Westphal. (Scottsdale, AZ: Great Potential Press, 2001).
This book discusses a family's year of living in the Czech Republic. It offers some good information regarding living abroad with children as well as about sending children abroad on intercultural exchanges that involve living with native families.

A Journey of One's Own: Uncommon Advice for the Independent Woman Traveler, 3rd edition, by Thalia Zepatos. (Portland, OR: The Eighth Mountain Press, 2003).
Engaging account of spending time abroad sprinkled with bits of wisdom that apply to any sort of travel — solo, family, or otherwise.

A Moveable Marriage — Relocate Your Relationship Without Breaking It by Robin Pascoe. (North Vancouver, BC: Expatriate Press, 2003).
Advice for couples and families regarding the psychological challenges of relocating abroad.

Adventuring With Children: An Inspirational Guide to World Travel and the Outdoors by Nan Jeffreys. (Ashland, OR: Avalon House Publishing, 1996).
Primarily focused on adventure travel with children and roaming in out-of-the-way areas.

Choose Mexico: Travel, Investment, and Living Opportunities for Every Budget, 8th edition, by John Howells and Don Merwin. (Guilford, CT: Globe Pequot Press, 2003).
General guide to retiring in Mexico with good information for those interested in living in Mexico long-term. Not specifically geared for families but includes bits of advice on every subject of expat life in our neighbor to the south.

Culture Shock! Successful Living Abroad: A Parent's Guide by Robin Pascoe. (Portland, OR: Times Editions, 1993).

Good solid information about parenting children somewhere other than home.

Family Travel: The Farther You Go, the Closer You Get by Laura Manske. (San Francisco: Travelers' Tales Guides, 1999).

An inspiring travelogue about traveling with kids for shorter adventures. A good book to read before taking any day trips with your kids.

Gutsy Mamas: Travel Tips and Wisdom for Mothers on the Road by Marybeth Bond. (San Francisco: Travelers' Tales Guides, 1997).

Basic information on health and keeping children entertained and parents sane while on the road.

Have Kid, Will Travel by Claire and Lucille Tristram. (Kansas City: Andrews McMeel Publishing, 1997).

Aimed at parents traveling with babies and young children.

Living Simply With Children: A Voluntary Simplicity Guide for Moms, Dads, and Kids Who Want to Reclaim the Bliss of Childhood and the Joy of Parenting by Marie Sherlock. (New York, NY: Three Rivers Press, 2003).

The title says it all. Well worth reading before and again after any family sabbatical.

Lonely Planet Travel With Children, 4th edition, by Cathy Lanigan. (Oakland, CA: Lonely Planet Publications, 2002).

Concise nuts and bolts information about traveling with kids (especially young ones), including packing suggestions, medical advice, transportation, finding short-term lodging, and keeping children entertained. The book also includes brief travelogues written by Lonely Planet employees detailing their adventures of traveling abroad (to rather exotic locales) with their children.

Mexico Health and Safety Travel Guide by Robert H. Page, M.D. and Curtis P. Page, M.D. (Tempe, AZ: MedToGo, 2005).

Guide to the Mexican health system and a detailed directory of English-speaking doctors and hospitals in cities throughout Mexico. Informative website as well.

One Year Off: Leaving It All Behind for a Round-the-World Journey With Our Children

by David Elliot Cohen. (San Francisco: Travelers' Tales, 2001).
This relates the author's year spent traveling with his wife, a nanny, and three small children. It's a compilation of email correspondence that details this family's many experiences during their 12-month, 7-country odyssey. Entertaining and can spur some discussion about a special adventure or two you might want to take with your kids.

Spanish – Live It and Learn It! by Martha Racine Taylor. (Fort Bragg, CA: Cypress House, 2006).
This is a city-by-city guide to Spanish-language immersion schools in Mexico. It has detailed information on programs, prices, locations, and contact information for the many schools listed. Aimed at adults and older children.

Staying Healthy in Asia, Africa and Latin America, 5th edition, by Dirk Schroeder. (Emeryville, CA: Avalon Travel Publishing, 2000).
Specific health information related to travel in more remote areas or places where access to Western medicine is limited.

Take Your Kids to Europe, 7th edition, by Cynthia Harriman. (Guilford, CT: Globe Pequot Press, 2005).
Detailed guide to traveling with kids in Europe. Includes sightseeing, accommodations, budgeting, and much more. An excellent resource if you're going to be living in Europe.

The Expert Expatriate: Your Guide to Successful Relocation Abroad, Moving, Living, Thriving by Melissa Brayer Hess and Patricia Linderman. (London: Nicholas Brealey Intercultural, 2002).
Aimed at business people relocating abroad with their families. The emphasis is on working abroad and how to help achieve a smooth transition from working life here to working life there. Worth reading and it has an excellent bibliography.

The Family Travel Guide: An Inspiring Collection of Family-Friendly Vacations, edited by Carole Terwilliger Meyers. (Berkeley, CA: Carousel Press, 1995).
First-hand family travel accounts.

The Grown-Up's Guide to Running Away from Home by Rosanne Knorr. (Berkeley, CA: Ten Speed Press, 1998).
Excellent and detailed information for retirees interested in chucking it all and living outside the United States. Although not specifically geared for families

with children, it includes invaluable advice regarding packing and preparations for leaving the States, specific costs of living abroad in different countries, how to pay for your life abroad, dealing with pets abroad, cutting costs, handling finances, obtaining visas, and so on. Excellent resource.

The People's Guide to Mexico, 13th edition, by Carl Franz and Lorena Havens. (Emeryville, CA: Avalon Travel Publishing, 2006).
The definitive travelers' guide to Mexico. A must-get if you're going to be traveling anywhere south of the border (or anywhere for that matter) with advice that runs the gamut from treating scorpion bites and camping with your kids to staying healthy while sampling the local cuisine. Worth the price just for the last chapter, "For More Information," which includes an extensive bibliography, a list of maps, and a well-researched guide to Internet resources for travelers abroad.

The Pocket Doctor: A Passport to Healthy Travel, 3rd edition, by Stephen Bezruchka, M.D. (Seattle: The Mountaineers, 2005).
A good medical reference book.

The Practical Nomad Guide to the Online Travel Marketplace by Edward Hasbrouck. (Emeryville, CA: Avalon Travel Publishing, 2001).
Useful book on how to use the Web to research travel destinations, buy tickets, find housing, keep connected, work over the Net, and much more.

Work Your Way Around the World, 12th edition, by Susan Griffith. (Oxford, UK: Vacation Work Publications, 2005).
This is the bible on how to find temporary work in nearly every country in the world.

Your Money or Your Life: Transforming Your Relationship with Money and Achieving Financial Independence by Joe Dominguez and Vicki Robin. (London: Penguin Books, 1999).
A step-by-step guide to taking control of money rather than letting it control you. This book offers concrete advice about how to achieve financial independence and make your dreams a reality. A great resource for putting your work and home life into perspective and giving you a way to see options when it seems that there may not be any.

Some helpful magazines and catalogs

International Living • www.internationalliving.com
This is a magazine geared primarily for people interested in purchasing property and living/retiring abroad, but it has some good general information about interesting places to check out.

Magellan's • www.magellans.com • Phone: 800-962-4943
Travel store and catalog offering clothing, luggage, safety items, and more.

Transitions Abroad Magazine • www.transitionsabroad.com
Excellent resource for teaching, employment opportunities, language learning, health insurance, and much more. The July/August 2005 issue is devoted to family travel and has one of the most complete resource guides I've seen.

TravelSmith • www.travelsmith.com • Phone: 800-950-1600
Fun travel catalog with lots of expensive but cool clothes and gadgets.

Walkabout Travel Gear • www.walkabouttravelgear.com • Phone: 800-852-7085
This is a fantastic product catalog as well as a source of critical travel information. Get the catalog even if you don't plan to order anything because the catalog itself is a wealth of well-researched nuts and bolts info about safety, electrical needs, computer stuff, and so on, presented on a country-by-country basis along with highly useful tips on travel, health insurance, time zones, and such. A great (FREE!) resource. Check out their website too.

Internet Guidebooks, Message Boards and General Information

www.aafsw.org
Associates of the American Foreign Service Worldwide website with many links and articles for expats.

www.bookpassage.com
Bookstore offering many travel books, among other interesting topics.

www.cheaptickets.com
Offers discount tickets to destinations abroad.

Internet Guidebooks, Message Boards and General Information, cont'd.

www.customs.ustreas.gov
U.S. Customs information.

www.escapeartist.com
Has articles and links for those looking to live, work, and invest overseas.

www.expatexchange.com
A great website for expats to exchange information on everything from how to move to politics, schooling, etc.

www.expatforums.org
This site has many links and resources as well as a message board.

www.expatnetwork.com
This features a job board for international jobs and an expat forum.

www.expatriates.com
This site offers an extensive resource directory and a discussion board.

www.familytravelforum.com
This subscription service provides chat boards, travel advice, articles of interest, great links and custom trip planning with an emphasis on traveling with children. Definitely worth checking out.

www.fawco.org
The Federation of American Women's Clubs Overseas, Inc. is an international network of independent groups that support American women living and working abroad. Has a very good links page.

www.independenttraveler.com
Useful site for general information and products such as electronic adapters, passport info, insurance, travel bargains, etc.

www.interculturalpress.com
Intercultural Press is a publisher offering a wide range of books related to living overseas.

www.lonelyplanet.com
The Lonely Planet folks have an interactive website with travelers' comments,

which can provide a useful personal perspective on different aspects of travel.

www.mexconnect.com

This site hosts many excellent discussion groups for everything to do with living in or visiting Mexico and other Latin American countries. A terrific resource.

www.overseasdigest.com

A vast range of articles about legal issues, emergency and security tips for overseas travel, finances, moving, insurance, and much more about overseas life.

www.talesmag.com

Tales from a Small Planet website offering firsthand articles and discussion on expat life in cities worldwide, plus a comprehensive list of international schools and other information.

www.travelwithyourkids.com

This website is written by parents and chock full of tips for traveling with children on both short and long trips.

Other Useful Internet Sites (listed alphabetically by topic)

ACCOMMODATIONS

www.directmoving.com

Links to overseas house-finding and moving services and other information on finding housing abroad.

www.exchangehomes.com

ExchangeHomes.com

www.homeexchange.com

International Home Exchange Network

www.intervac.com

Intervac is one of the largest home exchange organizations in the world.

www.vanpac.com

Vanpac International is a relocation specialist with information on moving services, pet shipping, rates, and links to other moving sites.

CURRENCY/FINANCES

www.irs.ustreas.gov

Tax forms for U.S. citizens living abroad. (Get IRS Publication 54: "Tax Guide for U.S. Citizens Abroad.")

www.oanda.com

Excellent currency converter and source for current exchange rates.

www.x-rates.com

Offers a currency calculator.

ELECTRONICS, COMMUNICATION EQUIPMENT, AND COMPUTER-USE INFORMATION

http://kropla.com

Highly detailed guide to voltage, television systems, telephone, and electric requirements world-wide. Excellent resource.

www.appliancesoverseas.com

An online store offering appliances and adapters for living overseas.

www.laptoptravel.com

An online store offering laptop mobility products and advice.

www.teleadapt.com

Website geared toward international business travelers offering products such as telephone and appliance adapters, modems, and an assortment of other communication equipment.

www.voltagevalet.com

Thorough discussion of computer and electronic products, adapters, and conversion requirements in countries around the world. Phone: 800-247-6900.

www.walkabouttravelgear.com

Highly detailed guide to international electricity and electronic requirements and source for adapters, converters, and transformers. Excellent resource.

EMPLOYMENT ABROAD

www.intemployment.com

Website of the *International Employment Gazette*, with links to international job openings.

EMPLOYMENT ABROAD, CONT'D.

www.livingabroad.com

The website for the Living Abroad International Resource Center features information and resources about visas, work permits, housing, insurance, schools, etc.

www.transitionsabroad.com

Site of *Transitions Abroad* magazine. Phone: 802-442-4827.

HEALTH AND SAFETY

www.amcenters.com

Site that provides information about American Medical Centers that operate in Eastern and Central Europe.

www.cdc.gov

U.S. Centers for Disease Control and Prevention. Get updated information about recommended vaccines and health precautions. Phone: 877-394-8747 for the Traveler's Health Hotline.

www.iamat.org

International Association for Medical Assistance to Travelers provides information about health warnings and concerns worldwide and helps travelers locate English-speaking doctors and hospitals overseas.

www.travel.state.gov

U.S. State Department website detailing hotspots, safety concerns, and warnings around the globe. Click on "international travel" and then "travel brochures" to check out "A Safe Trip Abroad" for some good basic traveling tips. The site includes links to the web pages of each embassy or consular office. Phone: 888-407-4747; from abroad: 202-501-4444.

HOMESCHOOLING

www.home-school.com

This is the website for *Practical Homeschooling* magazine.

www.nheri.org

National Home Education Research Institute. Phone: 503-364-1490.

www.usdla.org

United States Distance Learning Association

LANGUAGE LEARNING/SCHOOLING ABROAD

www.languagetapes.com

Website offering language tapes and courses in many different languages. Links to foreign language books and other resources as well.

www.state.gov/m/a/os/

U.S. overseas schools by region. Email address is OverseasSchools@state.gov. The site is hosted by the U.S. State Department.

www.travlang.com

Travlang's Foreign Language for Travelers includes translations, dictionaries, and pronunciation guides.

LEGAL FORMS

For creating a do-it-yourself will:

www.buildawill.com

A software program that is a bit easier to navigate than WillMaker (see below). However, it does not include programs for living wills or power of attorney.

www.legalzoom.com

Offers a variety of legal documents, including wills, which you can fill out and have LegalZoom staffers review. Will prices range from $69 to $119.

www.nolo.com

Offers the Quicken WillMaker Plus software programs. Nolo Press has been creating do-it-yourself wills since 1985 and offers excellent, inexpensive, and comprehensive programs.

For leasing your home:

www.findlegalforms.com
www.lawdepot.com
www.offcampusnetwork.com
www.smartformz.com

PASSPORTS AND VISAS

http://travel.state.gov/passport/about_contact_agencies.html

Website of the U.S. State Department's Bureau of Consular Affairs, which issues passports. Phone: 877-487-2778.

Passports and Visas, cont'd.

www.ppt.gc.ca
Passport Canada, which issues Canadian passports.

www.emb.com
  This is the website of the Embassy Network, with information about how to contact the embassies of any country in the world.

www.passportsandvisas.com
  This is a passport expediter. It will provide a passport in as little as one day for a steep price.

www.projectvisa.com
  Specific visa information on every country in the world.

www.us.cibt.com
  A travel document specialist and expediting service.

Travel Health Insurance

www.asaincor.com
  ASA Inc. offers health insurance worldwide. Phone: 888-ASA-8288, 480-753-1333; fax 480-753-1330; email asaincor@aol.com.

www.bupainternational.com
  One of the largest overseas healthcare insurers.

www.insuremytrip.com
  Insurance broker with easy-to-read comparisons among multiple insurance companies.

www.tenweb.com
  Traveler Emergency Network (TEN). Subscription service to emergency medical care around the world. Phone: 800-275-4836.

www.totaltravelinsurance.com
  Lets you compare prices from multiple insurance companies.

VoIP and Telephone Callback Services

http://voice.yahoo.com
  Offers PC to PC, PC to phone, and phone to PC services.

VoIP and Telephone Callback Services, cont'd.

www.callvantage.com

AT&T's VoIP service.

www.escapeartist.com/internet/callback.htm

Extensive listing of callback services of every stripe.

www.kallback.com

Phone: 800-516-9992 in the U.S. or +206-479-8600 overseas.

www.net2phone.com

Offers VoIP software, international calling cards, and PC-to-phone calling plans.

www.skype.com

A service similar to VoIP except it sticks to the Internet and doesn't use regular phone lines.

www.voicewing.com

Verizon's VoIP service.

www.vonage.com

Bills itself as the #1 U.S. provider of VoIP service.

INDEX

OTHER BOOKS FROM THE INTREPID TRAVELER

The Intrepid Traveler publishes money-saving, horizon expanding travel how-to and guidebooks dedicated to helping its readers make travel an integral part of their everyday life.

Please check with your favorite bookstore for other Intrepid Traveler titles. Or visit our website:

www.IntrepidTraveler.com

where you will also find a complete catalog, travel articles from around the world, Internet travel resources, and more.

If you are interested in becoming a home-based travel agent, visit the Home-Based Travel Agent Resource Center at:

www.HomeTravelAgency.com